WOMEN AND URBAN LIFE IN EIGHTEENTH-CENTURY ENGLAND

Women and Urban Life in Eighteenth-Century England

'On the Town'

Edited by

ROSEMARY SWEET and PENELOPE LANE

ASHGATE

Published by
Ashgate Publishing Limited
Gower House
Croft Road
Aldershot
Hampshire GU11 3HR
England

Ashgate Publishing Company
Suite 420
101 Cherry Street
Burlington, VT 05401-4405
USA

Ashgate website: http//www.ashgate.com

British Library Cataloguing in Publication Data
Women and urban life in eighteenth-century England : "on the town"
1.City and town life - England - History 18th century
2.City and town life - England - History 19th century
3.Women - Social conditions - England - History - 18th century 4.Women - Social conditions - England - History - 19th century 5.Women - Economic conditions - England - History - 18th century 6.Women - Economic conditions - England - History - 19th century
I.Sweet, Rosemary II.Lane, Penelope
307.7'6'082'0942'09033

Library of Congress Cataloging-in-Publication Data
Women and urban life in eighteenth-century England : on the town / edited by Rosemary Sweet and Penelope Lane.
p. cm.
Papers of a conference held at the University of Leicester in May 1999.
Includes bibliographical references and index.
ISBN 0-7546-0730-5 (alk. paper)
1. Women--England--History--18th century--Congresses. 2. City and town life--England--History--18th century--Congresses. I. Sweet, Rosemary. II. Lane, Penelope.

HQ1599.E5W624 2003
305.4'0942'09033--dc21 2002042679

ISBN 0 7546 0730 5

Printed and bound in Great Britain by MPG Books Ltd, Bodmin, Cornwall

Contents

Notes on Contributors

Hannah Barker is a senior lecturer in history at the University of Manchester. She is author of *Newspapers, Politics and Public Opinion in Late Eighteenth-Century England* (1998) and *Newspapers, Politics and English Society, 1695-1855* (1999). She is also co-editor of *Gender in Eighteenth-Century England* (1997), with Elaine Chalus; *Language, Print and Electoral Politics, 1790-1832* (2001), with David Vincent; and *Press, Politics and the Public Sphere in Europe and North America c.1760-1820* (2002), with Simon Burrows.

Helen Berry is lecturer in Early Modern British History at the University of Newcastle. She has published a number of articles on social and cultural history in seventeenth- and eighteenth-century England. She won the Royal Historical Society's Alexander Prize (2000) for an essay on Moll King's coffee house and the use of 'flash talk', a form of street slang in early Hanoverian London. Her book *Gender, Society and Print Culture in Late-Stuart England* was published by Ashgate in May 2003. Her next project will be a survey of cultural change, viewed through the history of English coffee houses between circa 1650 and 1850.

Elaine Chalus is a lecturer in the School of Historical and Cultural Studies at Bath Spa University College. She is the co-editor of *Gender in Eighteenth-Century England: Roles, Representations and Responsibilities* (London, 1997). Her most recent publications include 'Women, Electoral Privilege and Practice' in Kathryn Gleadle and Sarah Richardson (eds), *Women in British Politics, 1760-1860: The Power of the Petticoat* (London, 2000); and '"To Serve my Friends": Women and Political Patronage in Eighteenth-Century England', in Amanda Vickery (ed.), *Women, Privilege and Power* (Stanford 2001). She is currently working on a monograph on eighteenth-century women's involvement in English political life.

Denise Fowler is a speech and language therapist. She completed her doctoral thesis entitled 'Social Distinction and the Written Word: Two Provincial Case Studies, Warwick and Draguignan, 1780-1820' at the University of Warwick in 1999. She has published in local history journals in England and France on topics in reading and writing, and is currently involved in research on the iconography of women in reading and writing.

Karen Harvey is research fellow at the AHRB Centre for the Study of the Domestic Interior, Royal College of Art, and honorary research fellow at the Bedford Centre for the History of Women, Royal Holloway. She has published articles on erotic culture, masculinity, spatial metaphors and bodies. She is completing *The Pleasures of Merryland: Bodies and Gender in Eighteenth Century*

Erotic Culture for Cambridge University Press, and editing the collection *The Kiss in History* for Manchester University Press. Her current research project explores male authority and the household in England, 1650-1850.

Sylvia Pinches is a freelance historical researcher and the House Curator for the 78 Derngate Trust, Northampton. She recently completed her doctoral thesis entitled 'Charities in Warwickshire in the Eighteenth and Nineteenth Centuries' at the Centre for English Local History at the University of Leicester.

David E. Shuttleton is a lecturer in English at the University of Wales Aberystwyth. He has published on eighteenth-century medico-literary themes, especially the influence of Dr George Cheyne. He co-edited *De-centering Sexualities; Politics and Representations Beyond the Metropolis* (Routledge, 2000), and is currently co-editing a volume entitled *Punk to Poetess: Women's Poetry 1660-1750.* He is a contributing editor to the forthcoming Cambridge edition of Samuel Richardson's 'Correspondence and Works' and recently held a Clark Memorial Library Fellowship to research a monograph on smallpox literature.

Rosemary Sweet is a lecturer in History and deputy director of the Centre for Urban History at the University of Leicester. Her publications include *The Writing of Urban Histories in Eighteenth-Century England* (Oxford, 1997) and *The English Town. Government, Society and Culture 1680-1840* (1999). She is currently writing a book on antiquarianism in the eighteenth century.

Christine Wiskin teaches history part-time at the University of Warwick where she completed her doctoral thesis 'Women, Credit and Finance in England, c. 1780-1826' in 2000. She has contributed articles on eighteenth-century English businesswomen to the New DNB and to Business Archives: Sources and History.

Preface

This collection of essays arose out of a conference 'On the Town: Women and Urban Life in Eighteenth-Century England' held at the University of Leicester in May 1999. At the time we felt that there was little published material which dealt directly with the varied experiences of women in the eighteenth-century urban milieu, particularly in a non-metropolitan context. We hoped both to open up discussion upon the contribution of women to urban economy, society and culture, and to consider the impact of these economic, social and cultural changes taking place upon women, rather than generalising from the experience of men. A few years have passed and many more publications have come out since that conference was planned, but the relative void in the literature remains to be filled. It is hoped that this volume will contribute in a small measure towards that end.

The editors are extremely grateful to Dr Huw Bowen and Dr Peter Musgrave of the School of Historical Studies and Professor Peter Clark, formerly of the Centre for Urban History at the University of Leicester for their support of the conference.

Chapter 1

Introduction

Rosemary Sweet

As an area of historical research the eighteenth-century town has been attracting considerable attention: in the past two years, no less than three studies have been published in addition to the monumental *Cambridge Urban History of Britain.*[1] Urban history has become the focus of considerable attention, not least because it was within the urban framework that some of the most significant changes of society in the eighteenth century are commonly held to have taken place. Between 1700 and 1800 the proportion of the English population living in towns and cities (over 2,500) had increased from 18.7 per cent to 30.6 per cent; in per capita terms there was an increase from approximately 970,000 to 2,725,000 urban inhabitants. The number of towns is estimated to have increased from 68 to 188.[2] Such rapid population growth was both a response and a stimulus to economic expansion and diversification. Towns became the loci of new trends in consumption and leisure; the public sphere was largely the product of urban space, and the process of class formation occurred against the backdrop of urban society.[3]

However, the contribution of women to urban society and the urban construction of gender and gender roles is hardly mainstream in any of the recent publications. Even in *The Cambridge Urban History*, which represents an exhaustive overview of research in eighteenth-century urban history, discussion of women's work and women's experience is largely peripheral. The structure of the volume embodies the tendency in much urban history to award a higher priority to those aspects of urban history which were predominantly masculine, or at the very least to discuss the issues from a masculine perspective. Economic growth, urban politics and urban government, are represented as the product of largely masculine agency. Women, where they feature at all, appear as the purveyors of culture and sociability, the recipients of poor relief or the victims of sexual exploitation. Eighteenth-century associations between urban life and the definitively feminine

---

[1] Chalkin, C. (2000), *The Rise of the English Town, 1650-1850*, Cambridge; Ellis, J. (2001), *The Georgian Town, 1680-1840*, Basingstoke; Sweet, R. (1999), *The English Town: Government, Society and Culture*, Harlow; P. Clark, (ed.) (2000), *The Cambridge Urban History of Britain. vol. II, 1500-1840*, Cambridge.

[2] Corfield, P.J. (1982), *The Impact of English Towns 1700-1800*, Oxford, pp. 8-9.

[3] Borsay, P. (1989), *The English Urban Renaissance*, Oxford; McKendrick, N., Brewer, J. and Plumb, J.H. (1982), *The Birth of a Consumer Society: The Commercialisation of Eighteenth-Century England,* London; Earle, P. (1989), *The Making of the English Middle Class: Business, Society and Family Life in London, 1660-1730*, London.

vices of vanity, luxury and unruly sexuality have exercised a pervasive and insidious influence upon subsequent conceptualisations of the position of women in urban society. It is an overstatement, but not a complete distortion, to suggest that much of the literature on women in eighteenth-century towns has been conceived in terms of the polarities of, on the one hand, the sociable, extravagant girl about town, the stuff of which patriarchal moralists' nightmares were made of, who found in the greater freedom and anonymity of urban life opportunities to engage in sexual liaisons or to run up enormous bills, and on the other, the Hogarthian gin soaked harridan, with breasts hanging out and baby spilling from her arms, embodying a life of sexual exploitation, immiseration and degradation.[4]

In the recent historiography of the eighteenth century there has been no shortage of studies informed by the history of gender, but historians of gender seem to be as reluctant to address the urban variable as the urban historians are to deploy gender as a category of historical analysis. There is a much greater willingness to examine class formation, which is generally presented as the defining feature of urbanised society. Most studies which analyse the emergence of class in the urban context do so with at best implicit recognition of its gendered aspects and the role of women in the process. Class formation as described in the context of Leeds, Bradford or Halifax, for example, is an almost wholly masculine experience.[5] There are exceptions, however: the ground breaking study in this area was Leonore Davidoff and Catherine Hall's *Family Fortunes*, published in 1986. Although not framed as a specifically urban study, the volume's emphasis on the formation of the middle class gave it a strong urban dimension. The period covered, from 1780-1850 included a considerable part of the 'long' eighteenth century with which this volume is concerned. However, the trajectory of the argument and much of the research was heavily weighted towards the latter end of the period. Their interest in the eighteenth century went only so far as it was necessary to trace back the processes by which the model of feminised, bourgeois domesticity, with which they identified middle class culture of the mid nineteenth century, had emerged. Just under ten years later, Margaret R. Hunt's monograph examined similar questions starting at the other end of the eighteenth century: *The Middling Sort. Commerce, Gender and the Family 1680-1780*. Hunt's analysis, like that of Davidoff and Hall, makes the family central to the construction of a middling identity and therefore enhances the visibility of women and allows them a more active and creative role. Her findings demonstrated the manifold disadvantages under which women operated in the eighteenth-century urban economy, but also uncovered far more extensive participation by women than reliance of the prescriptive and descriptive sources (largely generated by men) would imply. In general, the tendency of nineteenth-century historians to search the eighteenth century for the origins of class formation has encouraged an

---

4 The classic description of the latter being in George, M.D. (1992), *London Life in the Eighteenth Century*, reprinted London.

5 Koditschek, T. (1990), *Class Formation and Urban-Industrial Society: Bradford 1750-1850*, Cambridge; Morris, R.J. (1990), *Class, Sect and Party: The Making of the British Middle Class, Leeds 1820-1850*, Manchester; Smail, J. (1994), *The Origins of Middle-Class Culture, Halifax, Yorkshire, 1660-1780*, Ithaca and London.

approach which has concentrated on the construction of *class* identities than *gender* identities in urban society. Women have generally been treated as passive objects in the process of urbanisation: manipulated, exploited and excluded, rather than being allowed the capacity for influence and active participation in urban economy and society.[6]

Although not directly concerned with specifically urban history, advances in our understanding of the legal position of women have considerable bearing upon the urban fortunes of early modern women. Susan Staves's recent publications on married women's property and women investors in chartered companies, have been very suggestive of the possibilities available for women to operate within a world of business and finance, which was nominally male and closed to them, whilst work by Amy Erikson has alerted historians to the opportunities which existed for early modern women to circumvent the restrictions of common law and exercise greater economic and legal autonomy than had previously been thought possible.[7] Erikson's study concluded in 1720, by which time, she suggests, some of the legal loopholes were already being closed off, as a falling age of marriage left women with fewer years of autonomy, and a decline in the relative value of marriage portions and the elevation of romantic love and surrender within the marriage undermined the position of women within marriage.[8] Research by Margot Finn suggests that Erikson's rather pessimistic prognostications were not necessarily justified. Finn argues that the difficulties inherent in a system which excluded so many of the adult population in a time of rapid economic expansion meant that the law of coverture was often ignored in practice. Married women were able to exploit the law of necessaries, which allowed them to make contracts pledging their husbands' credit to purchase 'necessary' household goods, in order to trade, do business and even as a means to secure independence when locked into a failed marriage. In the rapidly expanding commercial world the urban court of requests became an essential institution for settling small debts: amongst the most frequent litigants were women, using the courts to contest debts, even if the husband was ultimately liable.[9] In Whitehaven Christine Churches has found that customary law allowed women not only to hold and bequeath property but to exert a tangible influence upon the economic development of the town.[10] It is becoming increasingly apparent that the trend towards economic withdrawal and marginal-

---

[6] The nineteenth century is better served in this respect than the eighteenth, see for example Kidd, A. and Nicholls D. (eds) (1999), *Gender, Civic Culture and Consumerism: Middle Class Identity in Britain 1800-1940*, Manchester.

[7] Staves, S. (1990), *Married Women's Separate Property in England, 1660-1833*, Cambridge Mass., Staves, S. (1998), 'Investments, Votes and "Bribes": Women as Shareholders in the Chartered National Companies', in H.L. Smith (ed.), *Women Writers and the Early Modern British Political Tradition*, Cambridge, pp. 259-78.

[8] Erickson, A.L. (1993), *Women and Property in Early Modern England*, London, pp. 231-2.

[9] Finn, M. (1996), 'Women, Consumption and Coverture in England', *Historical Journal*, 39, pp. 703-22.

[10] Churches, C. (1998), 'Women and Property in Early Modern England: a Case Study', *Social History*, 23, pp. 165-80.

isation, which Erikson's conclusion indicates and which forms a basic premise of the argument put forward by Davidoff and Hall, needs to be modified, if not substantially revised.[11]

If legal restrictions were becoming more prohibitive in some areas, in others the eighteenth century represented unique opportunities in that the restrictive regulations of guilds and companies had been greatly weakened (enabling women to participate in framework knitting and tailoring, for example), whilst the advent of more rigorously gendered notions of what constituted suitable employment for women had yet to be fully developed in a number of areas, whether in the professions or in manufactures, commerce or industry. Evidence of female solicitors in early eighteenth-century London has recently been uncovered, for example, challenging the common assumption that the legal professions were invariably barred to women and raising the question at what stage the professions were definitively closed off to women. Similarly, Penelope Lane has demonstrated the active involvement of women in the economies of Leicestershire towns and their environs. She illustrates how women aided by industrial development broadened their range of wealth creating and income generating activities which included the letting of knitting frames, money lending, owning real estate and running businesses.[12] A recent study of women and work in eighteenth-century Edinburgh has highlighted the wide range of occupations in which women across the social strata were engaged and has emphasised their capacity for independent action. Edinburgh women were more likely to retain the use of their maiden name even after marriage than their English counterparts, and the official records are more informative as to their occupations. There was clearly a culture in Edinburgh which was more accepting of female employment, particularly amongst the married middling sort, than in many English towns, but it would appear improbable that such local customs represented a radical divergence from those south of the border: it certainly does not appear to have been a matter upon which contemporary visitors saw fit to comment.[13] Thus the emerging consensus tends to corroborate the view of Ellis that the urban world offered opportunities in the interstices of society, which women could exploit and develop to their own advantage.[14]

---

11 See also Berg, M. (1993), 'Women's Property and the Industrial Revolution', *Journal of Interdisciplinary History*, 24, pp. 233-50; Lane, P. (2000), 'Women, Property and Inheritance: Wealth Creation and Income Generation in Small English Towns, 1750-1835' in J. Stobart and A. Owens (eds), *Urban Fortunes: Property and Inheritance in the Town, 1700-1900*, Aldershot, pp. 172-194.

12 Prest, W. (1994), 'One Hawkins, a Female Solicitor: Women Lawyers in Augustan England', *Huntington Library Quarterly*, 57, pp. 353-8; Lane, 'Women, Property and Inheritance'; Shoemaker, R.B (1998), *Gender in English Society: The Emergence of Separate Spheres?*, Harlow.

13 Sanderson, E.C. (1996), *Women and Work in Eighteenth-Century Edinburgh*, London. Comparable studies have yet to be undertaken for other Scottish towns.

14 Ellis, J. (1995), '"On the Town": Women in Augustan England, 1688-1820', *History Today*, 45, pp. 20-27. A synthesis and overview of recent literature is provided in Shoemaker, *Gender in English Society*.

The relative shortage of material dealing specifically with women in urban society is explicable partly by the opacity and paucity of the records, but is somewhat surprising given the readily acknowledged preponderance of women in eighteenth-century towns. It has become something of a truism that the only town not to show a majority of female inhabitants in the 1801 census was Oxford, with its high number of unmarried college fellows and single undergraduates. Tellingly, the most extended consideration given to the experience of women and issues of gender in the recent *Cambridge Urban History* comes in Pamela Sharpe's analysis of migration patterns in her chapter on population and society, where, almost by subterfuge, the issue of gender is introduced.[15] Sharpe explores some of the factors behind this striking demographic imbalance. There were clearly push factors behind the steady flow of girls and young women to the capital and provincial towns and cities: the changes in agricultural employment in many areas diminished the demand for female agricultural labour and created a ready supply of young females looking for work.[16] On the pull side, urban employers favoured these country girls, who were reputedly stronger and better workers than their town bred sisters. The seemingly insatiable demand for domestic servants amongst the newly affluent urban middling sort ensured that, in the capital at least, wages for domestic labour were considerably higher than what these migrants could hope to earn elsewhere and offered higher levels of security.[17] As Sharpe suggests, domestic service 'was the way in which most females moved to urban areas and increased their chances of "making shift"'.[18] Domestic service allowed women relative economic independence and enabled them to exercise a higher degree of autonomy over their own lives than in rural society. Dale Kent's analysis of domestic service

---

15 Sharpe, P. (2000), 'Population and Society', in P. Clark (ed.), *The Cambridge Urban History of Britain. Volume II 1500-1840*, Cambridge, pp. 491-500.

16 Ankarloo, B. (1979), 'Agriculture and Women's Work: Directions of Change in the West 1700-1900', *Journal of Family History*, 4, pp. 111-20; Sharpe, P. (2000), *Adapting to Capitalism: Working Women in the English Economy, 1700-1850*, 2nd edn, Basingstoke; Kussmaul, A. (1981), *Servants in Husbandry in Early Modern England*, Cambridge; Snell, K.D.M. (1985), *Annals of the Labouring Poor: Social Change and Agrarian England 1660-1900*, Cambridge, pp. 270-319; on the impact of enclosure, Humphries, J. (1990), 'Enclosures, Common Rights and Women: the Proletarianisation of Families in the Late Eighteenth and Early Nineteenth Centuries', *Journal of Economic History*, 1, pp. 17-42; Neeson, J. (1993), *Commoners: Common Right, Enclosure and Social Change in England, 1700-1820*, Cambridge, pp. 176-7, 183-4, 198, 200-21, 329.

17 Meldrum, T. (2000), *Domestic Service and Gender 1660-1750: Life and Work in the London Household*, Harlow; Earle, P. (1989), 'The Female Labour Market in London in the Late Seventeenth and Early Eighteenth Centuries', *Economic History Review*, 2nd series, 42: 3, pp. 328-53; Earle, P. (1994), *A City Full of People: Men and Women of London, 1650-1750*, , chs. 3 and 4, London (1994); Hill, B. (1996), *Servants: English Domestics in the Eighteenth Century*, Oxford; Hecht, J.J. (1956), *The Domestic Servant Class in Eighteenth-Century England*, London; Kent, D.A. (1989), 'Ubiquitous But Invisible: Female Domestic Servants in Mid-Eighteenth Century London', *History Workshop Journal*, 28, pp. 111-28; Schwarz, L. (1999), 'English Servants and their Employers During the Eighteenth and Nineteenth Centuries', *Economic History Review*, 2nd series, 52, pp. 236-56.

18 Sharpe, *Adapting to Capitalism*, pp. 28-9.

in London suggests that the average age of marriage amongst servants was considerably higher and that there was a higher proportion of single, older women who had, one may suppose, exercised their independence in preferring a life of service to a married life.[19] Similarly, the industrialisation of the textile trades towards the end of the eighteenth century created demands for female labour in those sectors and often offered higher wages, encouraging female migration over longer distances and to larger towns.[20] If employment was not to be found, towns represented a stronger likelihood of gaining poor relief or charity (as Pinches' essay in this volume illuminates in the case of Birmingham) than did many rural areas.

Such studies which do focus upon the lived experience of urban women are almost all based upon metropolitan evidence. Two of the most recent publications in this area are Tony Henderson's study of prostitution in London and Tim Meldrum's account of domestic service.[21] Meldrum's exhaustive analysis has confirmed that it was heavily gendered and represented a crucial means of induction for adolescent girls to urban life. What became of all these domestic servants after leaving service is less clear (the victualling trade and lodging houses were clearly one avenue), but the temptation to make the connection with prostitution is not substantiated by Henderson's research.[22] However, Henderson's findings have done much to refine the historical image of prostitution as managed by pimps. He reveals instead a world where single women worked the streets and exercised considerable independence and control over their livelihoods. How far these findings can be paralleled in the towns of provincial England is extremely difficult to asses; the literature on prostitution and domestic service in towns outside London would appear to be thin or non-existent.[23]

An encouraging development in urban historiography is to be found in *Londinopolis*, edited by Mark Jenner and Paul Griffiths. In this collection of essays on the history of early modern London, the editors assert the importance of moving away from metanarratives of urban growth and positivist accounts of economic expansion, which privilege the male experience over the female. Their history of London is presented as a composite of overlapping narratives which reflect the fragmented and partial reality of urban life for those who inhabited London during the roughly 200-year period which the volume covers. Two of the

---

[19] Kent, 'Ubiquitous But Invisible', pp.115-17.

[20] On the problems of conceptualising migration see Feldman, D. (2000), 'Migration', in M. Daunton (ed.), *The Cambridge Urban History of Britain. Vol. III. 1840-1950*, Cambridge, pp. 185-97.

[21] Meldrum, *Domestic Service and Gender*.

[22] Sharpe, 'Population and Society', p. 497, comments that London migrant women appear to have been absorbed into the city, whereas in Scottish and continental towns there was a pattern of returning home to marry after a spell of working in the city. There is little evidence to indicate whether this was the case in other provincial English towns.

[23] Sharpe, *Adapting to Capitalism*, gives a brief discussion of prostitution in Colchester and its vicinity from the evidence of Vagrancy Acts, pp. 131-3. Despite the major importance of Leah Leneman's work on sexuality and social control in eighteenth-century Scotland, none of it deals with prostitution or sexuality in a specifically urban context.

essays in this volume deal directly with the experience of women: Margaret Hunt finds convincing evidence that 'city women were more independent and less likely passively to accept the blandishments of tradition than their rural counterparts'.[24] She draws on the records of the Court of Exchequer to show how London women and their families were able to redress a sense of being 'wronged' by their husbands and constructed a notion of 'rights' within marriage. Laura Gowing's perceptive essay on the 'freedom of the streets' alerts us to how the meaning of urban spaces was both gendered and mutable; how constructions of gender were inflected by the urban place.[25] Gowing's essay covers the period 1560-1640 and it would be stretching the boundaries of the long eighteenth century too far to incorporate it for our own eighteenth-century purposes. However, her argument that 'The rhetoric of enclosure and the identification of female mobility with sexual and economic disorder shaped female identities and women's use of space' is no less true of the eighteenth than the seventeenth century. Gowing's material on the treatment of female street traders around the area of Covent Garden parallels the findings of, for example, Wendy Thwaites on women traders in Oxford, whose use of space was similarly subject to gendered notions of propriety.[26]

The London-centric approach is a problem which afflicts almost any area of eighteenth-century cultural and social history. The gargantuan size of the metropolis exerts an enormous influence over the historiography; and it was, of course, productive of far more records for the modern historian than was any other place. But even at the peak of its eighteenth-century influence, London accounted for no more than 10 per cent of the population of England. There is a need for studies which examine the experience of women in a variety of different towns: the character of urban society, as contemporary commentators were acutely aware, varied markedly from place to place; not least in the freedom of action allowed to women, whether it be traditions of local customary law which allowed married women to dispose of property or trade independently of their husbands, or the local custom of allowing ladies the management of the assembly.[27] Different economic

---

[24] Hunt, M.R. (2000), 'Wives and Marital "Rights" in the Court of Exchequer in the Early Eighteenth Century', in P. Griffiths, and M.S.R. Jenner (eds), *Londinopolis. Essays in the Cultural and Social History of Early Modern London*, Manchester, p. 107; as further evidence for this 'independence', she cites Shoemaker, R. (1991), *Prosecution and Punishment: Petty Crime and the Law in London and Rural Middlesex c. 1660-1725* (Cambridge: Cambridge University Press, 1991), pp. 207-16 and Gowing, L. (1996), *Domestic Dangers: Women, Words and Sex in Early Modern London*, Oxford.

[25] Gowing, L. (2000), '"The Freedom of the Streets": Women and Social Space, 1560-1640', in P. Griffiths, and M.S.R. Jenner (eds), *Londinopolis. Essays in the Cultural and Social History of Early Modern London*, Manchester, pp. 130-53.

[26] Gowing, '"Freedom of the Streets"', p. 145; Thwaites, W. (1984), 'Women in the Market Place: Oxfordshire, c. 1690-1800', *Midland History*, 17, p. 26.

[27] Churches, 'Women and Property in Early Modern England' shows how customary law in Whitehaven allowed women to exercise a degree of financial and economic autonomy which was theoretically impossible under common law; in a number of towns, such as Colchester, 'borough custom' allowed a married woman the trading privileges of femme sole. Sanderson, *Women and Work*, highlights the factors peculiar to Edinburgh which facilitated women's involvement in trade.

structures and patterns of employment determined patterns of migration with obvious consequences for social structure and gendered identities: Birmingham and Sheffield, as Berg points out, had similar industries, but very different social structures and correspondingly different patterns of employment and structures of property holding for women.[28] Merthyr Tydfil, with its miners and beer shops held far fewer attractions for women, who would have inhabited a very different place in the urban community to the female domestic servants, who were such a numerous presence in Bath, or the lace workers of Honiton, who commanded some of the highest wages amongst female workers in the country.[29]

No-one has ever denied that some women were involved in the urban economy; there has always been plenty of evidence, from Defoe's recommendations in the *Complete English Tradesman* to the less eloquent testimony of trade directories and newspaper advertisements. However, the obstacles which stand in the way of recovering their activities are considerable; middling women seldom kept diaries or correspondence and unlike men their names were subject to change and were recorded in the documents with far less frequency. In general there has been relatively little effort to bring such disparate sources as there are together and to assess the full extent of female participation in business. For the most part, women's engagement in the eighteenth-century economy has followed in the path forged by Ivy Pinchbeck, and has been considered from the perspective of industrialisation and the impact of factory modes of employment upon women's lives and the construction of gendered identities.[30] Although it is now nearly ten years since Maxine Berg asked the question, 'What difference did women's work make to the Industrial Revolution?' attempts to follow up the implications of her suggestions in the urban context, in terms of the female contribution to manufactures, commerce and trade, have been slower to emerge.[31] We know rather more about the economic lives of the urban poor and labouring sort in industrialising towns than we do about the lives of women in towns with more diverse economies. It was not an area which Davidoff and Hall, for instance, pursued in any detail: in *Family Fortunes* there is only a mention, for example, of the fact that in Birmingham women had been involved in many aspects of the button and related industries, but such participation had effectively disappeared by the nineteenth century, a victim of the middle class quest for respectability.[32] However, their point that although the trade directories of Birmingham published

---

[28] Berg, 'Women's Property and the Industrial Revolution'.

[29] Sharpe, 'Population and Society'.

[30] Pinchbeck, I. (1930), *Women Workers and the Industrial Revolution, 1750-1850*, London; Honeyman, K. (2000), *Women, Gender and Industrialisation in England, 1700-1870*, Basingstoke; Sharpe, *Adapting to Capitalism*; Rendall, J. (1990), *Women in an Industrialising Society: England 1750-1880*, Oxford.

[31] Berg, M. (1993), 'What Difference Did Women's Work Make to the Industrial Revolution?', *History Workshop Journal*, 35, pp. 233-50. Shoemaker, *Gender in English Society*, offers a succinct summary of the variety of female employments to be found in eighteenth-century towns, pp. 160-67, 171-75.

[32] Davidoff, L. and Hall, C. (1987), *Family Fortunes: Men and Women of the English Middle Class, 1780-1850*, London, p. 304.

between 1800 and 1830 make no mention of women merchants, whereas the evidence of wills from the same period makes it quite clear that a number of merchants left their widows in charge of the business, is full of implications.[33]

In keeping with the findings of Davidoff and Hall, Wendy Thwaites has shown that fewer women were involved in the market place, particularly the corn trade, by the end of the century and argues that changes in the legal regulation of trade, and a shift away from the open market to the seclusion of a room in the inn where samples were exchanged, operated against the interests of women traders: 'The changes which the 18th century brought were therefore combining effectively to destroy many of the traditional roles women had been able to adopt.'[34] Thwaites' material is drawn largely from the grain trade which characteristically demanded large amounts of capital which were unlikely to have been available to women; other businesses and occupations, however, do not appear to have been equally inflexible for female entrepreneurs. Margaret Hunt working on London and Shani D'Cruze on Colchester have both shown that throughout the eighteenth century women were dominant in the millinery trades and running their businesses independently of men, taking on apprentices, making out bills and filling a highly respectable role in society.[35] Hannah Barker with Karen Harvey and Christine Wiskin all show convincing evidence of a substantial minority of female businesswomen continuing and expanding their trade in a range of other occupations throughout the eighteenth and into the nineteenth century.

The participation of women in urban business defies easy generalisation; nowhere did they participate on equal terms with men, but the degree to which they were excluded varied enormously as did the chronology of change, and there is a clear need for empirical studies based on particular towns. The two essays in this volume, both based upon non-metropolitan sources, dealing directly with middling women's involvement in trade and the urban economy, represent an important development therefore in redressing this imbalance. Future research, it is hoped, will continue to build on this trend: attention to the locally specific circumstances, rather than the retreat into generalisation, has the advantage of throwing the contribution of women into sharper perspective. The decline of regulated trades coupled with the new opportunities which opened up in retailing and victualling allowed enterprising women such as Elizabeth Raffald 'seemingly unhindered by gender' to build up a small business empire satisfying the demands of the urban

---

[33] The evidence of trade directories can never be taken as a fully comprehensive picture of the economic structure of a town, and is particularly unreliable for locating the presence of female traders.

[34] Thwaites, W., 'Women in the Market Place', p. 26.

[35] Contemporaries recognised that the millinery trades offered one of the few options for women to support themselves. See, for example, Campbell, R. (1747), *The London Tradesman*, London and Collyer, J. (1761), *Parents & Guardians Directory and the Youth's Guide in the Choice of a Profession or Trade*, London. See also D'Cruze, S. (1986), '"To Acquaint the Ladies": Women Traders in Colchester c. 1750-1850', *Local Historian*, 17:3, pp. 158-61. Millinery appears to have been the single most important trade for women in all eighteenth-century towns.

masses.[36] As Sara Pennell has recently argued, extra domestic provisioning was a fact of life in London, with its high population of inhabitants in lodgings, domestic servants on free days, and other 'floating' elements. The same would have been true, albeit to a lesser extent, of any of the major provincial towns of the eighteenth century. A life of family domesticity would never have been the norm for thousands of urban men and women, and eating became a socio-economic and organisational phenomenon, contracted out to victuallers and innkeepers, many of whom, whether in London, or as Barker, Harvey and Wiskin show, in the provinces, were women.[37] Cumulatively these studies demonstrate that women were a significant presence in the eighteenth-century urban economy, if less numerous than their male counterparts, and were well able to take advantage of the rapid expansion in consumer trades which were so marked a feature of urban life.[38] More work needs to be done, however, to establish the patterns of local variation and the chronology of change towards the more rigid differentiation of spheres to be found in Davidoff and Hall; or to establish whether that model should be comprehensively revised for the nineteenth as well as the eighteenth centuries.[39]

It has recently been argued that the key to industrial growth in urban society lay not so much in the accumulation of fixed capital or the development of industrial plant, but in the creation of knowledge and social capital. The unique advantage of urban society lay in the density of networks of kinship or neighbourhood; the rapid transmission of news, the ability to mobilise resources and to command credit through personal reputation, or to bring together a large work force.[40] This shift towards a less tangible and quantifiable perspective than that of capital formation is one which is sympathetic to acknowledging a greater role for women, as Christine Wiskin suggests, in her analysis of the contribution of women to business. It should also be acknowledged that many of the spaces in which knowledge or social capital were created, such as taverns, inns or coffee houses, were presided over or managed by women, such as Elizabeth Raffald of Manchester.[41] Moreover, in the informal networks of gossip, neighbourhood and market place women were not excluded as they had been from the formal institutions of guild, committee or corporation. This approach can be fruitfully applied to other dimensions of urban life: women were marginal to the 'public' world of urban politics and governance, but that did not preclude them from gaining an informed appreciation of patterns of

---

[36] See the chapter by Barker and Harvey in this volume.

[37] Pennell, S. (2000), '"Great Quantities of Gooseberry Pye and Baked Clod of Beef": Victualling and Eating Out in Early Modern London', in P. Griffiths and M.S.R. Jenner (eds), *Londinopolis: Essays in the Cultural and Social History of Early Modern London*, Manchester, p. 228.

[38] This corroborates Hunt's findings for the metropolis in the earlier part of the century, see *The Middling Sort*.

[39] For a critique of the separate spheres argument see Vickery, A.J. (1993), 'From Golden Age to Separate Spheres: a Review of the Categories and Chronology of English Women's History', *Historical Journal*, 36, pp. 383-414; see also Shoemaker, *Gender in English Society*, pp. 305-18.

[40] Reeder, D. and Rodger, R. (2000), 'Industrialisation and the City Economy' in, M. Daunton (ed.), *Cambridge Urban History. Vol. III. 1840-1950*, Cambridge, pp. 553-61.

[41] Barker and Harvey in this volume.

power and patronage which formed the hidden threads holding together the formal and masculine institutions of urban government and politics as the essays in this volume collectively demonstrate.

Politics has never stopped at the door of the town hall, any more than at the door to the House of Commons, and as a range of recent studies of eighteenth-century political culture continues to demonstrate, our understanding and definition of what constitutes politics and political behaviour has to be broadened to encompass the popular politics of the crowd, the canvass and the petition.[42] The elite women, such as Lady Susan Keck or Judith Baker and their ilk, were well informed on politics at both the national and the local level and used their patronage and influence within urban society to political effect.[43] Middling women were not allowed more than the most indirect participation in civic culture, but that should not stop us from asking what opportunities they had for influencing the course of urban politics and to what extent it was possible for them to share in the urban political culture. The involvement of women in chapel politics, for example, was essentially silent and subordinate, but has been characterised as a 'potent weapon' which took the form of non-attendance, gossip and the choice of whom to call upon.[44] The informal politics of gossip, social calls and networks would not have been confined to membership of nonconformist congregations, but would have applied equally to the Anglican parish, and in matters civil as well as ecclesiastical. This is a point which has been implicitly acknowledged by Patricia Crawford, commenting upon the problematic impact that membership of a dissenting body would have had upon women in early eighteenth-century society: they would have been debarred from membership of the social elite in most places and would have been excluded from the social networks of kinship and gossip, which would have left them at a disadvantage in day to day business and in household crises.[45] The positive implications which membership of the community of the parish would have held for women who *did* belong are seldom explicitly articulated. In this volume the ability of women to exploit these networks of knowledge is examined from a different perspective by Elaine Chalus's analysis of the Oxford Rag Plot of 1754. Possession of a parliamentary franchise, it has long been recognised, is not a necessary precondition for politicisation or political activity during this period, and the actions of Mrs Mary Carnell, the doughty protagonist of the Rag Plot, demonstrate how women such as she were not lacking in political knowledge, and that their networks of gossip and personal contact formed an important channel of political communication within an urban political

---

42 Dickinson, H.T. (1995), *The Politics of the People in Eighteenth-Century Britain*, Basingstoke, especially chapters 3 and 4; Innes, J. and Roger, N. (2000), 'Politics and Government 1700-1840', in P. Clark (ed.) *The Cambridge Urban History of Britain. Volume II 1500-1840*, pp. 555-65; on women's involvement see Bohstedt, J. (1988), 'Gender, Household and Community Politics: Women in English Riots, 1790-1810', *Past and Present*, 120, pp. 88-122.

43 See chapters by Berry and Chalus in this volume.

44 *Family Fortunes*, p. 136.

45 Crawford, P. (1993), *Women and Religion in England 1500-1720*, London, p. 191. See Hunt, *The Middling Sort*, for the importance of such networks for urban women.

culture which was still only partially literate, where printed word and word of mouth played complementary roles.

It is well established that female literacy rates were higher in urban than rural areas (the outcome of the Rag Plot would have been considerably different were this not the case) and the growth in the provision of female schooling has been well charted, notably by Susan Skedd.[46] The ability to read, write and cast accompts represented an important means by which women were able to contribute to the family economy, through keeping accounts or through earning additional income by school teaching.[47] Elizabeth Raffald represents a particularly impressive case of a woman who exploited the growth of urban literacy in her publication of the first Manchester trade directories. Literacy also lay at the heart of many of the occupations and activities which occupied the more leisured women of urban society and, as Denise Fowler shows, their possession of literate skills not only shaped their leisure hours, but enabled women to assume a role as educators in urban society and to make a positive contribution to the religious life of the town.

The women of the Warwickshire towns studied by Fowler, who compiled the scrapbooks of urban life, read the library books and wrote the novels, were living seventy years or more later than Mary Chandler, the poetess of Bath, whose topographical poems written in the 1730s are the subject of David Shuttleton's chapter. Chandler, who was eminently successful as a milliner and the proprietor of a lodging house, suffered from physical deformities and never married; she occupied, therefore, a somewhat anomalous position in Bath, a society which was geared to securing a husband. Her poetry reveals a woman who was actively engaged with the urban environment and acutely aware of the social changes which were consequent upon the rapidly evolving economy of the resort. Her 'pastoral' poems, which dwell on the pleasures of a rural retreat, defy the conventional equation between feminine pleasure and urban society, and modify the (masculine) conventions of the pastoral tradition in a distinctive manner. Chandler's rural ideal is presented as a productive investment and an escape from the pressures of shopkeeping, rather than the traditional corruption of the court, giving a distinctively bourgeois and pragmatic twist to the poetic conventions of the day. Despite the obvious disparities in the media which these women employed, and the very different language with which they expressed themselves, the writers who are the focus of both these essays illustrate a range of ways in which women used their literary skills to articulate their relationship to the urban community in which they lived, to demonstrate their sense of proprietorship in the town, and in turn to shape and influence that same urban society.

The impact of urban consumption and consumerism upon society's values has been largely examined through male writers and Shuttleton's analysis of Mary

---

[46] Skedd, S. (1997), 'Women Teachers and the Expansion of Girls' Schooling in England, c. 1760-1820', in H. Barker and E. Chalus, *Gender in Eighteenth-Century England: Roles, Representations and Responsibilities*, London, pp. 101-25; Reeves, M. (1997), *Pursuing the Muses: Female Education and Non-conformist Culture 1700-1900*, London; Watts, R. (1998), *Gender, Power and the Unitarians in England, 1760-1860*, Harlow, pp. 13-32.

[47] Hunt, *The Middling Sort*, pp. 87-9.

Chandler is also a welcome step towards an appreciation of the female response to the growth of consumer society and luxury. The on-going interest in the act of consumption has, of course, directed considerable attention to women's roles as consumers, although not invariably in a specifically urban context. Amanda Vickery's study of Lancashire gentlewomen opened up lines of inquiry which others have not been slow to follow.[48] Helen Berry's analysis of Judith Baker's shopping habits begins to answer some of the questions left unanswered by Vickery and produces evidence which directly contradicts the caricature of the female urban shopper as the extravagant victim of luxury and commercial manipulation.[49] Judith Baker exercised 'prudent luxury'; she demonstrated a highly rational approach to expenditure and financial management (book keeping skills were not confined to women of the middling sort) and showed a shrewd ability to exact the most from the tradesmen with which she dealt and to secure additional terms of credit. Berry shows that shopping was far more than an exercise in household management or even personal gratification, but could be used to cement social ties and loyalties and to create personal networks within an otherwise unfamiliar urban environment.[50]

Even though Baker was not a permanent resident of Durham, participation in the urban milieu of both Durham and London consumed a significant element of her attention in her daily responsibilities of managing her household, as well as being a source of sociability and entertainment. In Durham she was closely involved in the political life of the town and conducted much of her day-to-day business there; her close attention to tradesmen's bills and careful patronage complemented an astute political sense. Her control of the household budget would have opened up opportunities for indirect political management of the Durham tradesmen, of the kind which Elaine Chalus has described so convincingly in the actions of other aristocratic women.[51] Baker clearly took a close interest in the course of Durham politics; an interest which is recorded in her scrap book of political ephemera and her chronological account of the major political events in

---

[48] Vickery, A.J. (1998), *The Gentleman's Daughter*, Yale and New Haven.

[49] Walton, J. (2000), 'Towns and Consumerism', in M. Daunton, (ed.), *The Cambridge Urban History of Britain. Vol. III, 1840-1950*, Cambridge, p. 739 where Walton challenges the crude bipolarity with which has generally informed consideration of female consumer behaviour.

[50] See the chapter by Berry in this volume and her 'Consuming Passions: Shopping and Politeness', in *Transactions of the Royal Historical Society* (forthcoming 2002).

[51] Chalus, E. (1997), '"That Epidemical Madness": Women and Electoral Politics in the Late Eighteenth Century', in H. Barker and E. Chalus (eds), *Gender in Eighteenth Century England: Roles, Representations and Responsibilities*, London; Chalus, E. (1998), '"My Minerva at my Elbow": The Political Roles of Women in Eighteenth-Century England', in R. Connors, C. Jones and S. Taylor (eds), *Hanoverian Britain and Empire: Essays in Memory of Philip Lawson*, Cambridge; Chalus, E. (2000), 'Women Electoral Privilege and Practice in the Eighteenth Century', in K. Gleadle and S. Richardson (eds), *Women in British Politics, 1760-1860: The Power of the Petticoat*, Basingstoke; Chalus, E. (2000), 'Elite Women, Social Politics, and the Political World of Late Eighteenth-Century Britain', *Historical Journal*, 43, pp. 669-98; see also Richardson, S. (2000), '"Well-Neighboured Houses": The Political Networks of Elite Women 1780-1860' in, K. Gleadle and S. Richardson (eds), *The Power of the Petticoat*, Basingstoke, pp. 56-73.

Durham over a thirty year period. She never went to the extremes of active intervention of Lady Susan Keck, who, whether or not she was behind the Rag Plot of 1754, was the most formidable figure amongst the Oxfordshire New Interest. Lady Susan and Judith Baker were essentially outsiders, but they had considerable power to shape the course of urban politics, and their political agency, although less willingly recognised than that of men, is far easier to detect than that of the middling women, tradeswomen, and those on the margins of society. However, the importance attached to courting the ladies of the corporation by the politicians and their wives, such as Lady Susan, Judith Baker, or Mrs Montagu was a readily acknowledged feature of urban life; numerous election squibs directed at the women of the town testify to the fact that they were expected to use their influence over their husbands. In a political system which was widely accepted to be grounded upon influence, patronage and personal connection, and where the majority was not actively enfranchised, women of all ranks had a significant role to play.[52]

'I am actually an inhabitant of Newcastle, and am taking out my freedom, not out of a gold box, but by entering into all the diversions of the place.' So wrote Elizabeth Montagu to her aunt; given her otherwise anything but enthusiastic comments on Newcastle and provincial urban life, we may suppose that she was being something less than ingenuous in making this comment.[53] However, by 'entering into the diversions' that is participating in the social life of the Newcastle inhabitants, frequenting their race meetings, assemblies, musical occasions and taking tea with the dreaded aldermanesses, she felt that she had some kind of proprietorship in Newcastle which was the equivalent to if, not better than that bestowed by the gift of the freedom of the city in a gold box.[54] This brings us to the problem of urban identity and citizenship: although it is apparent that women had been able to take up freedom in certain towns, it is equally clear that such women had never, even in the supposed medieval golden age of equal opportunities, been anything more than a small minority.[55] Although fleeting

---

[52] Skinner, G. (2000), 'Women's Status as Legal and Civic Subjects', in V. Jones (ed.), *Women and Literature in Britain 1700-1800*, Cambridge, pp. 91-110 argues that women were unequivocally excluded from citizenship in the eighteenth century. Her argument takes citizenship as a concept in political theory, rather than considering it as a lived experience in the urban context.

[53] Climenson, E.J. (ed.) (1906), *Elizabeth Montagu: The Queen of the Bluestockings. Her correspondence from 1720-61*, 2 vols, London, ii, p. 205.

[54] On the participation of women in the social and cultural life of towns see Borsay, *The English Urban Renaissance*; Brewer, J. (1997), *The Pleasures of the Imagination: English Culture in the Eighteenth Century*, London, pp. 56-122; Ellis, 'On the Town'; Girouard, M. (1990), *The English Town. A History of Urban Life*, New Haven and London, pp. 127-44; Langford, P. (1989), *A Polite and Commercial People: England 1727-83*, Oxford, pp. 99-121; Shoemaker, *Gender in English Society*, pp. 276-82; Vickery, *The Gentleman's Daughter*, pp. 225-84.

[55] Roberts, M. (1990), 'Women and Work in Sixteenth-Century English Towns', in P.J. Corfield and D. Keene (eds), *Work in Towns 850-1850*, London, pp. 87-103. Two rather older works are still of value here: Carmichael Stopes, C. (1894), *British Freewomen: Their Historical Privilege*, London; Graham, R. (1929), 'The Civic Position of Women at

glimpses have been found of female participation in parliamentary or civic elections, women never took on civic office themselves, and were never more than an auxiliary presence in the occasions of civic ritual and ceremony.[56]

To what extent, therefore, did women share a sense of citizenship; how was it formed, and through what means was it given expression? Rosemary Sweet examines the role of women amongst the civic elite, where their visibility is in most records only marginal. Civic office was not something which could be inherited and continued by a widow, as was so often the case in trade and business, although fragmentary evidence does suggest that it was not unknown for women to act in a civic capacity on behalf of a husband or brother in case of emergency. Women are most visible in the kinds of situation to which Mrs Montagu was referring, at occasions of polite sociability and recreation. In many towns there was a formal role for them to play here, such that a mayor who had no wife to fulfil that office would have to persuade some female relative to take it on. It is easy to dismiss the role of lady mayoress or aldermaness as peripheral and incidental to the distribution of power and influence within urban society; but that is to conclude that the only structures of power were masculine ones. For urban women the social recognition which went with being the mayoress, the respect which was paid to her (particularly by politically astute gentry and aristocracy) would have enhanced her standing and reputation amongst the other women of the town.[57] Moreover, the legal requirements for freeman status were becoming increasingly redundant in most English town during the eighteenth century, and many of the most flourishing urban centres, had never been chartered. The formal lines of exclusion which could be drawn between male and female citizenship in an incorporated town had no equivalent in these unincorporated centres. Citizenship and urban identity therefore depended on factors other than the possession of freemen's rights and privileges, powerful though these might be. Citizenship was generally taken to be masculine, but could be employed in an inclusive sense which comprehended the female inhabitants of a town and the possibility of exploiting the ambiguity in words such as citizen or householder was always present.[58] Hence occasional instances arose when women were appointed to

---

Common Law Before 1800', in R. Graham (ed.), *English Ecclesiastical Studies: Being Some Essays in Research in Medieval History*, London, pp. 360-77.

[56] These issues are discussed at greater length in the chapter by Sweet.

[57] A similar point has been made by Gail Malmgreen, who refers to an 'emerging parallel hierarchy of women' amongst the wives of Methodist ministers, 'wherein fine gradations of social status, with appropriate niceties of dress and manner, counted for much.' Malmgreen, G. (1986), 'Religion and Family Life', in G. Malmgreen (ed.), *Religion in the Lives of English Women 1760-1930*, London, p. 66.

[58] Hilda Smith has characterised the problems arising from this type of vaguely inclusive language as the 'false universal'. See Smith, H.L., 'Women as Sextons and Electors: King's Bench and Precedents for Women's Citizenship', in H.L. Smith (ed.), *Women Writers and the Early Modern British Political Tradition*, Cambridge, p. 330. A number of these issues have been explored in the context of the early modern German town, see Roper, L. (1987), '"The Common Man", "the Common Good", "Common Women": Gender and Meaning in the German Reformation Commune', *Social History*, 12, pp.1-21.

positions within the parish such as overseer or churchwarden.[59] In cases of acute pressure, the gender distinctions which excluded women from political participation could be modified or laid aside; political crisis could create a situation in which women's participation became desirable, and the lack of precision which still existed at law on points such as the right of women to vote in parish matters, could be exploited.[60]

However, it remains the case that this is somewhat insubstantial evidence from which to argue for a positive sense of belonging or citizenship on the part of urban women. More practical evidence of identification with a particular town or urban community can be traced in the charitable gifts and benefactions with which so many towns were endowed. Although married women rarely enjoyed the financial freedom with which to dispose of large sums of money, they were able to exercise discretion in their smaller donations. Sylvia Pinches' essay examines the patterns of female charity in Birmingham, an unincorporated town, with comparatively weak traditions of charitable giving. Nevertheless, there were a number of charities which were specifically directed at the inhabitants of the town, to which the women of Birmingham directed their generosity and their activities. It was not simply the growth of the auxiliary branches of national institutions such as the SPCK which attracted female sponsorship, but also ventures which were wholly local in their scope and organisation. Charity, as a number of historians have reminded us, was one of those areas in which women were acknowledged to have a role to play beyond the confines of the household or the domestic sphere.[61] However, the involvement of women in urban institutions such as the charities described by Pinches, or the numerous female charity schools and friendly societies which were being established across provincial England and Scotland in the late eighteenth and early nineteenth centuries, have yet to be examined on a comprehensive basis.[62] From the perspective of the poor, the provision of relief within a town and the sense of entitlement to relief and other forms of charity in the mixed economy of welfare to which their urban residence made them eligible,

---

Sanderson, *Women and Work*, p. 7 notes that women were only regarded as burgesses in that they had no right to trade; there is no evidence that they played any part in civic administration.

[59] Graham, 'Civic Position of Women', and Carmichael Stopes, *British Freewomen*, pp. 79-83.

[60] See also Davidoff and Hall, *Family Fortunes*, pp. 135-6. Women at the New Meeting House in Birmingham were occasionally called upon to cast their votes at the vestry meeting as a means of overcoming opposition.

[61] Prochaska, F.K. (1980), *Women and Philanthropy in Nineteenth-Century England*, Oxford; Davidoff and Hall, *Family Fortunes*.

[62] For examples of such activity in York see Gray, Mrs E. (ed.) (1927), *Papers and Diaries of a York Family*, London; and Cappe, C. (1799), *An Account of Two Charity Schools for the Education of Girls, and of a Female Friendly Society in York*, York; Cappe, C. (1805), *Observations on Charity Schools, Female Friendly Societies, and Other Subjects Connected with the Views of the Ladies Committee*, York; Cappe, C. (1817), *On the Desireableness and Utility of Ladies Visiting the Female Wards of Hospitals and Lunatic Asylums*, York; Cappe, C. (1822), *Memoirs of the Life of the Late Mrs. Catharine Cappe, Written by Herself*, London.

would have been a fundamental feature of urban living and would have constituted in itself a sense of 'belonging' to that town.

There is one area which represents a significant gap in this volume, and that is the question of religion. The essays which are presented here give a very secular view of urban life, yet religion was a crucial component in the peculiar composite of urban society, informing and influencing politics, cultural life, education, charity and philanthropy, as well as spirituality more narrowly defined.[63] It has already been hinted that dissenting women would have inhabited very different social networks from their Anglican sisters, and it is in the study of dissenting communities that the most work has been done towards the analysis of the relationship between religion and gender in the urban context. However, the volume of literature is hardly enormous, and there is even less which addresses such issues from the perspective of the Church of England.[64] There is only one published article which specifically takes women and urban religion as its focus, and valuable though it is, it is a case study of a single town, Bristol.[65] *Family Fortunes*, which has much to say about gender and religion in Birmingham and Colchester, is focused upon nineteenth-century developments, and reactions to what the authors perceive to have been happening in the eighteenth century. Such studies as there are of urban religion and the problems and opportunities which the urban environment presented to religious institutions, do not examine the particular role of women in any detail, and thus the whole topic of religion, gender and towns has been seriously under-researched. One reason for this lacuna must be the assumption that urbanisation is connected with secularisation: a view to be found in, for example, A.D. Gilbert's influential study, *Religion and Society in Industrial England*.[66] Jonathan Clark has succeeded in putting religion back into English Society, but the recent historiographical emphasis on the 'polite and commercial' characteristics of the eighteenth century has done little to challenge the easy association between urbanisation and secularisation.[67] Again, the thematic divisions in the *Cambridge Urban History* are revealing on this point: although there is a chapter devoted to religious change and the reformation town in the first

[63] I am very grateful to Jeremy Gregory whose comments have provided the basis for much of the following paragraphs.

[64] The paucity of research in this field was the reason why, despite strenuous efforts to avert such a situation, it proved impossible to include a chapter on women and religion in an urban context in this collection.

[65] Dresser, M. (1996), 'Sisters and Brethren: Power, Propriety and Gender Among the Bristol Moravians, 1746-1833', *Social History*, 21:3, pp. 304-29.

[66] Gilbert, A.D. (1976), *Religion and Society in Industrial England. Church, Chapel and Social Change 1740-1914*, London; religion is not a dominant theme in Corfield, *The Impact of English Towns*; there is a short discussion in Sweet, *The English Town*, pp. 207-18 and passing references in Ellis, *The Georgian Town*.

[67] Clark, J.C.D. (2000), *English Society 1660-1832*, revised edn, Cambridge; Brewer, *The Pleasures of the Imagination*; Porter, R. (2000), *Enlightenment: Britain and the Creation of the Modern World*, London. However, Paul Langford's eponymous, *A Polite and Commercial People* is far less secular than the title might imply.

half of the volume up to 1700, in the second half, religion is relegated to being simply another dimension to urban culture.[68]

If we are to take Ellis's basic premise that the urban environment was attractive to women because of the different and varied opportunities which it offered, in the context of religion, it must be asked whether towns provided women with different religious opportunities from the countryside. The evidence we have to answer this question is probably slightly mixed and contradictory, and in the later eighteenth century is complicated by the rapid growth of industrialising villages which blurred the distinctions between urban and rural society. Nevertheless it can be argued that urban centres, and especially the larger ones, were more likely to have a greater variety of religious denominations on offer, giving women to some extent a choice in the religious market place. There has been little attempt seriously to address the question of whether religion in the eighteenth century became feminised as it became urbanised, as would appear to be the case in American society.[69] The evidence suggests that this was the case and there are clearly important implications which need to be explored here for the construction of gender and for the cultural significance of religion in urban society. Madge Dresser has found that the membership of the Bristol Moravian Brethren shifted towards a heavy female preponderance between 1770 and 1828.[70] Gail Malmgreen's analysis of the Methodist membership lists for East Cheshire suggests that the proportion of women in the congregation in mid-eighteenth century roughly matched that in the town overall, but that in Manchester in the early nineteenth century the ratio of women was higher. More conclusively, her findings suggest that the proportion of single women was far higher than that of single men. Malmgreen concludes that participation in religious services had different and gendered meanings; for men, it was something in which they participated along with female relatives. Women showed a different motivational pattern in which their married status made little difference.[71]

Viewed frivolously, going to church allowed women another opportunity for conspicuous display, to show off their finery, or to gossip.[72] Churches and dissenting chapels represented another space where gradations of hierarchy could be established and social status asserted. In Macclesfield Mrs [Jabez] Bunting was regarded as the queen of methodist society, and behind the facade of religious

---

[68] Harding, V. (2000), 'Reformation and Culture 1540-1700', pp. 263-88; Clark, P. and Houston, R.A. (2000), 'Leisure and Culture 1700-1840', pp. 575-614, all in P. Clark (ed), *Cambridge Urban History. Vol.II. 1500-1840*, Cambridge.

[69] Sheils, R.D. (1983), 'The Feminisation of American Congregationalism, 1730-1835', *American Quarterly*, 33, pp. 46-62.

[70] Dresser, 'Sisters and Brethren', pp. 304-5. Adult female membership stood at 46 per cent in 1770 and 68.5 per cent in 1828. See also C. Field (1993), 'Adam and Eve: Gender in the English Free Church Constituency', *Journal of Ecclesiastical History*, 44, pp. 63-79. More generally similar conclusions have been reached by Mcleod, H. (1981), *Religion and the People of Western Europe, 1789-1970*, Oxford, ch. 2.

[71] Malmgreen, 'Religion and Family Life', pp. 60-61.

[72] Vickery, *The Gentleman's Daughter*, p. 253 describes how Elizabeth Shackleton's diaries passed more comment on other members of the congregation and their appearance than the content of the sermon.

propriety, fierce rivalry existed amongst the ministers' wives.[73] Membership of a church or chapel allowed women the opportunity to meet potential husbands and also presented chances of bettering themselves through the provision of Sunday Schools – a factor which would have been of much less significance for men, who generally enjoyed higher literacy rates and better access to education.[74] The emphasis which many of the dissenting congregations placed upon education for both sexes would appear to be reflected in Fowler's essay, which finds strong connections with traditions of literate activity amongst women and the Unitarians in Warwickshire towns. Mary Chandler, the poetess of Bath, was also, one should note, from a nonconformist background. It is also clear that notions of Christian duty and conscience inspired certain women to lay claim to a more proactive role, not just in the preaching ministry but in political activity, whilst simultaneously subscribing to notions of domestic womanhood, seeing their actions as an extension of their moral obligations as Christians. Elizabeth Heyrick and Susanna Watts, active in Leicester in the late eighteenth and early nineteenth centuries, both used their religion as a platform from which to comment upon a range of issues, from urban politics and political corruption to the condition of framework knitters or the abolition of the slave trade.[75]

The little we do know does suggests that women played a significant role in towns both within the Church of England and within nonconformist denominations. Some of the most interesting work concerns the role of women in the rapid growth of the nonconformist denominations in the late eighteenth and early nineteenth centuries, in the industrialising townships of the midlands and the north, where the lack of organised institutional structures created spaces in which women could take on active roles of ministry and preaching.[76] Nonconformity clearly allowed women opportunities which were not available to them within the established church, but the peculiarities of the particular urban environment have also to be taken into account. In this respect it would be desirable to have comparisons not just between dissent and the Church of England, but between religion in an industrial town such as Manchester and a polite and historical cathedral city such as Canterbury. The Church of England would not allow women to preach, but wives and daughters, such as Elizabeth Carter, offered vital assistance to husbands, fathers and brothers in the work of the parish, although few went as far as Susanna Wesley who held services in her kitchen in the absence of her husband. By the early nineteenth century clergy wives could benefit from

---

73 Malmgreen, G. (1985), *Silk Town: Industry and Culture in Macclesfield 1750-1835*, Hull, p. 168.

74 Malmgreen, *Silk Town*, pp. 62-3.

75 Corfield, K. (1986), 'Elizabeth Heyrick: Radical Quaker', in G. Malmgreen (ed.), *Religion in the Lives of English Women, 1760-1930*, London, pp. 41-67. On women's involvement in the anti-slavery campaign more generally, see Midgley, C. (1992), *Women Against Slavery:The British Campaigns, 1780-1870*, London.

76 Valenze, D. (1985), *Prophetic Sons and Daughters: Female Preaching and Popular Religion in Industrial England*, Princeton; Dews, D.C. (1986), 'Ann Carr and the Female Revivalists', in G. Malmgreen, (ed.), *Religion in the Lives of English Women, 1760-1930*, London, pp. 68-87; Malmgreen, *Silk Town*, pp. 166-8.

manuals which outlined the sphere of their duties in educating the female parishioners, visiting the sick, distributing charity and organising Sunday Schools.[77]

The involvement of women in religion — as with philanthropy — complicates the pattern of public and private spheres.[78] If going to church and participating in church life was a public activity, then the church-going activities of women in eighteenth-century towns indicate that woman were very much part of public life. After all, it could be argued that the sermon delivered from the town (and rural) pulpit and listened to by both women and men was the prime source of political information in the period. Participation in church services, particularly the rites of passage or baptism, marriage and burial, brought membership of the parish community, whether or not women were permitted to participate in vestry meetings or take on parish offices.[79]

The literature on women, gender and urban society is still patchy, but some clearer patterns are beginning to emerge. Whilst it is fair to say that women in all parts of Britain were disadvantaged by the prevailing constructions of femininity and were excluded to a greater or lesser extent from large sectors of politics, social life, business and the economy, the degree to which this exclusion was enforced shows considerable variation from place to place, and fluctuated over time. The clinical separation of public and private suggested by the terms separate spheres is hardly helpful in trying to delineate the contours of women's involvement in urban society and gives no indication of the far more complex arrangements which evolved in different urban communities in response to the locally specific economic conditions and customary traditions. The chronology of change remains frustratingly unclear; it has long since been acknowledged that women's history follows a very different pattern to that of 'traditional' economic and constitutional development, but locating points of definitive change, at which, for example, middling women withdrew from assisting in business to a life of leisure in the drawing room, is deeply problematic. The sometimes contradictory findings which further research into women's participation in urban life throws up, highlight the difficulties in treating urban society as a constant. This collection has proceeded upon the assumption that the urban experience was both gendered and qualitatively different from that of other communities; these essays illustrate and confirm that assumption, but also demonstrate the extent to which the diversity of local economies, structures and customs which existed within the urban system renders attempts to draw generalisations a hazardous undertaking.

---

77 Myers, S.H., *The Blue Stocking Circle: Women, Friendship and the Life of the Mind in Eighteenth-Century England*, Oxford, pp. 159-71; Gregory, J. (1998), 'Gender and the Clerical Profession in England, 1660-1850', *Studies in Church History*, 34, pp. 262-6.

78 Vickery, *The Gentleman's Daughter*, pp. 254-7, Andrew, D.T. (1996), '*Noblesse Oblige*: Female Charity in an Age of Sentiment', in J. Brewer and S. Staves (eds), *Early Modern Conceptions of Property*, London, pp. 275-300; Prochaska, *Women and Philanthropy*.

79 Gregory, 'Gender and the Clerical Profession', p. 257.

Chapter 2

Women and Civic Life in Eighteenth-Century England*

Rosemary Sweet

In 1766, the mayor of Norwich, John Patteson, was confronted with a city convulsed with bread rioters. Rather than delegating his mayoral authority to an alderman, he deputed his sister in law, the mayoress, to act for him, leaving her with his chain of office.[1] What she did with this delegation of authority, history does not relate, but it opens up the possibility that this might not have been an isolated incident and that it was perhaps possible for wives — or lady mayoresses — to represent their husbands in an official capacity *in extremis*. This incident may have been an isolated emergency, but it allows us to raise the question of the nature of female participation in the civic culture of eighteenth-century towns. We should not only question the extent of women's exclusion from the masculine world of civic governance and civic culture, but we should also attempt to consider the meaning of civic culture and citizenship more broadly defined for eighteenth-century women.

Women as Citizens

The 'civic' culture of a town is one which would appear to be wholly dominated by men during the eighteenth century. Whilst contemporaries and historians have confidently recognised the place of women in the burgeoning areas of sociability and consumption, women have not featured in discussions of urban governance, citizenship, civic identities and what one might term the political culture of the town.[2] This might be stating the obvious, given that the records which would be

---

* In this essay 'civic' will be used to refer to the culture or identity of incorporated towns. When discussing citizenship and urban culture in towns more generally, including those which did not have charters of incorporation, the word 'urban' will be used.

[1] Cozens Hardy, B. and Kent, E.A. (1938), *The Mayors of Norwich, 1403-1835: Being Biographical Notes on the Mayors of the Old Corporation*, Norwich, p. 130.

[2] Brewer, J. (1997), *The Pleasures of the Imagination: English Culture in the Eighteenth Century*, London; Ellis, J. (1995), '"On the Town": Women in Augustan England, 1688-1820', *History Today*, 45, pp. 20-27; Vickery, A. (1993), 'Women and the World of Goods: a Lancashire Consumer and her Possessions, 1751-81' in J. Brewer and R.

used for such a study — the minutes of the corporation in particular, but also the vestry and the improvement commission — are formulaic, factual and firmly grounded in a political culture which was entirely masculine in its formal structures. Civic identities and civic politics were almost always constructed in masculine terms; the citizen was a definitively male subject. Women were excluded by their gender from active participation in both the traditional urban corporations and the newly established improvement commissions. The language of urban politics was such that women's presence or influence could not be acknowledged.

Women did, however, represent slightly over half the urban population. They were, as recent research is making increasingly apparent, active participants in the urban economy; not just as consumers or as providing low paid, low-skilled labour, but as entrepreneurs and business women also.[3] There is no shortage of evidence to show that women belonged to guilds and craft companies and could wield influence within these organizations. It is one thing to show that women were seldom made free of a town or that they were only permitted to exercise a trade by virtue of their husband's position, and to argue thereby that women were excluded from the civic body and from citizenship except vicariously through their husband.[4] However, this is to use a very narrow definition of citizenship, based upon membership of the freeman body, and one which was of diminishing relevance in many eighteenth century towns. It also precludes the possibility that those outside the freeman body could have identified with the urban community in which they lived: an assumption which is made difficult to sustain both by the declining proportion of freemen in incorporated towns, and the rise of a significant number of towns, without corporations, but which clearly were not lacking in a sense of urban identity, albeit not one which was based upon the traditional status of chartered rights and freemen's privileges. This essay attempts to explore what the civic identity might have meant to women and the contexts in which they might have participated in and

Porter (eds), *Consumption and the World of Goods*, London, pp. 264-301; Vickery, A. (1998), *The Gentleman's Daughter: Women's Lives in Georgian England*, New Haven and London.

[3] See in particular essays by Barker and Harvey, Lane and Wiskin in this volume and Barker, H. (1997),'Women, Work and the Industrial Revolution: Female Involvement in the English Printing Trades, c. 1700-1840', in H. Barker and E. Chalus (eds), *Gender in Eighteenth Century England: Roles, Representations and Responsiblities*, Harlow, pp. 81-100; Hunt, M. (1996), *The Middling Sort: Commerce, Gender and the Family in England 1680-1780*, London, pp. 125-46, whilst Davidoff, L. and Hall, C. (1987), *Family Fortunes: Men and Women of the English Middle Class, 1780-1850*, London, have played down the active role of women in business.

[4] This is essentially the view put forward in most discussions of early modern citizenship. See, for example, Rapapport, S. (1983), *World Within Worlds Structures of Life in Sixteenth-Century London*, Cambridge, pp. 36-41; Phythian Adams, C. (1972), 'Ceremony and the Citizen: The Communal Year at Coventry, 1450-1550', in P. Clark and P. Slack (eds), *Crisis and Order in English Towns, 1500-1700: Essays in Urban History*, London, pp. 57-85.

been conscious of a civic and, looking at towns more generally, an urban identity. It is not proposed to attempt to argue that women were actually pulling the strings behind the scenes in some covert way, previously undetected by historians. Rather, it is intended to consider how and to what extent women were integrated into the civic life of a town, how far they shared in the expression of urban identity, and what membership of the civic and the urban community might have meant and entailed for them.

In the only study devoted to freewomen, *British Freewomen. Their Historical Privilege*, Charlotte Carmichael Stopes attempted to argue that female participation in urban political culture was more widespread in the early modern period and that the terms freeman, freeholder and inhabitant had yet to be defined in exclusively male terms. Stopes claimed to have found evidence for the extensive participation of women in the civic political culture of towns up until the seventeenth century – from which point there was a process of steady decline until women were explicitly written out of the Great Reform Act, which defined the franchise as belonging to all male householders.[5] Stopes, a polemicist on behalf of women's enfranchisement, produced examples of women being admitted to guilds and companies and being made free of the city, exercising trading privileges, taking on apprentices, and even establishing guilds and voting in parliamentary elections;[6] the Hostmen of Newcastle for example were explicit in their inclusion of women in their membership: their records refer to 'sisters' as well as 'brothers'.[7] However, Stopes was a follower of the Alice Clark model of women's history, which argued that the position of women in society had been steadily undermined since a supposed Golden Age located in the medieval and early modern periods, during which men and women had enjoyed a more equal relationship and when roles and occupations had yet to acquire rigidly gendered definitions.[8] By the eighteenth century however, legal opinion had deemed that

---

[5] Carmichael Stopes, C. (1894), *British Freewomen: Their Historical Privilege*, London.

[6] Stopes cites the precedent of women voting for members of Parliament in their capacity as burgesses in London, Worcester, Bath and Newcastle. She also points to their involvement in guilds and the London livery companies, and cases where women were explicitly recorded as having entered into the membership of the corporation: p. 90 'that the 11th September 1593, Rose Cloke, single woman, (according to the order and constitutions of the town and parish of Maidstone aforesaid) was admitted to be one of the corporation and body politique of the same town and parish; from henceforth to enjoy the liberties and franchises of the same in every respect, as other the freemen of the said town and parish. And she was also then sworn accordingly, and for some reasonable causes and considerations then stated she was released from paying any fine, other than for her said oath, which she then paid accordingly.'

[7] Dendy, F.W. (ed.) (1901), *Extracts from the Records of the Company of Hostmen of Newcastle upon Tyne*, Surtees Society, Newcastle.

[8] Clark, A. (1992), *Working Life of Women in the Seventeenth Century*, A.L. Erickson (ed.), 3rd edn, London. For more recent assessments of the position of women in

no woman could exercise the parliamentary franchise directly, and further, that civic duties which had in earlier times been performed by women were 'inappropriate' to the female sex.[9] More recently, historians have been rather more sceptical about the real extent of female participation in the guilds, and the trading companies of medieval and early modern towns. However, Stopes was right to highlight the fact that, albeit occasionally, women could and did take up the freedom and become members of trade companies, these being defining experiences of being an urban citizen, and would thereby have been in a position to participate in the civic culture of the town.

Nor do we have to adopt the Alice Clark/Carmichael Stopes thesis of inexorable retreat into the private domestic sphere to acknowledge the fact that women's participation in various aspects of civic or urban life did become more circumscribed from the seventeenth century — although the process by which this happened was much more uneven and indefinite than the traditional teleology, outlined by scholars such as Clark, would suggest. As in so many areas, we are reliant upon records largely written by men, for men, and we are left to guess the extent of slippage between the everyday reality of more flexible relations between the sexes and the rigid gendered differentiation which we find in the texts of legal pronouncements and civic records. Occasionally a chink in the masculine carapace of public life appears and a hint of feminine participation breaks through.

Lady Mayoresses and Corporate Sociability

The most frequent references to the presence of women, and lady mayoresses in particular, in the civic and ceremonial live of the town, come, not surprisingly, from those with the longest history of corporate government and the richest traditions of civic ceremonial. Contemporary sources such as civic histories and also the report of the Royal Commissioners for Municipal Reform of 1835 bear witness to the continuity of traditional practices into the eighteenth century.[10] In these towns it is clear that the mayoress and the wives of the aldermen — the women of the civic

---

medieval urban life see for example, Uitz, E. (1990), *Women in the Medieval Town*, London.

[9] Stopes blamed Coke for this shift in legal thought, and argued that 'his experience as the youngest son with seven sisters probably made him overvalue his own sex. His well-known matrimonial disputes probably helped to increase his prejudice against the other sex.' (p. 103). For a case study of the implications of this kind shift in legal thought, see Smith, H. (1998), 'Women as Sextons and Electors: King's Bench and Precedents for Women's Citizenship' in H. Smith (ed.), *Women Writers and the Early Modern Political Tradition*, Cambridge, pp. 324-42.

[10] On urban histories, see Sweet, R. (1997), *The Writing of Urban Histories in Eighteenth Century England*, Oxford.

elite — were definitely perceived as part of the corporate body. Corporation minutes record fines for aldermen's wives as well as their husbands for failure to wear scarlet on red letter days. They had their special pews in church. At civic funerals they too processed, equipped with gloves at the corporation's expense.[11] Charles Deering, the historian of Nottingham, described how the mayoress was entitled to a shilling from every freeman at the annual bullbaiting in return for providing the rope, and joined in the civic processions on Easter Monday; in Oxford, the mayoress by tradition appointed the mayor's sergeant; in York she received a fee of five shillings for every admission to the freedom, whilst in Norwich she had the privilege of nominating individuals to vacancies in three of the hospitals whose funds were managed by the corporation and in Bristol, Mrs Mayor received 20s to buy her a muff and 40s p.a. out of a piece of ground called the Mayor's Paddock.[12]

One should not, of course, make too much of such anecdotes; it is unlikely that many ladies of Bristol, for example, would have been pressing their husband to take up the mayoralty (an office which entailed considerable financial losses for the incumbent) purely for the thrill of being presented with a special muff. Nor would one want to suggest that the mayoress's choice of rope had much long term significance for the economic fortunes of the Nottingham butchers. These examples demonstrate the reality of female involvement in the ceremonial life of the town, rather than 'hard core' government and administration. However, ceremonial was a very important part of the civic culture of towns, and was the fulcrum around which the civic identity of the town revolved. Although excluded from much of the activities of the corporation, the women of the town did participate in some of the most crucial and defining points in the civic calendar. When they died they recognised this relationship in bequests to the civic community and their membership of the urban community was commemorated amongst the lists of benefactors. These women were, at least intermittently, a part of the corporate body politic. To argue that their presence was intermittent and ornamental and therefore of little significance is to perpetuate a male-centred interpretation of such events. It fails to consider what such civic culture meant both to the women those who were involved on these occasions and who were spectators.

However, it has been forcefully argued that by the eighteenth century the ceremonial activities of the corporation had become something of an empty shell. They had lost their communal links and were essentially nothing more than

---

[11] Gloves symbolized freeman status, see Tittler, R. (2001), *Townspeople and Nation: English Urban Experiences, 1540-1640*, Stanford, pp. 91-2.

[12] Deering, C. (1751), *Nottinghamia Vetus et Nova*, Nottingham, p.125; Hobson, M.G. (ed.) (1942), *Oxford Council Acts, 1752-1801*, Oxford, p. xxi; Oxford City Archives (hereafter OCA) Common Council Minute Book, B 4 1, entry for 17 July 1826; Barrett, W. (1789), *The History and Antiquities of Bristol*, Bristol, p. 121; *Report of the Commissioners for Municipal Reform*, P.P. (1835), xxv, p. 1742; xxvi, p. 2464.

occasions for private sociability at the expense of the town.[13] Similarly, it is often assumed that corporations were becoming increasingly detached from the urban community whose interest they were supposed to protect, and were nothing more than self selected and self interested oligarchies, which had forfeited the goodwill and support of the wider urban community. However, corporations were certainly not as irrelevant to civic life as some of the traditional accounts, influenced by the Webbs' critique, would suggest, and membership of the corporation still carried considerable prestige and influence within most towns.[14] Leaving aside the issues of whether ceremonial had ever been as participatory and socially inclusive and cohesive as has sometimes been suggested, the significance of these 'private social rituals' can be dismissed too quickly. The boundaries between the social and the political spheres were far from being rigidly drawn, and it would be unwise to assume that the feasting and sociability which figured so largely in corporation accounts did not serve some broader political purpose as well, by forging links and contacts amongst the better sort of urban society. Few if any corporations were wholly representative of the wealthiest members of the community, or could claim to be commensurate with the social elite and the increasing numbers of gentlemen and their families, who whilst they may not have been resident, were often heavily involved in urban life for cultural, political or business purposes. In no town was the urban elite a single, cohesive body; rather it was composed of interlocking spheres representing different social and economic groups. Corporate hospitality then was an important means of consolidating the position of the corporation in the leadership of the town.

If we award a weightier importance to the rituals of polite sociability, it has implications for the women whom we last saw being restricted within the bounds of domesticity, for in this socio-political aspect to civic life the potential for female participation in the public life of the urban elite deserves greater recognition. Whilst women's opportunities in some areas were being increasingly restricted by a more rigidly gendered interpretation of the law, their social role was arguably acquiring a greater significance as the role of the corporation was thus modified in

---

[13] This was certainly the perception of the Commissioners for Municipal Reform who made their report in 1835. For a more sensitive interpretation of the shifts in meaning of civic ritual see Borsay, P. (1984), '"All the Town's a Stage": Urban Ritual and Ceremony, 1660-1800' in P. Clark (ed.), *The Transformation of English Provincial Towns*, London, pp. 228-56.

[14] The Webbs' (1908) account of municipal government in the eighteenth century, *English Local Government from the Revolution to the Municipal Corporations Act: the manor and the borough*, London, remains the most comprehensive and has heavily influenced most other accounts. It is however, deeply unsympathetic to the unreformed system. For a more recent survey of urban government in this period see Sweet, R. (1999), *The English Town: Government, Society and Culture, 1680-1840*, Harlow.

response to broader shifts in urban society.[15] The examples to be used here might easily be challenged on the grounds of selectivity and atypicality, but in the absence of more formal records and a more sustained period of research, anecdotal evidence has been used to suggest preliminary lines of inquiry rather than to state categorical findings. The examples are drawn from geographically diverse areas, and from different ends of the long eighteenth century. They are also drawn predominantly from the records of incorporated towns, which were not, of course, representative of towns as a whole over the long eighteenth century, but they do throw up more evidence in the form of lady mayoresses, aldermanesses and other members of the civic elites.

During the late seventeenth century one Samuel Newton of Cambridge kept a detailed diary of his involvement in corporation affairs.[16] He noted not just the formal meetings of the corporation, those which would have been minuted in the official records, but also the far more numerous informal meetings — at the local tavern, or at private houses — which brought urban governance into a 'domestic' sphere, where women could also be present. For example on 14 December 1663/4 he wrote that 'Wednesday, this night I supped at Alderman Crabbs, where alsoe then supped the Aldermen, Bayliffs, and Treasurers *but none of their wives.* Mr Mayor was then at London, the Serjeants invited the guests: noe woman supped with the company but Mrs Crabb; *Mr Chapman at this time Dep. Maior.*' Newton clearly thought it worth commenting on the absence of 'wives', which could be taken to mean that the presence of women at such gatherings was commonplace. Given that his notes were not formal records of those present, the fact that women were not noted on other occasions need not be taken as conclusive proof that they were not there. What is clear is that the wives of the mayor and aldermen did attend at least the more convivial elements of informal corporate meetings which in turn opens up the possibility that they were informally involved in or contributed to discussion or debate.

The presence of women is most apparent in the passing references to them in records and descriptions of the more formal civic occasions: the mayor making and civic funerals and the social entertainments which followed upon these exclusively male ceremonies, such as the balls and assemblies, which were increasingly held to

---

[15] Stopes, *British Freewomen*, pp. 79-132; Smith, 'Women as Sextons and Electors', p. 329; Mendleson, S. and Crawford, P. (1998), *Women in Early Modern England*, Oxford, pp. 418-30.

[16] Forster, J.E. (ed.) (1890), *The Diary of Samuel Newton: Alderman of Cambridge 1662-1717*, Cambridge, pp. 6-7. The practice of calling on the mayor after his election was clearly common in a number of towns. Barrett, *History and Antiquities of Bristol,* p. 120 described similar rituals, but did not specifically mention the presence of women. Silence on this point, however, need not be assumed to indicate their absence.

mark any notable occasion in the urban calendar.[17] Some towns, it is true, did exercise very rigid separation of the sexes, even in their more social gatherings. In Bury St Edmunds social segregation extended to the dining arrangements before balls, and the ladies and gentlemen only met once all the company had arrived at the ballroom. The *Oakes Diaries*, a rich source for the lifestyle of a family which can fairly be said to have moved easily between the social spheres of the town's merchant elite and the neighbouring gentry and nobility, give no indication that women were ever present at any corporation events.[18] However, for all that Bury St Edmunds was a centre of polite society, it should not be assumed that such a rigid differentiation between the sexes was the norm in other towns — in fact, practice varied significantly from town to town. By way of contrast, Francois la Rochefoucauld, a French visitor to East Anglia in 1784, was struck by the practice of the ladies dining with the gentlemen at the corporation feast of another East Anglian town, Kings Lynn: they had their own table presided over by the two mayoresses in the same room as that of the mayor and men. In Kings Lynn at least, the ladies were not excluded, by virtue of their gender, from the most significant social statement of the corporate body.[19]

Another variation on this theme comes from Reading, where in 1722 the mayor, John Watts, decided to invite the ladies of the town to the mayoral feast, after inquiring what the usual procedure was from the outgoing mayor:

> The Mayor told me that the usual Fee was fifty pounds if I invited men only, but if I would invite men and women (as formerly they used to do) it had been the usual custom to allow ten pounds extraordinary to defray that charge. I replied, that since it had been a custom that had been formerly practised by several Mayors my predecessors, I was willing to revive that laudable custom of inviting the ladies as well as the gentlemen.

The ladies 'sate at one long table' and the gentlemen at another. However, this change provoked intense disapproval from his colleagues within the corporation:

> Thus I passed through the office of Mayor for the first time, though looked upon by some of my brethren with an evil eye, as is plain by what one of them said who lives in St Mary's Parish. He was pleased to tell a reverend person at my first Feast that I was certainly Made, and that I was drawing such expences upon the Mayors as could not be

[17] Borsay, P. (1989), *The English Urban Renaissance*, Oxford, pp. 150-62; Girouard, M. (1990), *The English Town*, London, pp. 75-100, 127-44.

[18] Fiske, J. (ed.), (1990), *The Oakes Diaries: Business, Politics and the Family in Bury St Edmunds,* Suffolk Record Society, 32, Woodbridge, p. 267, entry for 30 September 1790.

[19] La Rochefoucauld, F. (1995), *A Frenchman in England in 1784*, J. Marchand (ed.), translated S.C. Roberts, London, pp. 240-41.

> coped with, and that these extravagancies was to make others look little in their office.

Disapproval arose, not in protest against the presence of the female sex *per se* at the dinner, but on grounds of cost: the additional numbers made it all too expensive.[20] It is unclear whether the opposition arose from genuine financial pressures or whether it was simply sullen opposition to a mayor who was a relative newcomer to the town from London and clearly had an agenda to sweep the corporation clean with a new broom. Whatever the reasons, it was never suggested that women should be disqualified from being invited simply because of their sex.

Polite Rituals

In the expanding world of polite sociability and leisure, in the new rituals of assemblies, tea drinking and dining, women naturally participated and found themselves new roles.[21] The mayoress and the aldermen's wives were present at important social and civic occasions in their capacity as women of the civic elite; although how far this transient social involvement translated into more substantive influence within the civic elite is much harder to ascertain. The role of the mayoress in eighteenth-century towns had yet to be invented as the kind of figure who opens church fetes and visits schools. However, the role of mayoress was one which had a recognised and official capacity and nowhere more so than in the City of London.

London was, of course, unique, and its corporation enjoyed a far higher political profile than that of any other town, but as a result of this, the role of the mayoress is less obscure for London than it is for any other city. Evidence from London may be rejected as being atypical and *sui generis*, but it is arguable that parallels may have existed in provincial towns, which did not attract the same kind of attention from contemporary observers. The lady mayoress of London occupied a well-defined role in the Corporation. John Wilkes, famously besotted with his daughter, Polly, made her Lady Mayoress during his mayoralty of 1774-5, being estranged from his wife, but this was not just the whim of a doting father.[22] Other occupants

---

[20] Burton, K.G. (ed.) (1950), *The Memorandums of John Watts Esq.: Mayor of Reading 1722-23 and 1728-29*, Reading, p. 18.

[21] Dain, A. (1997), 'Assemblies and Polite Leisure in East Anglia', *Suffolk Review*, 28, pp. 2-22. In eighteenth-century Sheffield the subscription society which ran the assemblies was also under female leadership: Leader, R.E. (1901), *Sheffield in the Eighteenth Century*, Sheffield, p. 114. Female leadership was also to be found at the Derby Assembly (Girouard, *The English Town*, p. 134) and at Edinburgh (Youngson, J.A. (1966), *The Making of Classical Edinburgh*, Edinburgh, pp. 250-52).

[22] The most recent biography Thomas, P.D.G. (1996), *John Wilkes: A Friend to Liberty*, Oxford, is curiously silent about Wilkes' relationship with his daughter and her place in his social life.

of the mayoralty who were similarly placed also equipped themselves with substitute lady mayoresses for the duration of their term of office. The main role of the mayoress was one of hospitality and entertainment. Her biggest day was on Easter Monday when by tradition she and the aldermen's wives joined in a procession to St Pauls. In the evening she held a rout at the Mansion House. That held by Polly Wilkes was particularly splendid (as were all the social events of Wilkes' mayoralty). Polly Wilkes' entertaining clearly had a political slant; she opened the ball by dancing with Wilkes' political ally Lord Mountnorris and followed it by partnering a succession of his cronies.[23] Wilkes' diary for the rest of his mayoralty records him dining on many occasions with other members of the mayoralty and their wives, amongst whom Polly was included.[24] Given that during this period they were living in close proximity to each other, their otherwise copious correspondence dries up and reveals little of the extent to which Polly was involved in her father's tenure of the mayoralty.[25] Polly Wilkes was of course the exceptional daughter of an individual who had revelled in challenging conventions. Yet by this point he was shifting towards the respectable conformity with which he was to end his career, and his behaviour in this respect was mirrored by other holders of the mayoralty. Richard Clarke, the mayor in 1784, was on the whole a less exceptional incumbent of the office. He stands out, however, amongst eighteenth-century mayors of London, in that he kept an extremely detailed diary of his term of office. This shows that his wife was no less important to his mayoralty than had been Polly Wilkes to that of her father. She gave the same routs, and attended Clarke on numerous social occasions, not least when they were presented at court. Clarke recorded that on 16 December he 'Went to Kensington Gore to Governor Johnston's who with his Lady accompanied me and Lady Mayoress to the Drawing Room where Lady Mayoress was presented to their Majesties and I was presented to the Queen, they received us graciously and conversed familiarly – the princess Royal and princess Augusta were present and spoke to Lady Mayoress and myself.' [26]

The example of Polly Wilkes, or indeed Mrs Clarke, shows many parallels to work which has been done on the involvement of women within elite 'social politics', most notably by Elaine Chalus. The conclusions which she draws concerning the ability of women to influence patronage, their place in social politics, and above all their participation in the electoral process, must raise questions as to how far there was a comparable world of social politics in which towns women performed a crucial role as social networkers, participated in

---

[23] See the description of this occasion in Guildhall MS 332, ff.287-8.

[24] British Library (hereafter BL) Add MS 30,866 diary of John Wilkes, 1770-1797.

[25] BL Add MS 30,879 correspondence between John and Polly Wilkes. Letters of a later date, after Wilkes' mayoralty, show that Polly was certainly well informed concerning her father's political affairs and was a crucial link in his political as well as social networks.

[26] Guildhall MS 3385, f.16.

discussions, exercised their judgement and influenced their menfolk.[27] The obvious disparities of class make it difficult to draw similar conclusions for urban women of the middling sort. The differences in their education and their socially constructed roles are significant. More prosaically, the correspondence which forms such a rich source for the study of aristocratic women does not exist. As with electoral politics, where it is clear that many women were shrewd operators and fully conversant with the machinations of the electoral world, operating through the more informal channels of conversation and letter writing, it would appear where evidence does survive that corporation wives could be similarly conversant with civic affairs.

Middling women were not in the habit of such frequent epistolary communication; or if they were, the letters do not survive. The cultivation of literacy was not so significant a part of their education, and their life style was less peripatetic. Hence their social networks would have been essentially locally based, therefore precluding the need to exchange news and views by letter. Moreover, their family and household commitments did not allow them the same kind of leisure for literary composition. Nor are there plentiful journals; the diary of Abigail Gawthern would appear to be a notable — and fascinating — exception. Gawthern's husband was a leading figure of Nottingham corporation for eight years, and whilst she did not apparently make any efforts to pull strings in corporation affairs, it is clear that she was well aware of the identities and the political affiliations of the various members of the corporation and habitually noted events such as civic elections and processions.[28]

Social Politics

The correspondence of the nobility and gentry is not entirely redundant however, given that there were frequent occasions upon which the surrounding gentry families, if not the nobility, interacted in urban society and politics. The attractions of the town brought gentry families into the sphere of the social elite; the rise of

---

[27] Chalus, E. (1997), '"That Epidemical Madness": Women and Electoral Politics in the Late Eighteenth Century', in H. Barker and E. Chalus (eds), *Gender in Eighteenth Century England: Roles, Representations and Responsibilities*, Harlow; Chalus, E. (1998), '"My Minerva at my Elbow": The Political Roles of Women in Eighteenth-Century England', in R. Connors, C. Jones and S. Taylor (eds), *Hanoverian Britain and Empire: Essays in Memory of Philip Lawson*, Cambridge; Chalus, E. (2000), 'Women Electoral Privilege and Practice in the Eighteenth Century', in K. Gleadle and S. Richardson (eds), *Women in British Politics, 1760-1860: The Power of the Petticoat*, Basingstoke and see also her essay in this volume; Richardson, S. (2000), '"Well-Neighboured Houses": The Political Networks of Elite Women 1780-1860', in Gleadle and Richardson, *The Power of the Petticoat*, pp. 56-73.

[28] Henstock, A. (ed.) (1980), *Diary of Abigail Gawthern of Nottingham 1751-1810*, Nottingham.

borough mongering similarly necessitated significant levels of interaction between would-be political patrons and the leaders of urban society. It is at the interface of gentry and nobility involvement with the urban or civic elite that we may hope to find some indications of the activities of women which have gone unrecorded in other sources.

Aristocratic and gentry women were clearly involved at this level – their participation in electioneering is particularly noteworthy, and all the more so in that it was often conducted specifically woman to women. Susannah Centlivre satirised this trend in 1715 in the play *The Gotham Election*, in which the wife of Sir John, the sitting MP, having quarrelled with him over a matter of religion, took her marriage portion of £1000 and resolved to spend it on unseating her husband at the next election. The landlord, Scoredouble, described her tactics thus: 'so she veasts the good Wives, d'ye mind, and so secures all those Husbands Votes, whose Wives wear the Breeches.'[29] Centlivre's satire is hardly empirical evidence, but Judith Milbanke, wife of Ralph Milbanke MP, inveterate snob and social climber, used to complain to her aunt Mary of the tedium of entertaining the aldermanesses of Newcastle to tea; however, she continued to do so, being fully aware of how important it was for maintaining one's position and her husband's interest in local society.

> I have had Mrs Mayoress & divers Aldermen's Wives to visit me, more vulgar than any thing you can conceive! But they mean to be civil therefore I certainly shall be so to them, as I hold it to be very bad Policy to be at variance with the Inhabitants of a Place you are obliged to live at; they seem to be very hospitable & Invitations to Dinner come so thick that this is the first day that Mr Milbanke has been able to dine at home since we came, but it is not the Ton to have mixed Dinners of Gentlemen & Lady's.[30]

Mrs Elizabeth Montagu, wife of the wealthy Newcastle landowner and industrialist Edward Montagu, was less bored by socialising with the Newcastle worthies, but she too assumed an air of amused condescension: 'I behave very prettily, make visits duly, and have been this evening to make my compliments to the wife of the sheriff elect; and I think if Mr Montagu had the honour to be made an alderman of Newcastle, I should become the station very well.'[31] The Duchess of Northumberland commented tartly upon the lack of breeding of the Lady Mayoress of London upon whom she was required to call, and Lady Rockingham

[29] Centlivre, S. (1968), *The Gotham Election*, in *Collected Works*, 3, reprinted London, p. 158.

[30] Elwin, M. (ed.) (1967), *The Noels and the Milbankes: Their Letters for Twenty-Five Years*, London, p. 108, 2 June 1778.

[31] Historical Manuscripts Commission (HMC) 30 Fortescue (1894), II, p. 144.

was hardly more enthusiastic.[32] Whilst husbands were expected to do their political duty by becoming 'elevated' at the corporation feast, a political wife underwent the trials of rounds of visiting and tea drinking with the ladies of the corporation. Remarks such as Judith Milbanke's outburst to her aunt are fairly uncommon; the former made it quite clear that she found the whole business tiresome and the women intolerably vulgar (and herein may lie one reason why it was seldom commented upon: it was not worthy of record, and the vulgarities of the corporation wives were not, as a rule, an amusing topic for letter writing).

It may be argued that such an approach tells us little about the role of urban, middling women and does nothing more than highlight yet again the distinctive role of aristocratic women, illustrating the common place eighteenth-century assumption that women must be courted as they could influence the votes of their male relatives. However, it should also be allowed that social connections were never merely auxiliary to the conduct of politics and the brokerage of power, and from this it must follow that urban politics, and indeed any politics, was conducted on a much broader front than has hitherto often been suggested, and be acknowledged that women could be active as well as passive agents. As 'political culture' displaces the primacy of aristocratic political brokerage as a topic of historical research, our perception of who participated in the political process has been considerably broadened. In 1767, Lord Harcourt addressed the assembled company at the Mayor's feast at Abingdon, announcing the pleasure he felt 'to see a glow of happiness playing on Mrs Mayoress's plenteous countenance when she gives both hands in the conclusion of the minuet, or receives her fan from some humble relation who can never aspire to equal dignity.'[33] Harcourt's patronising description of Mrs Mayor suggests a role that was purely ornamental and peripheral, but the rounds of sociability and display of the civic elite should not be denuded of their political significance. The presence of the wives, of lady mayoresses and aldermanesses, their social rituals and the courtesies shown to them were part of the complex interplay of society and the negotiation of influence. Courtesy shown to the wives of the civic elite was more than a gallant display to the 'fair sex' but represented honour also to the town, whose identity was embodied in the membership of the corporation. Mayoresses, and to a lesser extent aldermen's wives, clearly still occupied a defined and valued role in civic life. In terms of the individual experience of women themselves, the status conferred by association with civic office should not be ignored. Such women would have been aware of their position within the urban community as wife to the mayor, or an alderman or any other position of civic office and would have been conscious that it was by virtue of this that they were being courted. In terms of the feminine social networks

---

[32] Chalus, E. (1997), 'Women in English Political Life, 1754-1790', unpublished University of Oxford D.Phil thesis and see note 26 above.

[33] *The Harcourt Papers,* vii, 271: 14 July 1767, quoted in Langford, P. (1990), *Public Life and the Propertied Englishman*, Oxford, p. 552.

within the town, and the pecking order of status, the role of mayoress endowed the holder with considerable status, by virtue of her connection through her husband with the civic persona of the corporation, and by virtue of the standing it gave her in her own right as a woman to be courted by the aristocracy and the landed elite.[34] Some idea of the social consequence which was attached by women to their association with civic office is given in Smollett's (admittedly satirical) creation Mrs Grizzle, sister to Peregrine Pickle, who 'seemed to have renounced all the ideas she had acquired before her father served the office of sheriff; and the era which regulated the dates of all her observations, was the mayoralty of her papa.'[35] The masculine world of corporation business and politics and feminine world of family and social networks cannot be neatly prised apart and should be restored to their mutually complementary partnership.

A natural corollary to such an argument would be to identify evidence which indicated whether or to what extent wives, sisters, mothers — or any other women with connections to those with influence with the urban elite — were approached by those wishing to procure corporation patronage. Direct evidence is hard to come by. A few mayoresses did have limited patronage in their own right, such as the right to nominate to certain charities or appoint minor civic officers such as the mayor's sergeant, but of much greater significance would have been the potential for tapping corporation patronage through the influence of wives over their husbands: corporations frequently controlled charitable bequests which represented a considerable financial resource, they had the right to bestow the freedom, they controlled significant amounts of property and could award very considerable contracts for building and maintenance work within the town – all of which in an age of urban development and improvement, could be of crucial import. The social politicking of the political patrons with the women of the civic elite was clearly one aspect of this, but there is also the almost entirely dark figure of patronage which was courted from below, yet given the commonplace assumption that women could be persuaded to influence their husbands over the casting of a vote, it does not seem illogical that they should not also have been approached to exert their persuasive powers in other directions.[36] The following example from Manchester is

---

[34] Chalus, 'Women in English Political Life', p. 189, cites the example of the mayoress of Exeter calling upon Lady Chatham in 1771: 'The Mayoress of Exeter and Mrs Walker present their most respectful compliments to Lady Chatham and they will do themselves the Honor of Waiting upon Her Ladyship if it is Agreeable.' Public Record Office (PRO), 30/8/66, pt1, f.43, 22 Aug 1771.

[35] Smollett, T. (1904 repr. 1951), *Peregrine Pickle*, London, p. 9.

[36] Shani D'Cruz's study of 'brokerage' amongst the middling sort in eighteenth-century Colchester suggests that women could have been involved as brokers in administrative areas and particularly in negotiations with overseers of the poor over poor relief. See D'Cruz, S. (1990), 'The Middling Sort in Provincial England: Politics and Social Relations in Colchester 1730-1800', unpublished University of Essex PhD thesis, p. 79.

illustrative of the kind of behaviour which it is argued might have taken place and is suggestive of much more widespread practices. A pamphlet published in 1800 attacking the administration of poor relief singled out in particular the activities of certain women, complaining that 'Overseers wives acted as magistrates, they signed passes, relieved the poor, and gave under their own signatures, no less than from *five to six hundred tickets a year,* upon the governor of the workhouse for *cloathing*'.[37] It might be argued that this was simply another instance of a patriarchal society tracing back any identifiable ill to female culpability, the complaint does have a semblance of plausibility about it.

The example just cited was taken from Manchester, which unlike the examples from the rest of the discussion was not an incorporated town, nor did it enjoy parliamentary representation. Manchester was governed by a combination of the court leet, the vestries, and latterly the paving commissioners; and as with corporations there is little evidence of women acting in a formal or official capacity in any of these bodies. However, in Manchester, citizenship cannot be said to have been predicated upon civic rights and the franchise in the way that it was in incorporated towns, which raises the question of what exactly constituted the civic, or in this context *urban* identity of Manchester, and whom did it comprehend? It was not necessary to be 'free' of a town, to exercise the civic or parliamentary franchise or to be a member of the corporation in order to play an active role in the urban community and to experience a strong sense of identity with that town.[38] Citizenship has often been defined in terms such that it carries with it a sense of political activity; however, parliamentary politics were far from constituting the sum total of the political culture of eighteenth-century towns.

Citizenship and Urban Improvement

The following example from Derby, although an isolated example, provides an illustration of the circumstances in which women were permitted, albeit temporarily, to participate in an active political sense in urban citizenship. By 1792 Derby had undergone considerable growth and the public amenities and urban infrastructure were held by many to be no longer in keeping with Derby's position as a wealthy manufacturing town and county centre. Proposals for urban improvement were made comprising provision for paving and lighting, and new

---

[37] [Battye, T.] (1800), *A Concise Exposition of the Tricks and Arts used in the Collection of Easter Dues, with a List of Items which Compose this Divine Tax.* By TB, Manchester, p. 26.

[38] For a fuller discussion of the issues surrounding urban identity and pride see Barry, J. (1990), 'Provincial Town Culture, 1640-1780: Urbane or Civic?' in J.H. Pittock and A. Wear (eds), *Interpretation and Cultural History*, Basingstoke; and Sweet, *The Writing of Urban Histories,* pp. 198-234.

building developments.[39] The question at issue was how this project should be funded. Should the unenclosed, common land, Nun's Green, which belonged to the inhabitants of the town, be sold off to pay for the improvement scheme, or should it be financed by a rate upon property? The debate was one which split the town. As the pamphlet debate progressed, specific appeals were made to the female inhabitants to exert their influence over their male relatives, in a series of broadsides purporting to be written by a 'lady' of the town.

> Ladies, there is no part of the community so much interested in the designed improvements of the town by paving and lighting the streets, and by altering the projecting spouts, as ourselves. Rugged and sharp stones and dirty kennels beneath, with water clattering on our heads from above, confine those of us within doors many months of the year; who do not possess the convenience of chaises or chairs. Day after Day have I often look'd in vain at the morning clouds, hoping for fine skies and dryer streets; that I might share the delight of gossiping and shopping; but have not been able to walk about the town for weeks together to visit the new caps, and hear the new scandal; and to be seen as well as to see.

At one level this extract merely reinforces the stereotype of eighteenth-century ladies who shopped, and who had no thought in their heads but for gossip and clothes, and of course there was never any question of women being allowed to give their vote in the decision over Nun's Green. Political propaganda at a local and national level was always framed on the assumption that the role of women would be to influence the votes of their husbands or male relatives. There is more to this episode, however, than a superficial gesture towards a constituency which was normally excluded from urban political culture. Whilst women were excluded from formal participation in the act of decision making itself, the prevailing tenor of the rhetoric was that as inhabitants of the town, and as householders, they were implicated in the affair as much as anyone else: the Green belonged to them as inhabitants, the improved town was a place in which they, as well as men, would take pride, and women as a group were appealed to as potential beneficiaries or losers from the proposed changes. Another pamphlet was written in the voice of a woman: 'Nun's green, say I, I hate the name of it! — What have we to do with Nuns in these days? — Besides, brother, it belongs to us, as well as to you; women have rights as well as men; and the act of parliament says, the Nun's green belongs to every inhabitant of Derby.'

---

[39] Elliott, P. (2000), 'The Derby Philosophers: Urban Scientific Culture and Society in Provincial England, c. 1750-1850', unpublished University of Leicester PhD thesis, section 5:3. I am very grateful to Dr Elliott for sharing his knowledge of Derby sources and history with me. See also Heath, J. (1979),'The Borough of Derby 1780-1810', *Derbyshire Miscellany*, 8, pp. 181-97 and Craven, M. (1988), *An Illustrated History of Derby*, Derby.

It should be acknowledged that the language of women's rights alluded to in this passage is due in some measure to the influence of radical thought in reformist circles in Derby at this time. However, the radical flavour of the language must not obscure a reality which should not be underestimated: women's involvement in the economic and social and life of the town would have stimulated an active interest in affairs of common concern, such as local improvement. This is borne out in the petitions which were signed by those who were against the sale and by those whose opinion was neutral. Of the 1406 people who signed the petition against the sale and the proposed mode of taxation, 276 were women, that is, nearly 20 per cent. Of the 203 signatories to the petition expressing neutrality, fifty-six were women (27.6 per cent). We might compare these figures with the 567 subscribers for rebuilding two of the town's bridges in 1790 which included a combined total of thirty-five women (7.5 per cent of the total signatories). [40]

It was not unusual for women to invest their money, or for male relatives to invest on their behalf, in schemes of public improvement.[41] This episode in Derby, however, illustrates that women could be pressed into service in the political debate at a particularly acute moment of crisis when the issues were being actively debated, rather than simply investing money in an undertaking which had the sanction and security of Parliamentary statute or the consensus of the community behind it. It is also established that women who were rate-payers could and did participate in vestry meetings and elections. It was not necessarily the norm, but they could be drawn in when occasion demanded, for example, at a contested election or a controversial decision. Women were amongst those who signed their names in the first year of elections for paving commissioners in the parish of Holy Trinity, Cambridge in 1788.[42] They do not appear thereafter which might be taken to indicate that they did not exercise their votes as householders again, but it is equally clear that the minutes did not list all those present each year, which leaves open the possibility that the presence of women and their votes went unrecorded. On other occasions we find their participation on occasions of emergency when extra votes had to be drummed up, as in the case of a contested election to sexton in

---

[40] Derby Local Studies Library, collection of broadsides.

[41] The contribution of female investors to urban improvement awaits a systematic analysis. In Bath, for example, 46 per cent of the capital for building projects during the 1770s derived from women, ranging from gentlewomen to servants, Davies, G. and Bonsall, P. (1996), *Bath: A New History*, Bodmin, p. 39. Chalkin, C.W. (1998), also notes a growing number of female investors in eighteenth-century public building, *English Counties and Public Building 1650-1830*, London, p. 65. On the financing of urban improvement more generally see Chalkin, C.W. (1980), 'Capital Expenditure on Buildings for Cultural Purposes in Provincial England', *Business History*, 22, pp. 51-70.

[42] Cambridgeshire Record Office, P22/8/1 and see also Langford, *Public Life and the Propertied Englishman*, pp. 230-1. Other parishes also elected commissioners, but the minutes for the parishes of St Giles, St Edward and St Andrew the Great do not record the names of those voting.

the parish of St Mary's in Nottingham in 1805, or an election for Churchwardens in East Looe in 1825, when all the single women and widows of the parish were marshalled in to sway the vote.[43] Even in 1835, three years after the political subject had been redefined as exclusively male, in the debates over the proposed bill for municipal reform one speaker, Mr Borthwick, called for removing the adjective male from the word householder in clause six of the bill, which laid down the qualification for voting for the town council, as he feared that the ladies of Bath would lose their right of voting in Vestry.[44] As Susan Staves has recently remarked, *a propos* of women's participation in the world of joint stock companies, 'the socialization of women not to act was more powerful than a legal regime entitling them to full participation.'[45]

The ambiguity surrounding women's citizenship and their status as householders and inhabitants meant that in moments of pressure such as this, their influence could be of considerable significance. In strictly legal terms citizenship may have been narrowly defined, but beyond the narrow definition the understanding of citizenship, in the sense of belonging to and identifying with a town and an urban community was one which comprehended women, and which clearly carried meaning for women, however difficult it may be to recover it. Elizabeth Montagu commented to her aunt that 'I am actually an inhabitant of Newcastle, and am taking out my freedom, not out of a gold box, but by entering into all the diversions of the place' but her comment, despite its deliberate facetiousness, acknowledges that there was much more to the public life of the town than simply membership of the corporation.[46]

---

[43] Nottinghamshire Archives Office (NAO) DD TS 1610, ff. 11-16. The two candidates (one of whom was Sarah Johnson, the widow of the former incumbent) issued pamphlets appealing for the support of the parishioners, addressed to 'Ladies and Gentlemen'. The records only include a simple breakdown of the votes cast so it is impossible to ascertain how many women voted on this occasion: Keast, J. (1989), *A History of East and West Looe*, Chichester, p. 73.

[44] *Hansard* 3rd series, lxix (1835) p. 646: 'He begged to move, that from line one in Clause 6, the word "male" be omitted. The House would see his object was to qualify the ladies to vote for Members of the Town Council. In Bath, for instance, ladies who were householders had the right of voting in Vestry. The clause therefore, as it now stood, would deprive those ladies of the right they had hitherto exercised. He hoped the noble Lord would, as a point of gallantry, agree to the Amendment.'

[45] Staves, S. (1998),'Investments, Votes, and "Bribes": Women as Shareholders in the Chartered National Companies' in H. Smith (ed.), *Women Writers and the Early Modern Political Tradition*, Cambridge, p. 277.

[46] Climenson, E.J. (ed.) (1906), *Elizabeth Montagu: The Queen of the Bluestockings. Her Correspondence from 1720-61*, 2 vols, London, ii, p. 205.

Conclusion

A more flexible definition of citizenship, which draws on the participation of the individual in various aspects of the public life of the town more broadly defined, allows for the possibility of women to share in it. If we approach the issue from the other direction, as it were, from the expression of civic pride, and develop a notion of citizenship which is based upon a different sense of pride, the *amor loci natalis,* it becomes a much less restrictive concept. It also makes it possible to accommodate within our understanding of citizenship and urban identities the increasing range of urban-centred activities which were taking place through associations and voluntarist activities (the Derby improvements being a typical example). These activities were generally considered by contemporaries to be amongst the foremost evidences of public spirit and 'civic' feeling.[47] Improvement commissions and other similar bodies were exclusively male in membership, but as the example from Derby has shown, the discussion of improvement was not confined to the executive body. Nor should 'urban improvement' be narrowly conceived simply in terms of the physical fabric of the town. Eighteenth-century citizens looked equally to the moral and social improvement of their fellow inhabitants and the growing range of urban charities, philanthropic organizations, and cultural associations through which improvement was achieved drew on female membership and support.[48]

Moreover, below the level of the civic elite some of the barriers which excluded female participation in civic life were more permeable; but it was a porosity which was intermittent and fluctuated, and could remain unexplored for considerable

[47] Barry, J. (1994), 'Bourgeois Collectivism? Urban Association and the Middling Sort' in J. Barry and C. Brooks (eds), *The Middling Sort of People: Culture, Society and Politics in England 1550-1800*, Basingstoke, pp. 84-112; Langford, *Public Life and the Propertied Englishman*, pp. 207-87; Morris, R.J. (1983), 'Voluntary Associations and British Urban Elites 1780-1850', *Historical Journal*, 26, pp. 95-118; Wilson, K. (1990), 'Urban Culture and Political Activism in Hanoverian England: the Example of Voluntary Hospitals' in E. Hellmuth (ed.), *The Transformation of Political Culture: England and Germany in the Late Eighteenth Century*, Oxford, pp. 165-84. On the importance of clubs and societies to urban culture more generally, see Clark, P. (2000), *British Clubs and Societies 1580-1800*, Oxford.

[48] See Sylvia Pinches' essay 'Women as Objects and Agents of Charity' in this volume. Other studies of women's involvement in philanthropy and anti-slavery agitation include Andrew, D.T. (1989), *Philanthropy and Police: London Charity in the Eighteenth* Century, Princeton, pp. 63-4, 72; Andrew, D.T. (1996), '*Noblesse Oblige:* Female Charity in an Age of Sentiment' in J. Brewer and S. Staves (eds), *Early Modern Conceptions of Property*, London, pp. 275-300; Midgley, C. (1992), *Women Against Slavery: The British Campaigns, 1780-1870*, London; Prochaska, F.K. (1980), *Women and Philanthropy in Nineteenth Century England*, Oxford; Shoemaker, R.B. (1997), *Gender in English Society 1650-1850*, Harlow, pp. 238-55; Vickery, *The Gentleman's Daughter*, pp. 256-7.

lengths of time. Civic and parish offices, which were positions of private rather than public trust, could be filled by women — sextons, bell ringers, workhouse keepers — all these and other similar positions were performed by women in towns across the country on an intermittent if not a regular basis. Leicester corporation even employed two female organists in succession to play at the city church of St Martins.[49] In most towns women were eligible for receipt of loans and other charities in the gift of the corporation, and were also the donors of gifts and benefactions intended for the good of the town.[50] Women were thus drawn into the civic community through employment and through the structures of charitable relief, and at this level of participation they would therefore have shared in the civic identity of a town.

Women could and did act in their capacity as householders and ratepayers, participating in the parish and holding various offices, and therefore, despite their inability to exercise the franchise, that defining feature of the freeborn Englishman and citizen, they were arguably equally citizens of a town alongside men. However, the rhetoric of urban citizenship which has shaped subsequent interpretations, was one which drew on the language of freemen's rights, historical traditions and urban identity and, despite its ostensible inclusiveness and appeals to the common good and community, was patently exclusive.[51]

The real extent of women's participation in the public life of the town and the civic elite is not easy to unravel, not least because the law itself was still ambiguous and ill-defined on many points. Women's participation was both less consistent and less proactive than that of their male relatives and conditional upon other factors, but it was not irrelevant. They held an established position in urban society, the potentials of which should be acknowledged on their own account, not simply with respect to their impact upon masculine governance. Amanda Vickery's recent book, based on the correspondence of Elizabeth Shackleton, describes the world of a genteel woman who moved easily between the society of the urban and county elites.[52] Vickery argues that urban affairs were of little interest to Mrs Shackleton,

---

[49] Chinnery, G.A. (ed.) (1967), *Records of the Borough of Leicester. Volume VI. The Chamberlain's Accounts 1688-1835*, Welwyn Garden City, pp. 245, 291. Miss Greatorex and Miss Valentine were paid £10 pa for their services.

[50] Withington, P. (2000), 'Citizens, Communities and Political Culture in Restoration England' in P. Withington and A. Shepard (eds), *Communities in Early Modern England: Networks, Place, Rhetoric*, Manchester, pp. 143-55.

[51] For a discussion of the meanings of civic identity see Sweet, R. (1998), 'Freemen and Independence in English Borough Politics, c. 1770-1830', *Past and Present*, 161, pp. 84-115 and Barry, J. (2000), 'Civility and Civic Culture in Early Modern England: The Meaning of Urban Freedom', in P. Burke, B. Harrison and P. Slack (eds), *Civil Histories. Essays Presented to Sir Keith Thomas*, Oxford, pp. 181-196 and Barry, J. (1995), 'I Significati della Libertà: La Libertà nell'Inghliterra del XVII e XVIII secolo', *Quaderni Storici*, 89, pp. 487-513.

[52] Vickery, *The Gentleman's Daughter*, p. 221.

who was, she suggests, ambivalent about 'inflated masculine rituals' of local government, was not involved in the sociability and 'disparaged the self-important ceremonies of county administration.' Where women were involved, it was as a civilising presence, tempering the masculine crudity and bringing a level of refinement and civility to the social gatherings which ornamented the hard core masculine business of government and administration. Shackleton of course, was not resident in a town, so it is not surprising that she felt little interest in urban affairs. No doubt many other women shared her view of the drunken excesses which were apparently inseparable from corporation business. But, rather than excluding women from the discussions of urban identity, there is a need to think in what contexts and on what occasions women might have felt conscious of, or expressed their sense of belonging to a town, a community with an identity and a tradition.

Chapter 3

The Rag Plot: The Politics of Influence in Oxford, 1754

Elaine Chalus

> *'Oxford is paved with Libels; and the very Stones in the Streets, whenever they open their Lips, speak Treason.' This is a Truth, which we have had sent down to us from the best Authority; and it is confirm'd by Fact, and every Day's Experience. One cannot pass through the most private Lane or Ally of this Town, but our Ears are stunn'd with the Cries of Hawkers and Ballad-singers, who are continually venting their Insults against his Majesty's Crown and Dignity ....*[1]

Mrs Mary Carnall stepped out of the doorway of her shop on the corner of Carfax into the hubbub of the Oxford marketplace.[2] It was Quarter Sessions week in July

---

[1] *Mr. Boots's Apology for the Conduct of the late H—h Sh—ff; In answer to a late Infamous Libel, intituled,* The Blackest of all Black Jokes (1754).

[2] This account of the Rag Plot, which followed the inconclusive scrutiny after the controverted 1754 Oxfordshire election and preceded the petition to Parliament, is drawn primarily from the surviving 'voluntary informations' taken from Mary Carnall and sixteen others between 29 July and 14 October 1754. Fifteen depositions were taken between 29 July and 22 August by various combinations of a solidly Old Interest (Tory) triumvirate: the Mayor of Oxford, Daniel Shilfox; the President of Trinity College and Vice-Chancellor of the University, Dr George Huddesford; and the famous jurist of All Souls College, Dr William Blackstone. Letters between the New Interest agent in Oxford, Dr Thomas Bray of Exeter College, and two of the leading New Interest peers, Lords Harcourt and Macclesfield, reveal that copies of these depositions were circulating in the county almost immediately. This may have been because the Secretary of State, Lord Holdernesse, had forwarded the depositions received from Shilfox and Huddesford to Macclesfield, who had then taken copies of them. Fearing that the Old Interest JPs would purposefully skew the depositions in order to discredit the New Interest with the public, the New Interest arranged for several of their JPs to take depositions from some of the leading witnesses for comparative purposes. These included depositions from Mary Carnall on 26 July and Mary West on 4 August. The discrepancies, especially between the two versions of Mrs West's 'information', confirmed their fears. Lords Harcourt and Macclesfield consequently advised Bray to arrange for a re-examination of willing witnesses in front of a panel of six New Interest JPs: Sir Edward Turner, Bart; the Master of Balliol, Dr Theophilus Leigh; John

1754, so there were more people at the midweek market than usual even though it was rainy. Mrs West, the cheesemonger, was keeping dry by sitting on her hampers under the awning over the shop window. On the ground next to her was a little pile of straw that she had used to pack her cheese, and, on top of that was a small parcel of linen rags tied up in a handkerchief. What caught Mrs Carnall's eye while she was chatting with Mrs West was that there was a thick piece of paper — like the endpaper from a book — among the rags. It appeared to be covered with writing. Curious, she stooped over and extracted it from the bundle. It was a longish piece of paper, wider than her hand and coloured like button paper, white on one side and buff on the other. She wiped it against her petticoat and began to read:

Britons shake off the Gloomy Veil
That clouds your Sight and Understanding
Take Sword in hand with Loyal Zeal
And meet Your Monarch at his Landing.

Too long We've bore the Service Yoke
Of false and flattering Usurpation
Now now's the Time One Loyal Stroke
Will fix a happy Restoration.

Lenthall, Esq.; Anthony Tracy Keck, Esq.; Paul Elers, Esq.; and John Travell, Esq. Of these men, three had a personal interest in the outcome of the election: Turner was one of the candidates; Leigh was closely related to Turner through marriage; and Keck had gone to significant expense and effort to support the New Interest candidates over the previous two years. He had also just been returned as the New Interest MP for the duke of Marlborough's borough of New Woodstock. The additional 'informations' obtained as a result of their efforts were given, ostensibly, to correct the errors of omission and commission in the Old Interest's version of events. More importantly, they provided the New Interest with yet another opportunity to cast aspersions on the Old Interest. Both sides were keen to keep the issue of the election alive in the period before the election petitions were tabled in Parliament. The Old Interest depositions were originally printed as *Informations and Other Papers Relating to the Treasonable Verses Found at Oxford, July 17, 1754* (1755). Two copies of this publication survive in the Bodleian Library. So, too, and rather confusingly under the same title, does a compilation volume which binds the Old Interest depositions together with most of the New Interest depositions. The pagination of the New Interest depositions suggests that they had originally been printed as a separate pamphlet. For the sake of simplicity, all references here are to this compilation volume. Transcripts of the depositions survive in both Holdernesse's and Bray's papers: see BL Egerton MS 3,440 (Leeds Papers), vol. cxvii; Exeter College Archives, Bray Papers, L.IV.7.D., Oxfordshire Parliamentary Elections, 1752–55, fos. 1–24. See the correspondence about the Rag Plot between Macclesfield and Hardwicke, Hardwicke and Holdernesse, and Macclesfield and Holdernesse, in BL Egerton MS 3,440. See also Bray's correspondence with leading New Interest figures, e.g., Harcourt to Thomas Bray [n.pl., September 1754], 8 September 1754; Richard Blacow to Thomas Bray [London?], 8 October 1754, Macclesfield to Thomas Bray, London, 14 October 1754. I would like to thank the Rector and Fellows, Exeter College, Oxford for permission to use the Bray Papers. I would also like to thank Professor Paul Langford for his generosity in sharing his knowledge of the Bray Papers with me.

Britons no longer Gazing Stand
But joyn great Charles your Lawful Hero
He soon will claim His Injured Land
From this devouring Cursed Nero.
Britons come on with Sword in hand
Let's push the Way for our Highland Laddie
May still Success his arm attend
Who wears no Armour but his Plaiddie.

The Golden Age draws on apace
And soon Corruption will be vanish'd
And Loyal Charles will never cease
Till he this Breed of Whelps has Banish'd.[3]

This was treason! Even though it was nearly a decade after the '45, Mrs Carnall was convinced that Oxford still harboured Jacobites; these verses confirmed her belief. What she wanted to know was how had they come to be under her window and who had put them there.

[3] Two copies of the verses survive in the Secretary of State's, Lord Holdernessse's, papers. One copy, in what appears to be Thomas Bray's handwriting, was sent to Holdernesse by Lord Macclesfield; the second is a copy in Holdernesse's secretary's hand: BL Egerton MS 3,440, vol. cxvii, fos. 71–2, 73–4. R.J. Robson, who devotes a brief dismissive chapter to the Rag and Watch Plots, appears not to have known of the existence of these verses. He quotes solely from a version of the verses that survives as handwritten marginalia in Bodl., G.P. 98(6): See Robson, R.J. (1949), *The Oxfordshire Election of 1754*, Oxford, p. 129. There are minor differences between the two versions, but either would have been considered treasonable at the time. In particular, the last line of the third stanza in the Holdernesse verses refers to 'this devouring Cursed Nero', and not 'a devouring Nero'; similarly, the last line in the Holdernesse version reads 'Till he this Breed of Whelps has Banish'd', whereas the other version refers more directly to 'Till he this breed of Guelphs has banished'. Mary Carnall's second 'information' on 10 October refers specifically to the Holdernesse version of the text, as she recounts Dr William Blackstone asking her, when she gave her first deposition, whether she believed 'Cursed Nero' to be treasonable (*Informations and Other Papers*, 32). It is highly probable that there was yet at least another version of the verses, as Mary Kirby — and not the widow, Jane Sims, as indicated by Robson — conflates the two versions in the line she quotes in her deposition on 17 August: 'Britains no longer gazing stand / take Sword in Hand' (Robson, *Oxfordshire Election*, p. 129; *Informations and Other Papers*, 35). In the Holdernesse text, the line is 'Britons come on with Sword in hand', while the other reads, 'Britons, no longer gazing stand'. The possiblity that multiple copies of the verses had been found on different dates was used at the time by Macclesfield to explain the seeming discrepancy between the date of discovery of 13 July, as indicated in the first advertisement, and 17 July, when Mrs Carnall actually 'discovered' the verses. BL Eg 3440, fos. 79–80, Macclesfield to Holdernesse, St. James's Square, 29 July 1754.

Mrs West told her that the rags belonged to Maria Duke, who she had sent off to deliver some cheese. Riah, as she was commonly known, eked out a living on the streets of Oxford selling fruit and buying rags.

Mrs Carnall was still on her doorstep with the verses in her hand when her maid, Mary Faulkner, came down from breakfast. She showed them to her and told her that they were high treason. Shortly afterwards, Riah returned from her errand and came in to the shop to reclaim her property. Mrs Carnall refused to return it and demanded instead to know where Riah had bought the rags. Riah refused to tell her and left the shop angrily, muttering accusations of theft.

A short time later, she returned. By this time, Robert Carnall and Lawrence Horner, a perruke-maker who ran a neighbouring shop, had joined Mrs Carnall and Mary in the shop. Riah tried again to get the paper back and Mrs Carnall tried again to get Riah to tell her where the rags had come from. Both efforts were futile. Mrs Carnall then took another tack. When she saw William Harris buying some cheese from Mrs West, she called him into the shop and read him the verses. Harris was a servant of the Kecks of Great Tew and frequently called at the shop to do their business. Surly and obstinate by this time, Riah tried to snatch the paper from Mrs Carnall's hand. Tauntingly, she announced that she would tell Harris everything she knew if he gave her a pint of ale. Mrs Carnall immediately countered with the offer of a quart. Riah refused contemptuously. Unfortunately, Harris could not stay to take up Riah's offer, as he had to rejoin the Kecks who were on their way out of town. It was at this point, Mary Faulkner later recalled, that Riah asked if the verses were about local politics, particularly if they were about the Blues (the county's Old Interest, i.e., Tories). It was only when Mrs Carnall told Riah that they had nothing to do with either the Blues or the Greens (the New Interest, i.e., Whigs), but that they were a treason against the king and the Protestant Succession, that Riah abruptly abandoned them: 'Then damn them'.

The Rag Plot

Thus begins what quickly became known as the Rag Plot. The Plot was an audacious attempt by the Oxfordshire New Interest to influence public opinion locally and nationally against the Old Interest — and with it Parliament's final determination of the 1754 county election.[4] It provides an intriguing insight into an eighteenth-century 'dirty tricks' campaign and demonstrates how long-standing personal and ideological animosities were interwoven into both university and

---

[4] For the most detailed account of the election, see Robson, *Oxfordshire Election*. Robson's coverage of the printed sources available in the Bodleian Library is impressive, but he does not appear to have consulted any manuscripts, even the Bray Papers. For an examination of the election and particularly the involvement of Lady Susan Keck, see Chalus, E. (2001), 'Lady Susan Woos the Voters', *BBC History Magazine*, (June), or my longer '"My Lord Lady Sue": Lady Susan Keck and the Great Oxfordshire Election of 1754', (forthcoming).

electoral politics in Oxford. Yet more importantly for the purposes of this book, it casts light on the operation of electoral politics at the community level and reveals that eighteenth-century urban women could and did play an active and influential part. While recent research has significantly expanded our understanding of the variety and extent of elite women's electoral involvement in the eighteenth century, that of women lower down the social scale has yet to receive similar attention.[5] Urban areas tended to have the most hotly contested elections in the eighteenth century and, while the political awareness of urban women is recorded in their testimonies as witnesses in controverted election cases, where they could serve as the electoral memory of their communities, little is known about their actual political involvement.[6]

The leading role in the Rag Plot was played by Mrs Carnall, an urban woman whose politicization and involvement was tacitly or openly acknowledged by both the men and women in her circles and by leading members of the local political elite. An examination of Mrs Carnall's part in the Rag Plot reveals a clear understanding and a knowing use of the politics of influence. It suggests that she used her networks of contacts knowingly and capitalized on her place at the heart of the marketplace to disseminate the verses, gossip about the Plot and spread rumours attributing it to the Old Interest. In doing so she took advantage of the highly personal, local nature of politics at the time. More significantly, her part in the Rag Plot grew out of an early modern tradition of treasonable or libellous verses which was particularly well suited to women's involvement.[7] Such verses aimed to discredit political opponents and influence local opinion. They were customarily placed in highly public places, such as marketplaces, where they could be ostentatiously 'discovered'. This guaranteed that they would become the gossip of the day and that news of their discovery, even transcripts, would be spread as

---

[5] See, for instance, Colley, L. (1992), *Britons: Forging the Nation, 1707–1837, London*; Foreman, A. (1998), *Georgiana: Duchess of Devonshire*, New York; Chalus, E. (1997), '"That Epidemical Madness": Women and Electoral Politics in the Late Eighteenth Century', in H. Barker and E. Chalus (eds), *Gender in Eighteenth-Century England: Roles, Representations and Responsibilities*, Harlow, pp. 151–78; Chalus, E. (2000), 'Elite Women, Social Politics and the Political World of Late Eighteenth-Century England', *Historical Journal*, 43:3, pp. 669-98. Two recently published collections of essays on women and British politics also add significantly to our general knowledge and go a long way towards dispelling previously held assumptions about women's withdrawal from politics at the end of the eighteenth century. See Richardson, S. and Gleadle, K. (eds) (2000), *Women in British Politics, 1760–1860: The Power of the Petticoat*, Basingstoke; also Vickery, A. (ed) (2001), *Women, Privilege and Power: British Politics 1750 to the Present*. Important information on the political activities of women of the 'people' can be found in Wilson, K. (1995), *The Sense of the People: Politics, Culture and Imperialism in England, 1715–1785*; also Rogers N. (1998), *Crowds, Culture and Politics in Georgian Britain*.

[6] Chalus, E. (2000), 'Women, Electoral Privilege and Practice in the Eighteenth Century', in Richardson, S. and Gleadle, K. (eds), *Women in British Politics 1760-1860*, Basingstoke, pp. 19–38.

[7] See, for instance, Cavanagh, D. and Kirk, T. (eds) (2000), *Subversion and Scurrility: Popular Discourse in Europe from 1500 to the Present*, Aldershot.

widely and as rapidly as possible. Since women had a strong presence in the marketplace as retailers and shoppers, and since they were assumed to gossip and spread rumours among their acquaintances, treasonable verses could provide them with a ready-made opportunity for informal but nonetheless influential political involvement.[8]

The Rag Plot occurred, however, at a transitional moment in popular political culture. Early modern political practices, such as libellous verses, which had emerged as a means of shaping local political opinion in a partially literate society, were by the mid-eighteenth century being replaced by the increasingly influential, literacy-dependent, national political press. While this transition would not have affected urban women's ability to use gossip and rumour for political ends, it may well have limited their ability to expand their political involvement or shape political opinion beyond their immediate communities. Even elite women, with their higher levels of literacy and their greater likelihood of being personally involved with the political men and issues of the day, contributed only infrequently to the political press — and then under pseudonyms. On 27 August 1756, for instance, when Lady Anson published a defence of the Admiralty after the loss of Minorca in the *Public Advertiser*, she did so under the pseudonym *Civicus*.[9] The odds against a woman of Mrs Carnall's rank doing something comparable are high. As the debate over the Rag Plot became more print-orientated and national, it was dominated entirely by men.

The Context

Although the Rag Plot was a direct result of the New Interest's defeat in the vitriolic and inconclusive 1754 Oxfordshire election, it also wove together a number of other, older concerns. Underlying the Plot as a whole was an assumption (which proved to be outdated) that the public still feared Jacobitism in the way that it had earlier in the century. Thus, the Plot built upon accusations of Jacobitism that had been levelled at the Old Interest throughout the election campaign. It also recalled the Tory country gentlemen's decidedly lacklustre support for the Hanoverian monarchy in 1745. At the outbreak of the rebellion, when 121 Oxfordshire landowners and clergymen subscribed to a loyal Association to preserve the constitution in church and state, only 15 per cent were identifiably Tory, despite the fact that Oxfordshire was a predominantly Tory county.[10]

---

[8] Fox, A. (1994), 'Ballads, Libels and Popular Ridicule in Jacobean England', *Past & Present*, 145, p. 63.

[9] BL 35,376, fos. 132–3, Lady Anson to Royston [Admiralty], [8? August 1756]; fos. 134–5, newspaper clipping of published letter from *Civicus*, *Public Advertiser* (27 August 1756).

[10] Robson, *Oxfordshire Election*, 1.

The Plot also drew upon the university's established reputation for Jacobitism and, over time, became increasingly implicated in settling a score between two old academic enemies — the Whig, Richard Blacow, Canon of Windsor and ex-fellow of Brasenose College, and the old Jacobite, William King, the Principal of St Mary's Hall. Although the university had been justifiably notorious earlier in the century for its Tory/Jacobite sympathies (and sympathizers), its day as a training-ground for Tories and Jacobites had already passed by the 1750s.[11] Thanks, however, as much to King's undisguised Jacobite sympathies and his immoderate use of language, as well as to the expression of similar sentiments by the Vice-Chancellor,[12] Blacow more than settled his score with the university. Not only did the university emerge from the Rag Plot with a reinforced reputation for Jacobitism, but also with the lowest enrolment figures for the entire eighteenth century.[13]

While the possibility of another Jacobite uprising was quickly discredited and the Plot was swiftly recognized to be just that — a plot — and attributed to the New Interest, it should not be seen as a failure. Indeed, instead of being depicted as it was by R. J. Robson as a poorly planned footnote to the Oxfordshire election, or as it was by Dame Lucy Sutherland as 'a ludicrous, even if somewhat sinister, conspiracy' intended to 'smear the university with the imputation of active Jacobitism',[14] it could justifiably be argued that the Plot was a success in that it met its goals and contributed significantly to the larger, eventually successful, New Interest political campaign. Locally, it aimed to keep the election fresh in the minds of the electorate and to discourage support for the Old Interest cause. Nationally, it made astute use of the press and political connections with the Whig Administration to raise awareness and support for the New Interest among the MPs who would be sitting in judgment on the Oxfordshire election petition. It succeeded in meeting both of these goals. Although it is true that by the autumn of 1754 Mrs Carnall's activities and the verses themselves had been superseded by a pamphlet duel between Blacow and King, the Plot, in this final manifestation, attracted significant attention right up until the opening of Parliament. Yet more importantly, the Plot was recognized by contemporaries as having been influential in securing the final New Interest victory. As one anonymous contemporary wrote

---

[11] Langford, P. (1986), 'Tories and Jacobites, 1714–1751', in L.S. Sutherland and L.G. Mitchell (eds), *History of the University of Oxford*, v, Oxford, pp. 99-128.

[12] See *Dr King's Apology or Vindication of himself from the several Matters charged on him by the Society of Informers, delatores, hominum genus pulicis exitiis repertum (1755)*; also Blacow, R. (1755), *A Letter to Dr King*. Others, including the Vice-Chancellor, George Huddesford also entered the fray. Huddesford's speech at Encenia in July and his speech at Convocation in October, as well as his subsequent pamphlets, did little to help the university's cause.

[13] Sutherland, L. (1986), 'Political Respectability, 1751–1771', in L. Sutherland and L.G. Mitchell (eds), *History of the University of Oxford*, v, Oxford, p. 142.

[14] Robson includes both the Rag and Watch Plots as unsuccessful New Interest addendum to the election. Robson, *Oxfordshire Election*, pp. 128-35; Sutherland, 'Political Respectability', p. 135.

below his transcription of the treasonable verses: 'They certainly had this effect, that Sr Edw. owed to them his Seat in Parliam^{t}. The K. was provoked. The Courtiers who had been indifferent about the Oxfordshire election, sided with S^{r}. Edw. and the consequence was, that he was declared duely elected'.[15]

The Plot was the New Interest's most daring salvo in a battle for political control of the county that lasted for more than two years. The election campaign had been notorious even at the time for its excess, violence and cost (reputedly £20,000 per side). It was also highly publicized, with some of the university's finest minds being employed as propagandists for each side. The electorate was inundated with poems, squibs, broadsides, satires, letters and essays, all filled with varying amounts of venom. The eagerness with which both sides turned to the press not only resulted in the publication of Oxford's first long-running newspaper, *Jackson's Oxford Journal*, but also spilled over regularly into the London newspapers. Since the county included a significant number of non-resident voters and since the politicians and activists on each side had close contacts in London, it was important to disseminate the latest developments in Oxfordshire or the most recent publications.

The poll of 17–23 April 1754 did little to resolve the situation or lower the political temperature. During the poll, an Old Interest mob blocked access to the polling booths on Broad Street in an effort to prevent the New Interest from voting. The New Interest was ingenious in circumventing the mob. Exeter College — one of the few strongly pro-New-Interest colleges in the university — very conveniently happened to have a side door that opened out on to the backs of the polling booths. New Interest supporters were consequently channelled through the college and out the side door to cast their votes. While such partisan behaviour met with approval from the New Interest leadership, it served to exacerbate pre-existing political tensions in the already ideologically divided university. It also contravened the Vice-Chancellor's directive, which had instructed colleges not to take part in the election.[16] Even so, it was not quite enough to secure a New Interest victory: at the end of the poll, the Old Interest candidates, Lord Wenman and Sir James Dashwood, Bart., came out ahead of the New Interest candidates, Lord Parker and Sir Edward Turner, Bart., by 114 and 95 votes, respectively.[17].

The New Interest immediately challenged the outcome by calling for a scrutiny. It was scheduled for mid-May, which gave each side the time it needed to gather witnesses and secure evidence of corrupt practices. Instead of resolving the situation, however, the scrutiny only increased the animosity between the two sides. A legitimate procedural decision taken at the start of the scrutiny granted the losing New Interest side the right to open the scrutiny by presenting its entire case of 347 votes; only when its case was complete would the Old Interest have the

---

15 Bodl. G. P. 98(6).

16 Bodl. Gough Oxf. 101(2), *Announcement of Guidelines for Election ... April 15, 1754*. This directive from Vice-Chancellor Huddesford stated, among other things, that all college gates were to be shut for the duration of the poll.

17 *Jackson's Oxford Journal*, 52, 27 April 1754, p. 3.

right to reply. As a result, the entire two-week scrutiny was dominated by the New Interest. In the end, the Old Interest had only a day and a half to requalify as many of its own votes as possible *and* present its case against the New Interest. Needless to say this was an impossible task and resulted in the High Sheriff judging the scrutiny inconclusive and making a double return (i.e., returning all four candidates instead of choosing a pair of winning candidates).[18] This meant that the final outcome of the election rested with the new, Whig Parliament, a fact that could not have inspired much confidence in the Old Interest.

Under normal circumstances, political tensions would then have eased during the summer. Immediately after the scrutiny, however, as a group of New Interest gentlemen were leaving Oxford, they were met on Magdalen Bridge by an angry Old Interest mob. In the fracas that ensued, the mob tried to throw some of the carriages into the river. One of the gentlemen who was being threatened shot into the crowd, hitting a chimneysweep who later died. This necessitated a coroner's inquest, which meant that each side had to arrange for yet more witnesses to come to Oxford to testify. The inquest quickly became as politicized as the scrutiny. Finally, in mid-June, in true tit-for-tat fashion, the Coroner who was an Old Interest supporter brought down a verdict of wilful murder. Since this necessitated presenting the case all over again at the Assizes, which were scheduled to begin in Oxford on 24 July, the political atmosphere remained highly charged. The New Interest appeared to be trailing in what looked set to become a war of attrition.

The Suspects

Such then was the situation when Mrs Carnall 'found' the verses outside her shop on 17 July, exactly a week before the Assizes. Although her part in the Plot was crucial, it seems unlikely that she played a part in its inception. Just who planned the Plot and who wrote the verses is now impossible to determine conclusively, as no definitive evidence survives. She was, however, considered to be one of the four suspects at the time. The others were the Oxford attorney, Cornelius Norton; the New Interest's outstanding female politician, Lady Susan Keck; and the government writer and influential New Interest propagandist, Richard Blacow (who after October 1754 would also be the editor of the pro-Administration *Evening Advertiser*).[19]

Of the four suspects, Norton is the least plausible. His involvement in the Plot seems to have been limited to two bit parts. Only one of these demanded any effort from him, and even that he did not supply. He appears first in name only in the *London Evening Post* advertisement of 23 July which announces the discovery of the verses in Oxford. It advised anyone wishing to claim a reward of £50 offered by a 'certain Number of Loyal Subjects' to contact him with their information.[20]

---

[18] Robson, *Oxfordshire Election*, p. 123.
[19] Robson, *Oxfordshire Election*, p. 134.
[20] *London Evening Post*, 23 July 1754.

Blacow was behind the advertisement. Although Norton protested in his depositions that his name had been used without his consent, he did admit that he had been contacted immediately after the publication of the advertisement — presumably by Blacow — and had agreed to hold the reward. Norton's protestations may, of course, have been entirely fictitious. Even if he did not know about the Plot in advance, he must have been enough of a known New Interest supporter to have been assigned this role. Norton did little better with his second, more important task. He was trusted with the job of working together with Mrs Carnall to draw up the presentment to the Grand Jury. When he fell ill, his son, who was a London attorney, drew up the presentment instead. He also accompanied Mrs Carnall to the Grand Jury to present it on 26 July.[21]

Despite Mrs Carnall's importance to the Plot, it is highly unlikely that she instigated it. As a Carfax shopkeeper's wife, she simply did not have the requisite status or connections. It would have been impossible for her to hold the leadership position in a group made up of educated and aristocratic men. Indeed, her subordinate position in the Plot with regard to Bray and Blacow is made clear in a letter of 3 August. In it, Blacow cautioned Bray against giving her any compensation — yet — for loss of trade due to her involvement in the Plot, arguing that doing so at that stage would be 'of dangerous consequence with regard to the evidence she gives & will have reason to repeat'. Instead, he advised Bray to compensate her discreetly after the brouhaha had faded: 'answer, in whatever manner your prudence will direct, for an indemnity to be made hereafter'.[22]

Lady Susan Keck is a more plausible suspect. She certainly had the force of character, the social status, the connections at Court and the requisite local experience to be the driving force behind the Rag Plot. She was used to working with men and would have had no trouble heading a group of male conspirators; however, there is nothing in the surviving correspondence to suggest that she did. As one of the most dedicated activists in the New Interest, she was certainly no stranger to the murky depths of eighteenth-century electioneering. She had often connived with Bray during the election campaign to do whatever was deemed necessary to outmanoeuvre the Old Interest. She genuinely believed that the Old Interest sheltered Jacobites, so the idea of a Plot that played on this connection and influenced public opinion in favour of the New Interest would have appealed to her. In addition, she could also have supplied the link to the Carnalls, as their shop supplied her household. Other suspicious coincidences also make her a likely suspect: the verses happened to be discovered on a day when the Kecks were in Oxford; and, more fortuitously, one of their servants just happened to be at the Carnalls's shop at exactly the right time to corroborate Mrs Carnall's story.

Since very little happened in New Interest circles that Lady Susan did not know about, it would have been surprising if she had not known about the Plot in

[21] Cornelius Norton, 22 August 1754, in *Informations and Other Papers*, pp. 36-7; see also p. 7; Robson, *Oxfordshire Election*, p. 131.

[22] Bray Papers, L.IV.7.C/49, Richard Blacow to Thomas Bray [London], 3 August 1754.

advance. Her direct involvement, however, may have been limited. Her contemporaries assumed that either she or Sir Edward Turner wrote the verses. Both were known to write poetry.[23] Moreover, Lady Susan was known to have published at least one *Address to the Freeholders* and some squibs during the election.[24] She was also a Scot by birth, and the verses contained Scottish expressions. Finally, several depositions stressed that 'some Words of the same were mis-spelt, and seemed to be wrote by an indifferent writer, resembling a Woman's Hand-writing'.[25] Although this implies, rather curiously, that legitimate Jacobites would have had flawless spelling and a beautiful hand, these comments could well have been a simple statement of fact. They would certainly have described Lady Susan's hand-writing accurately: her script was 'indifferent' at best, and her spelling was consistently idiosyncratic.

Despite this circumstantial evidence against Lady Susan, it is much more likely that Richard Blacow was the instigator of the Plot. Blacow, a former fellow of Brasenose College, was an experienced government writer who had been electioneering for the New Interest since 1753. Often in London, he was ably assisted in Oxford by his Exeter College compatriots, Thomas Bray and Benjamin Kennicott. The *London Evening Post* identified this triumvirate as the instigators of the Plot from the outset.[26] As the New Interest's 'men of business', they were the perfect people to carry out such an undertaking. All three were experienced New Interest agents and some of its most avid propagandists. They were also ambitious men who were eager to better themselves and had grievances against the university. As Whigs in a Tory institution, their political views opened them to

---

[23] Bodl. Gough p. 39; Robson, *Oxfordshire Election*, p. 134.

[24] Old Interest publications identify Lady Susan as the author of *An Address to the Freeholders of the County of Oxford* (1753). This pamphlet was taken seriously enough to merit two detailed Old Interest responses. See Bodl. G.A. Oxon. 8° 39(2), *To the Right Honourable Lady Susan Keck* (23 March 1753), in *The Old and New Interest: or, A Sequel to the Oxfordshire Contest* (1753), pp. 68-72; also G.A. Oxon. 8° 39(6), *A Letter to the Printer; with A Letter to the Freeholders of Oxfordshire. Containing Some Few Candid REMARKS on a* NEW *PAMPHLET, intitled An Address to the Freeholders of the County of Oxford* (1753). She is also credited with being the author of *A Letter to an Old Interest Freeholder of Oxfordshire*, a MSS copy of which survives in Thomas Bray's handwriting in his papers: Bray Papers, L.IV.7.F, Oxfordshire Parliamentary Elections, 1752–55. Elsewhere, Lady Susan is referred to satirically as 'a celebrated poetess ... *the Sappho of Oxford*'. In *A Song*, she is also charged with delighting in writing 'Such verses ... / As all modest Women abash wou'd'. This last comment appears to refer to *A Double Metamorphis: A Letter from Lord* Sue *to* Lady *Jemmy*, in which Lady Sue agrees that she is a better man than Sir James Dashwood and claims his breeches. See Bodl. Vet. A5 d. 1724, *News Boys, News! More and More News! or, The Electioneering Journal with Improvements. By an Impartial Hand. Wednesday, April 25, 1753. Numb. II*, in *The Election Magazine; or, The Oxfordshire Register,....* (1753), p. 26; see also Bodl. G.A. Oxon. 8° 53(1), *A Song*, and *A Double Metamorphis: A Letter from Lord* Sue *to* Lady *Jemmy*, both in *The Oxfordshire Contest* (1753), 57, pp. 52-3.

[25] Cornelius Norton, in *Informations and Other Papers*, pp. 36-7. Bew and Carter also reiterate this pp. 27, 29.

[26] *London Evening Post*, no. 4169.

hostile attacks and made lucrative preferments unlikely. Consequently, their future success depended largely upon their ability to secure the favour and patronage of the Whig establishment. Blacow and Bray, in particular, had both the motives and the means to set up the Plot.

Blacow's grievance was the most long-standing. His uncompromising Whiggism had destroyed his university career.[27] Back in 1747 when he had been the university's Warden of the Streets, he had arrested a group of undergraduates spouting Jacobite slogans. One of these students had been a member of St Mary's Hall, where Dr William King, the Principal, was an avowed Jacobite. When the Tory university administration refused to press charges against the students, Blacow side-stepped it and took the case to one of the country's leading Whig politicians, the duke of Newcastle. Eventually, Blacow succeeded in forcing the students' prosecution in King's Bench — and won. This satisfied his political principals, but it did little for his university career. He had aroused such lasting animosity in the university that he eventually gave up his fellowship and left Oxford. Fortunately, he was able to use his Whiggism and his political connections to secure useful patronage. By 1754 he was Canon of Windsor and his friendship with the Secretary of State, Lord Holdernesse, gave him access to the inner circle of the Newcastle Administration.[28]

Bray's grievance was more recent. The Old Interest's propagandists — all fellow academics — had made a concerted effort to blacken his reputation during the election campaign. In the summer of 1753, an Oxford prostitute, Theodosia Cornel, swore her bastard on Bray. The charge gave the Old Interest hacks, particularly John Billstone of All Souls College, an excuse to launch a sustained attack on Bray just as the election campaign was beginning to heat up. By August 1753, Bray was having to take time out of electioneering to gather character witnesses while Lady Susan Keck was helping him by putting pressure on Cornel's gaoler in order to prevent her from having any contact with the Old Interest. When the case finally came up at the March Assizes in 1754, Bray was vindicated. Cornel was convicted of slander and imprisoned for a further three months.[29]

With Bray and Kennicott in Oxford, and Blacow in London, the triumvirate was well situated to ensure that whatever happened in Oxford received press

---

[27] Kennicott and Bray were both actively seeking preferment in 1754. In May, Kennicott's efforts in the New Interest cause were successful and he was made a preacher in the king's chapel at Whitehall. After the election, in recognition of his efforts, Bray was appointed to the rectory of Bixbrand (Bix) by Lord Macclesfield. Later, he would serve as Rector of Exeter College (1771–1785), and, when Lord Harcourt became Lord-Lieutenant of Ireland, he would appoint Bray Dean of Raphoe. Bray would exchange this in 1774 for a canonry at Windsor and the rectory of Dunsfold. In August 1754, Harcourt and Marlborough were working together to secure him a vacant prebendary of Canterbury. See Robson, *Oxfordshire Election*, p. 74; Stride, W.K. (1900), *Exeter College*, pp. 136–7; Bray Papers, L.IV.7.C/51, Harcourt to Thomas Bray, Cockthrop, 4 August 1754.

[28] Robson, Oxfordshire Election, p. 4.

[29] Bray Papers, L.IV.7.B/26, Lady Susan Keck to Thomas Bray, Great Tew, 12 August 1753; Robson, *Oxfordshire Election*, p. 75.

coverage and political attention in London. Blacow inserted the first advertisement about the Plot into the London papers himself. He also brought the discovery of the verses to the attention of the Administration through his friend, the Secretary of State, Lord Holdernesse.

As Lord Hardwicke's correspondence with Holdernesse reveals, both he and the duke of Newcastle, then First Lord, took the verses very seriously.[30] For Hardwicke, the verses transcended the local struggle between the Old and New Interests in Oxford: they were 'downright Treason & incitement to Rebellion' which 'stands clear of any Party'.[31] Thus, he believed that the Administration could not afford to dismiss them like other libellous papers; instead, he favoured inserting an advertisement in the newspapers in the king's name. This advertisement, which offered a £200 reward, was meant to show 'the Support & Encouragem^{t}. of the Governm^{t}. to those well-affected Persons, whose Zeal has induc'd them to take notice of it already'.[32] In fact, it served as an excellent piece of advertising and ensured that knowledge of the verses (and by implication the political situation in Oxfordshire) was spread rapidly around the country.

Mrs Carnall and the Politics of Influence

The immediate success or failure of the Plot rested upon Mrs Carnall's ability to stage-manage the discovery of the verses and make them appear credible for long enough to ensure that the news could spread through the county, and then, via the London press, across the country. She had to make sure that knowledge of the discovery, even the words of the verses themselves, reached as many people as possible. She also had to link the verses to the Old Interest in the public mind if they were to dissuade potential witnesses from supporting the Old Interest cause in Parliament. In each of these, she was successful. As such, it is arguable that the part that she played in the Oxford marketplace was at least as important to the outcome of the Plot as that played by Blacow among the politicians in London.

Mrs Carnall's activities are doubly interesting because so little is known about the political involvement of urban women in the eighteenth century. Many of these women left no personal records, and here Mrs Carnall seems to be no exception. Indeed, most of the information available about Mrs Carnall comes from the depositions. They indicate that in 1754 she was the wife of a shopkeeper whose shop occupied prime real estate in the centre of Oxford, fronting the marketplace. The shop was patronized by the county elite. The Carnalls had at least two servants, and at least one of these helped in the shop. While both of the Carnalls seem to have had comfortable social relationships with their neighbouring shopkeepers, Mrs Carnall's relationships with townswomen who were somewhat

---

[30] BL Eg MS 3440, fos. 77–8, Hardwicke to Holdernesse, Powis House, 24 July 1754.

[31] BL Eg MS 3440, fo. 77.

[32] BL Eg MS 3440, fo. 77–77d; Robson, *Oxfordshire Election*, p. 130.

below her in rank appear to have been fraught. If a tedious contemporary satire can be believed, this might have been because Mrs Carnall was attempting to distance herself socially from women who had once been her peers, or it might have been envy on the part of the townswomen. *The Ragged Uproar: or, The Oxford Roratory: A New Dramatic Satire*, suggests that the Carnalls were an upwardly mobile couple who had originally been stallholders in the market, but had risen to become successful shopkeepers. Portrayed as the Plotwells, the play presents the Carnalls as an ambitious and unscrupulous couple, primarily interested in self-advancement. Mrs Carnall is portrayed as the dominant partner — Lady Macbeth to Carnall's Macbeth.[33]

Although this depiction is undoubtedly exaggerated, it does seem to reflect the balance of power within the relationship. Mrs Carnall definitely took the leading role in the Plot; her husband played at best a supporting part. It may also help to explain why the Carnalls became involved in the Plot. They do not appear to have been motivated by money, as they seem to have received only compensation for loss of trade. It seems more likely that they were driven by a combination of ideology and self-interest. If, as the depositions suggest, the Carnalls were firm New Interest supporters and, as the play insinuates, they were also eager to improve their social status and attract more elite customers (and thus more wealthy business), then the Plot would have looked very tempting. As New Interest supporters in Oxford, they were decidedly in the minority and, as such, especially given the length and viciousness of the election campaign, they would likely have had to endure numerous insults from Old Interest crowds. The Plot would have offered them a chance to strike a telling blow in return. It would also have held out the possibility of improved business by providing them with useful connections among the political elite, which, if carefully nurtured, might be turned into new customers or additional trade. Finally, if they were a calculating couple, they would have realized that even moderate success in the Plot would place the New Interest leadership in their debt — and debts of this sort in the eighteenth century could provide avenues to lucrative patronage, and thus improved status, in the future. These factors may well have outweighed the risk of arousing the hostility of Oxford's Old Interest supporters. The extent to which the Carnalls did become the focus of crowd anger testifies both to their centrality to the Plot and to the impact that the Plot was believed to have had at the time. As a result of their involvement, the Carnalls were publicly cursed, they and their servants were insulted in the streets, posters were put up advising a boycott of their shop, and their shop was attacked by a mob bent on violence and destruction.[34]

---

[33] *The Ragged Uproar: or, The Oxford Roratory: A New Dramatic Satire* [1755?].

[34] For the probably somewhat exaggerated indignities suffered by the Carnalls as a result of their involvement in the Plot, see the depositions given by Mary Faulkner and Mary and Robert Carnall to the six New Interest JPs on 10 October 1754: *Informations and Other Papers*, pp. 20-31. Mary Faulkner, in particular, related an incident involving an Oxford tailor, a Mr Breach. At about 9 p.m. one evening he appeared at the Carnalls's door to curse the house. After repeating '*May God eternally damn this House for here the Plot began!*'

This violence may well be due to Mrs Carnall's success in managing the initial stages of the Plot, particularly through her consummate skill in using the early modern tradition of verse libel to advantage and her ease in making political use of urban women's networks of contacts and their ability to mix readily with men and women in the marketplace. She arranged the 'discovery' of the verses wisely: it took place in public, in the middle of the market place, on a day when because of Quarter Sessions the market would have been busier than usual. She made sure that it took place in front of a well-known market trader, the widowed Mrs West. This gave her a reliable witness. Although, in her deposition to the Old Interest JPs on 4 August, Mrs West was to claim that she had not seen a paper in Riah's rags when she put them down — suggesting, correctly, that Mrs Carnall had put the verses into the rags herself — it is important to note that she does not appear to have raised this concern at the time of the discovery.[35] Furthermore, while the Old Interest made an effort to counter Mrs Carnall's version of events as soon as possible by circulating copies of their depositions, it must be noted that this still left her with a two-week advantage in spreading her story.[36]

Perhaps more by good fortune than careful forethought, Mrs Carnall also chose well in 'pinning' the verses to Riah Duke. An illiterate girl who made her living by buying rags and selling fruit in the streets of Oxford, Riah had neither the status nor the capability to challenge Mrs Carnall's version of events effectively. Had the verses been real, she would have made an excellent courier, as she moved around the city freely and by necessity mixed widely with people of all classes. Moreover, it could have been argued that she had the necessary connections. She was known to associate with a fruiterer named Kate Robinson, who Mrs Carnall claimed had Jacobite leanings and from whom, according to Riah's aunt, she had learned 'all Manner of such Songs'.[37] She also had a useful network of contacts through which she could spread the story of the verses and her ill-treatment at Mrs Carnall's hands.

When Mrs Carnall discovered the verses, she made a show of both the discovery and her (horrified) response. This must have attracted the attention of at least some of the traders and shoppers in the marketplace at the time. If nothing else, it would certainly have given Mrs West something to talk about for the rest of the day. In either case, the story of the discovery would have become common knowledge very quickly and rumours would have begun to fly. Then, after dawdling noticeably on her doorstep with the verses in her hand, Mrs Carnall took

---

about twenty times, Mary stepped outside to challenge him by telling him that she knew who he was. Completely unconcerned — presumably because, as Robert Carnall's experience with a rioter had shown, the local Constables were Old Interest supporters and refused to come to the aid of the Carnalls — his only reply was, 'Then you scourge me, if you can'. *Informations and Other Papers*, p. 24, p. 27.

[35] Mary West, 4 August 1754, in *Informations and Other Papers*, p. 20.

[36] See Bray Papers, L.IV.7.D., fos. 1–24. See especially Bray's correspondence with Harcourt [September 1754] and 8 September 1754, Blacow, 8 October 1754, and Macclesfield 14 October 1754.

[37] Mary Carnall, 10 October 1754, *Informations and Other Papers*, pp. 31-2.

them in to the shop where she shared them with her customers and neighbouring shopkeepers. She also made a point of taking them over to the shops of at least two other nearby shopkeepers and the stalls of some traders who travelled in to Oxford from more distant towns. The potential for spreading the news of the Plot grew exponentially with each shopkeeper or stallholder she told.

Mrs Carnall was vigorous in circulating both her tale of the discovery and the verses themselves. Those who could read, like the Oxford perruke-maker, Lawrence Horner, or John Barker, a milliner and hosier from Bicester, were given the verses to read. She also ensured that they were left in no doubt about who was behind the Plot. As the cordwainer, John Sare, recalled, he learned about the verses when Mrs Carnall came up to John Barker's stall in the marketplace. She introduced the verses to them, saying: 'See what the Blues have done! or, See what the Blues will do!'.[38] Some people were also given the opportunity to copy the verses. They were left for hours, for instance, perhaps even over night, with her neighbours, the tinman, Edward Browne, and his wife, Elizabeth.[39] Once retrieved, they were passed on directly to the mercer, Richard Bew, who took a copy for himself.[40]

People who were illiterate, such as Mrs West, Riah Duke or the laundress, Jane Sims, learned about the Plot by having the verses read to them, or being regaled with the details. Mrs Sims's story is especially intriguing.[41] It suggests in passing that levels of female literacy in Oxford were changing generationally at mid-century, so that illiterate female employers, even laundresses, might have literate female servants. More particularly, it reveals the degree of interest that the Plot sparked among women well down the social scale. It is impossible to tell from the information that survives whether Mrs Carnall and her servant, Mary Faulkner, planned what happened, or whether it occurred by chance; however, it certainly does indicate that by Sunday, 21 July, if not before, the Carnalls had more than one copy of the verses in their household.

According to Mary Faulkner, she had begun to copy the verses on to a piece of paper soon after they had been discovered, presumably out of interest, although neither this nor why she wanted a copy are explained. She then inadvertently wrote the laundry bill on the other side of the paper and delivered it, along with the dirty laundry, to Mrs Sims on 21 July. It was not until the laundry was returned clean the following Friday, 26 July, that she saw the bill again. In the intervening period, Mrs Sims, who was illiterate, had had her literate servant, Mary Kirby, read the verses to her. Mrs Sims claimed later that she had not understood the verses and so paid little heed to them. Mary, however, clearly found them highly interesting and read them carefully. In addition to reading them aloud to Mrs Sims, she read them

[38] Lawrence Horner, 19 August 1754, *Informations and Other Papers*, p. 23.

[39] Elizabeth Browne, 17 August 1754, *Informations and Other Papers*, p. 25.

[40] Richard Bew, 17 August 1754, *Informations and Other Papers*, p. 27.

[41] The narrative that follows is compiled from the 17 August depositions of Jane Sims and Mary Kirby, and the 10 October deposition of Mary Faulkner: *Informations and Other Papers*, pp. 32-35, pp. 22-24.

aloud to herself on at least three other separate occasions. Considering that the verses were in the Sims household for the better part of a week, there would have been plenty of time for her to have taken a copy or copies, and/or to have shared them with other friends and servants. In any case, at the time of her deposition on 17 August, she still knew parts of the poem by heart.

Mary Faulkner, who seems not to have been concerned about the verses while they were missing, made such a show of relief at seeing the bill returned that she prompted Mrs Sims to ask for an explanation. Her curiosity was further piqued when Mary told her that the verses were treasonable. She consequently took the bill away with her and refused to return it to Mary, even when Mary followed her into the street to demand it. Mary then grabbed someone else's clean laundry from Mrs Sims's basket and refused to return it unless the verses were surrendered. Since all of this took place just outside Mrs Carnall's shop — i.e., in the middle of the marketplace — it must have attracted the attention of onlookers and focused yet more attention on the verses. Mrs Sims was only finally persuaded to return the verses when Mrs Carnall sent another servant, Ann Smith, to tell her that she would withdraw her custom if Mrs Sims did not return them. After such a fuss — whether intentional or not — it would have been surprising if Mrs Sims and Mary Kirby had not spread their story — and thus news of the Plot — through their own networks of clients and friends.

Conclusion

Mrs Carnall used her networks of contacts knowingly and capitalized on her place at the heart of the marketplace to mix easily with men and women in order to disseminate the verses, gossip about the Plot and spread rumours attributing it to the Old Interest. She expressed her political allegiance openly and, while she may have been more highly politicized than other urban women, it is obvious from the way that her political involvement was acknowledged and accepted that her 'type' was familiar to her contemporaries. Moreover, her ability to use the early modern tradition of the verse libel to good effect testifies to at least one way that urban women could maintain a visible and vocal political presence in their communities and achieve some degree of political influence. As Andy Wood has noted in his recent study of social conflict in the Peak Country, 'women's words were more frequently remembered as spoken within the open places and streets of the Peak's small towns ... The market place of Wirksworth town was one such site'.[42] While Wood may be correct in suggesting that 'the public world of plebeian politics' was increasingly coming to be defined as that of 'the settled, adult male' in the eighteenth century,[43] he is also correct in suggesting that there was a significant gap between the rhetoric and reality of women's political involvement at the

[42] Wood, A. (1999), *The Politics of Social Conflict: The Peak Country, 1520–1770*, Cambridge, p. 186.

[43] Wood, *The Politics of Social Conflict*, p. 127.

community level. While their formal political involvement might have been strictly limited, the extent and importance of their informal participation — personally or as members of female networks — could vary significantly according to community and local context.[44] This is worth bearing in mind and exploring in more detail if, as both Rosemary Sweet and Phil Withington have argued in slightly different ways, eighteenth-century towns did not descend into sloth and corruption but remained politically vital communities where 'a variety of cultural precepts and practices were sustained, contested, modified and appropriated'.[45] The nature of urban women's political involvement at the community level becomes increasingly important if, as Withington has argued — and Sweet would agree — eighteenth-century towns retained strong 'communal imperatives of citizenship' that were manifested in much more diverse forms of civic participation and governance than historians who have focused on civic office-holding have tended to assume.[46]

By the time that the Old Interest JPs began to take depositions, Mrs Carnall had spread the news of the Plot directly to at least nineteen named people. It is impossible to guess how many others remained unspecified or learned about the Plot at one remove. Even if she had told few others, the news would still have travelled widely. At the core of the named group were seven market traders or shopkeepers, four servants and a laundress — all people extremely well placed to pass the story on through their own extensive networks of contacts. The shopkeepers and market traders included: the cheesemonger, Mary West; the mercer and JP, John Austin; the perruke-maker, Lawrence Horner; Elizabeth Browne (whose husband presumably learned about the Plot from her and/or by reading the verses in the comfort in his own home); the milliner, William Carter, and his wife; and the milliner and hosier, John Barker. The mercer, Richard Bew, learned about the verses from Robert Carnall, but later made a special trip back to the Carnalls's shop to read and copy them. This second trip may have brought him into direct contact with Mrs Carnall. The servants included the Mary Faulkner, Ann Smith, William Harris, and Mary Kirby.

Ultimately, the success or failure of the Plot depended upon Mrs Carnall's ability to carry it successfully through the discovery and dissemination stages. This she did. By the time that the Plot itself had been exploded and the debate over it had degenerated into an internecine university squabble, it had largely met its goals. It succeeded in keeping the election fresh in the minds of the electorate over the summer and, judging from the anger it aroused in the Old Interest crowd, it had made an impact in the wider community and may well have discouraged support for the Old Interest. Through its use of the press and political connections, it was

---

[44] Wood, *The Politics of Social Conflict*, p. 87.

[45] Sweet, R. (1999), *The English Town, 1680–1840*; Withington, P. (2000), 'Citizens, Community and Political Culture in Restoration England', in A. Shepard and P. Withington (eds), *Communities in Early Modern England: Networks, Place, Rhetoric*, Manchester, pp. 135-6.

[46] Withington, 'Citizens, Communities and Political Culture', p. 136.

understood to have raised awareness and support for the New Interest cause among MPs. Perhaps Mrs Carnall was able to take just a little pleasure in hearing Old Interest supporters damn her as they passed her shop because 'she had *ruined the Old Interest* and the *Town*'.[47] When the eventual victory of the New Interest candidates was declared in April 1755, she must certainly have felt some sense of vindication.

[47] For the Old Interest response, see the final depositions given by Mary and Robert Carnall and their servant, Mary Faulkner, on 10 October 1754, in *Informations and Other Papers*, pp. 25-34.

Appendix: Rag Plot Chronology*

17–23 April, 1754	Poll;
9–28 May	Scrutiny: New Interest representations;
29–30 May (noon)	Scrutiny: Old Interest representations;
31 May	Writ to be returned; Sheriff Blackall makes a double return;
[31?] May	Chimneysweep shot by Col. Turton on Madgalen Bridge;
c.1.–16 June	Inquest;
16 June	letter from Marlborough to Newcastle indicates that the Coroner (an Old Interest supporter) has brought down a verdict of wilful murder; the case is referred to the Assizes;
17 July	Rag Plot begins with discovery of 'treasonable' verses by Mrs Mary Carnall at Carfax;
23 July	Richard Blacow's advertisement in London newspapers which misdates the discovery of the verses to 13 July and identifies Cornelius Norton as the contact for the £50 reward;
24 July	Assizes; presentment of verses to the Grand Jury by Norton's son and Mrs Carnall;
27 July	the Newcastle Administration's advertisement in London newspapers in the king's name offering a reward of £200 for further information about the perpetrators of the Rag Plot;
29 July–22 Aug.	Old Interest depositions are taken from witnesses in front of three Old Interest JPs: the Mayor, Daniel Shilfox, the Vice-Chancellor George Huddesford, and the jurist, William Blackstone; a few New Interest depositions are taken for balance in front of the New Interest JPs Paul Elers and John Lenthall; the Old Interest depositions are quickly circulated and are later printed;
10 Oct.	another set of New Interest depositions is taken from leading witnesses in front of six New Interest JPs: Sir Edward Turner, Bart.; the Master of Balliol, Dr Theophilus Leigh; John Lenthall, Esq.; Anthony Tracy Keck, Esq.; Paul Elers, Esq.; and John Travell, Esq.;

18 Nov.	three petitions regarding the Oxfordshire election are presented to Parliament;
3 Dec.	Oxfordshire's controverted election case begins in Parliament;
12 Dec.–21 Jan.	Old Interest counsel objects to between 530 and 548 votes; disqualifies 414;
28 Jan.–13 Feb.	the New Interest counsel deals with question of bribery and vindicates copyholders' right to vote;
13 Feb.–*c.* 1 Mar.	Old Interest motion/debate to disqualify all copyholders;
25 Feb.–mid-Mar.	New Interest counsel requalifies 264 of the votes disqualified by the Old Interest and then objects to 522 Old Interest votes; disqualifies 374.
week off	
29 Mar.	Old Interest counsel requalifies 50 votes; debate on conduct of the High Sheriff;
24 Apr.	New Interest victory: Hillsborough moves at midnight that Turner is elected; a subsequent motion declares Parker elected; the outcome of the election is finally settled.

* towards the end of 1754 there was another minor stir, when the butler at Exeter College was accused of trying to place a picture of the Old Pretender into the back of an Old Interest gentleman's watch; nothing however comes of this 'watch plot'.

Chapter 4

Women as Objects and Agents of Charity in Eighteenth-Century Birmingham

Sylvia Pinches

Ever since the exhortations in the New Testament 'to visit the fatherless and widows in their affliction', women have been seen as proper objects of charity. However, people were also aware of the parable of the widow's mite, when Christ extolled the poor widow for giving all she had, in contrast to the rich who only gave what they had to spare. The allegorical depiction of Charity was often a female figure and women were regarded as having a special affinity with works of mercy. This was seen as an extension of their domestic and maternal roles, yet the ministration of charity frequently took women out of their homes. Some charities were aimed exclusively at women, and many more were supported by women. As the eighteenth century wore on women moved from traditional neighbourly visiting and pious bequests to involvement with voluntary associations and with many reforming campaigns. Given the urban location of most of these associations and campaigns, charitable work, it could be said, was for many women a defining feature of urban life and constituted an important channel through which they could actively engage with and contribute to the urban community of which they were a part. Towns, with their higher concentrations of wealth, their traditions of charitable giving, and their networks of charitable associations, also offered more opportunities for women seeking to survive through the mixed economy of welfare. This chapter will explore the experiences of women as both donors and recipients of charity, through a case study of one eighteenth-century town, Birmingham.

The period covered by this study is the long century from the 1690s to the 1830s. Apart from David Owen's sweeping survey of 300 years of charitable effort in *English Philanthropy, 1660-1960*, it is only in recent years that much attention has been paid to the eighteenth century.[1] However, there have been detailed studies of certain categories of beneficiary, such as the physically and mentally ill, or 'fallen women'.[2] The lack of a general study is particularly true with regard to

[1] Owen, D. (1965), English Philanthropy, 1660–1960, London.

[2] For hospitals, see Berry, A. (1995), 'Patronage, Funding and the Hospital Patient, c. 1750–1815: Three English Regional Case Studies', unpublished University of Oxford PhD thesis; Borsay, A. (1991) 'Cash and Conscience: Financing the General Hospital at Bath, c. 1738–50', *The Social History of Medicine*, 4, pp. 219-20; Borsay, A. (1991),

female involvement with charity. There has been a considerable amount of research on female philanthropy in the nineteenth century but, as Amanda Vickery has put it for female history in general, 'the eighteenth century is the sketchy before picture'.[3] Those who have studied eighteenth-century female philanthropy have mostly concentrated on aristocratic women's patronage or have focussed on the role of evangelicalism at the turn of the nineteenth century.[4] Much has been written about philanthropy as essentially a feminine sphere of action, in the context of the debate over the 'separate spheres' of public and private, male and female, activity. However, Mary Martin, in a detailed study of the activities of elite women in the suburban parishes of Walthamstow and Leyton in the period 1740 to 1870, has challenged the assumption that female philanthropy was different from male, and that it reflected an increased separation of the sexes over the years.[5]

According to Penelope Corfield it is a 'firmly established fact that the majority of urban residents in eighteenth century England were female'.[6] It is therefore high time for a study of urban women and philanthropy, and Birmingham provides an appropriate locus for such a study. By the end of the eighteenth century Birmingham had grown from a busy market and manufacturing centre to the fourth largest town in England, after London, Liverpool and Manchester. The population of Birmingham expanded rapidly in the eighteenth century: it has been estimated that in 1700 it was between 5,000 and 7,000, in 1750 was 23, 688 and by 1775 had risen to 40,000. In 1801 the population was 73,670, including Aston and Edgbaston.[7] Situated as it was in the extreme north-west corner of Warwickshire,

---

'"Persons of Honour and Reputation": the Voluntary Hospital in an Age of Corruption', Medical History, 35, pp. 281–94; Lane, J. (1992), *Worcester Infirmary in the Eighteenth Century*, Worcestershire Historical Society, 6, Worcester; Porter, R. (1989), 'The Gift-Relation: Philanthropy and Provincial Hospitals in Eighteenth-Century England', in L. Granshaw and R. Porter (eds), *The Hospital in History*, London, pp. 149–80; Porter, R. (1987), *Mind-Forg'd Manacles: A History of Madness in England from the Restoration to the Regency*, London. For fallen women, see Lloyd, S. (1996), '"Pleasure's Golden Bait": Prostitution, Poverty and the Magdalen Hospital in Eighteenth-Century London', *History Workshop Journal*, 41, pp. 57–70; Nash, S. (1984), 'Prostitution and Charity: the Magdalen Hospital, a Case Study', *Journal of Social History*, 17, pp. 617–28.

[3] Vickery, A. (1993), 'Golden Age to Separate Spheres? A Review of the Categories and Chronology of English Women's History', *Historical Journal*, 36, pp. 393–401, p. 397.

[4] Andrew, D.T. (1995), 'Female Charity in an Age of Sentiment', in J. Brewer and S. Staves (eds), *Early Modern Conceptions of Property*, London, pp. 275–300; Larson, E. (1986), 'A Measure of Power: the Personal Charity of Elizabeth Montagu', *Studies in Eighteenth-Century Culture*, 16, pp. 197–210; Elliott, D.W. (1995), '"The Care of the Poor is Her Profession": Hannah More and Women's Philanthropic Work', *Nineteenth-Century Contexts*, 19, pp. 179-204; Prochaska, F.K. (1974), 'Women in English Philanthropy, 1790-1830', *International Review of Social History*, 19, pp. 426– 45.

[5] Martin, M.C. (1994), 'Women and Philanthropy in Walthamstow and Leyton, 1740– 1870', *London Journal*, 19, pp. 119–50.

[6] Corfield, P. J. (1982), *The Impact of English Towns, 1700–1800,* Oxford, p. 99.

[7] *Victoria County History of Warwickshire* (1964), VII, p. 8 (hereafter cited as *V.C.H.*); Hopkins, E. (1998), 'The Birmingham Economy During the Revolutionary and Napoleonic Wars, 1793–1815', *Midland History*, 23, pp. 105–20, p. 105.

bordering Staffordshire and Worcestershire, the built-up area of Birmingham soon included parts of neighbouring parishes over the county borders. This made a very complex set of problems for local government and the reality of parish boundaries was important both for poor relief and charity eligibility. Birmingham exerted a social as well as an economic influence over a wide region. Therefore, this study will include charities in the parishes of Aston, Birmingham, Edgbaston, Handsworth and Harborne, all of which became subsumed in the city of Birmingham, and will make occasional excursions to nearby urban centres, such as Coleshill.

Although there were economic fluctuations over such a long period as that under consideration here, and considerable regional variations, the eighteenth century was not, in general, an easy time for women. Bridget Hill has highlighted the particular difficulties facing single women, whether spinsters, unmarried mothers, or widows, whose livelihood depended on their own exertions. Not only did eighteenth-century society fail to acknowledge the problems facing single women, but there was a refusal to recognise that women had any real existence outside marriage. Single women not only had to struggle to support themselves, but were the objects of scorn for their unmarried state.[8] This led to the adoption of many strategies for survival, the manipulation of charitable funds being one of them.[9] In the mixed economy of welfare, charity played an important role: Peter Mandler's comment that charity was probably a more important resource for women than for men during the nineteenth century is likely to have been true of the eighteenth century, too.[10] To this extent, therefore, a large urban centre was potentially a more attractive environment for women who were in vulnerable positions than was rural and semi-rural society, where charitable provision was more limited.

The definitions of charity have been many and various, and have changed over time. As Hugh Cunningham wrote, 'in the seventeenth to nineteenth centuries the terms "charity" and "philanthropy", like the modern term "welfare", designated broad areas of concern, rather than particular modes of addressing those concerns'.[11] Although the relief of poverty is the first thing which springs to mind on hearing the word charity, it was by no means the only activity which was covered by that word. The promotion of religion, the support of education and the improvement of many aspects of public life have all been considered charitable. This study will take a wide interpretation of charity, encompassing endowments and voluntary associations operating in various spheres. The eighteenth century

---

[8] Hill, B. (1989), *Women, Work and Sexual Politics in Eighteenth-Century England*, Oxford, p. 263.

[9] Connors, R. (1997), 'Poor Women, the Parish and the Politics of Poverty' in H. Barker and E. Chalus (eds), *Gender in Eighteenth-Century England: Roles, Representations and Responsibilities*, London, pp. 126–47.

[10] Mandler, P. (1990), *The Uses of Charity: The Poor on Relief in the Nineteenth-Century Metropolis*, Philadelphia, p. 20.

[11] Cunningham, H. (1998), 'Introduction' in H. Cunningham and J. Innes (eds), *Charity, Philanthropy and Reform from the 1690s to 1850*, Basingstoke, p. 2.

also saw the rise of many societies for mutual benefit and, while they were not strictly speaking charitable, they were often sponsored and encouraged by members of the elite.

This chapter will begin by looking at women as objects of charity; examining charities through the different stages of the female lifecycle – children, women in childbirth and women alone – rather than by type of organisation. In the second section women's activities as agents of charity – as donors, trustees, subscribers and committees will be considered, bearing in mind the fact that individual women may well have been involved in more than one type of activity.

Women as Objects of Charity

Unfortunately few charities have left sufficiently detailed records for the eighteenth century to be able to identify individual recipients, still less to hazard a guess as to their reactions to their situation. The main documentary survivals for endowed charities are title deeds to properties and trust deeds nominating new trustees. Further evidence is provided by the Gilbert Returns of Charitable Donations, 1787–8 and the reports of the Commission of Inquiry under Lord Brougham, 1819–37. The latter reports give details of the history of the endowment as well as of its state at the time of the inquiry.[12] Voluntary associations and institutions have left minute books and printed reports, including lists of subscribers, and their activities were mentioned in local newspapers, but the individual beneficiaries are seldom evident. Therefore the various categories of beneficiary will be discussed as a group, with an outline of the help provided for them in Birmingham.

Female Children

There were few charities aimed specifically at female children, although girls were included in some general charities of an educational nature. For example, at the end of the seventeenth century George Fentham left £20 a year for the education of male and female children.[13] The trustees of the Birmingham charity decided to pay the Blue Coat School to educate a certain number of children, rather than employ a schoolmaster themselves. At the time of the Charity Commissioners' enquiry in 1828 the Fentham trust was paying £11 per child, usually between ten and twenty at

---

[12] Gilbert Returns of Charitable Donations, P.P. 1816 (511) XVIa (returns for Warwickshire, Warwickshire County Record Office (hereafter W.C.R.O) QS 69/4); Reports of the Commissioners to Inquire concerning Charities relating to the County of Warwickshire, 1819–1837 (published in one volume, 1843; London, 1890), hereafter cited as *Brougham*.

[13] By will dated 24 April 1690 and codicil dated 2 December 1697. George Fentham had been born in Hampton-in-Arden, Warwickshire and became a mercer in Birmingham, leaving money for the poor and for education and apprenticing in both Hampton and Birmingham. *Brougham*, pp. 245-52, 402-11.

a time, as well as £10 a year to the master and mistress of the school.[14] This kept the child fully clothed throughout the year, in a coat or gown of coarse green cloth, to differentiate them from the Blue Coat scholars. On leaving the school an apprenticeship was sought for them, without a premium, and they were given a set of clothes.[15]

The Blue Coat School had been established in 1722, subsequent to the Act of Parliament which established the new parish of St Philip's.[16] From the outset the school combined voluntary support with endowed income, and attracted the benefactions of women. Only three months later, in February 1722/3, Elizabeth White drew up her will, leaving an estate in Aston for the benefit of the charity school at Birmingham for the education of boys and girls.[17] Other endowments followed, as well as annual subscriptions and charity sermons.[18] By 1828 the annual endowed income amounted to £1028 18s. 4d., 'increased by subscriptions and casual benefactions to above £2000 per annum'. The education provided for 160 children, plus the Fentham children, and encompassed reading, writing and the 'principles of Religion according to the Church of England'.[19]

Other denominations, too, were concerned for the education of the young. Birmingham had a particularly strong dissenting tradition, and a Catholic minority which grew rapidly in the later eighteenth century. Just over ten years after the foundation of the Anglican Blue Coat School, Mrs Ann Crowley established a school for Protestant Dissenters. She left property in Birmingham, to provide £5 a year for the poor, the remainder for the use of a school run by some poor woman for ten poor children. From 1779 £6 a year was paid to a schoolmistress to teach ten girls in her own home to read, sew and knit. In 1804 Mrs Ann Scott, wife of Joseph Scott, a great supporter of Carr's Lane Independent Chapel, gave £100 to be invested for the benefit of this school, producing £5 5s. in dividends by 1828. This latter sum was used 'in the purchase of cloth and worsted, and other material, which are given to the girls, to be by them worked up into clothing for their own

[14] The income of the Birmingham trust was £298, of which some £190 was spent on education. *Brougham*, p. 410.

[15] *Brougham*, p. 395-7. For the uniform worn by the children of the Blue Coat School, Birmingham, including Fentham's Green Coats, see Cunnington, P. and Lucas, C. (1978), *Charity Costumes of Children, Scholars, Almsfolk and Pensioners*, London, pp. 157-61.

[16] Still, V.D.B. (1972), *The Blue Coat School, Birmingham, 1722-1972*, The Blue Coat School, Birmingham.

[17] *Brougham*, p. 396.

[18] In 1726 Benjamin Salusbury left £2 a year to the school and 15s. each to the rectors of St Martin's and St Philip's to preach a sermon for the benefit of the school on 1 November and 1 June respectively. *Brougham,* p. 397. In October 1789 Dr. Samuel Parr of Hatton took the opportunity of the charity sermon to castigate the citizens of Birmingham for their money-grubbing spirit and to remind them 'to do their duty by the children of the poor'. Derry, W. (1966), *Dr. Parr: A Portrait of the Whig Dr. Johnson*, Oxford, pp. 128-9.

[19] Analytical Digest of the Reports of the Commissioners of Inquiry, 1819-37, P.P. 1843 [433] [435] XVI, XVII, p. 283.

use'.[20] This emphasis on useful work was approved of by William Hutton when he wrote his *History of Birmingham* in 1783. He described the Dissenting Charity School as being established 'upon nearly the same plan as [the Blue Coat School], consisting of about eighteen boys and eight girls; with this improvement, that the boys are inured to moderate labour, and the girls to house-work'.[21] By the 1820s there was also a Girls' Lancasterian School in Birmingham.

However, many children were already gainfully employed and thus prevented from attending such schools as did exist. The rector of St. Martin's told the Commission on the Education of the Poor in 1819:

> As it is the practice in Birmingham to employ children at an early age, in the different manufactories, there will always be a large class of both sexes precluded from the advantages of Education, except on Sundays, and that if buildings (which are much wanted) could be provided in the most populous and necessitous districts of the town for instruction on that day they would most essentially promote the advantages of education; the expenses for teachers and books would be trifling, and might generally be provided for by local subscriptions and congregational sermons.[22]

Although not sufficient for the need, there were a number of Sunday Schools in Birmingham already, which also included girls in their care. Although often particularly associated with the dissenting sects, Sunday Schools were also provided by Anglicans and Roman Catholics. Birmingham in the 1780s offered an intriguing, if short-lived, example of an inter-denominational Sunday School under lay management.[23] Thereafter the various denominations ran their own Sunday Schools, imparting their own flavour of religion along with 'a tincture of learning to the poor and destitute offspring of the lower class'.[24] As with day schools, even when they took both sexes, Sunday Schools educated girls in separate departments under female instruction. The experience of the Catholic Sunday Schools established at St. Chad's Church shows that there were limits to the commitment of many women to the ideals of philanthropy: it was not always easy to find young women prepared to work so closely with the inhabitants of the slums of central Birmingham. At the first annual general meeting in 1810 it was resolved 'that the subscribers be requested to solicit the young ladies of the congregation to devote some little time to the most charitable work of attending the school' and they asked

---

[20] *Brougham*, pp. 414-15.

[21] Hutton, W. (1783; 1976), *The History of Birmingham*, Wakefield, p. 214.

[22] Report on the Education of the Poor, P.P. 1819 (224), IX Part II, p. 997.

[23] There were other examples in Norwich, Manchester and Coventry. 'The sordid details' of the break-up of the town-wide schools in Birmingham 'only emerged as part of Joseph Priestley's account of the high Church bigotry in which the King and Country Riots were but the last episode'. Laqueur, T.W. (1976), *Religion and Respectability: Sunday Schools and Working Class Culture, 1780–1850*, London, pp. 30, 70-1.

[24] Copy of an address to the Catholics of Birmingham, January 10th 1812. Birmingham Archdiocesan Archives (hereafter B.A.A.) P1/60/1 Journal of the Catholic Sunday School Established in Birmingham 1809.

Mr. Hardman, a leading member of the congregation and the first visitor of the Sunday School, 'to solicit his daughter to set the first example'. Such pleas were repeated over the next few years. It was not until 1815, after the first lady visitor, Mrs. Hunt, had been appointed that thanks were recorded to Miss Hardman and Miss Gray 'for their great attention to the children ... and for the plan they have laid down for their instruction which has very much contributed to the improvement of the school.'[25]

Women in Childbed

Although, or perhaps because, the experience of childbirth was so common an exigency, there were few, if any, endowed charities for the support of the nursing mother. It was during the middle years of the eighteenth century that the attention of philanthropists turned to women in childbed. The same fears about a debilitated nation and declining population that contributed to the establishment of the Foundling Hospital in 1739 also led to the establishment of lying-in hospitals and charities.[26] Due to the poor reputation which large towns such as Birmingham had for high mortality rates, this was a particularly pressing urban concern. As was often the case with philanthropic causes, this movement began in the metropolis and then was taken up in the provinces. The City of London Lying-in Hospital (later called the British Lying-in Hospital) was founded in 1750.[27] Seven years later, reflecting disquiet at both the cost and ineffectiveness of hospital deliveries, the Lying-in Charity for Delivering Poor Married Women in their own Habitations was established.[28] It was this latter type of charity which was more often emulated in the provinces, although for reasons which are not entirely clear, Birmingham was somewhat slow to do so. In Pye's *Description of Modern Birmingham* (1818) there is mention of the Female Benevolent Society, established in 1802 to 'relieve indigent married women when ill or confined', but it does not appear to have left any records.[29] However, the Birmingham Society for Administering Relief to Poor Lying-in Women, established in 1813, has done.[30]

Like most lying-in charities, the Birmingham society was only for the benefit of married women. It is interesting to compare the regulations with those of the Lying-in Charity at Coleshill, a market town some eight miles from Birmingham. This had been established in 1789 when a fund raising sermon was preached in the presence

[25] B.A.A., P1/60/1 Journal of the Catholic Sunday School ..., 1 Jan. 1810; 7 Jan. 1812; 16 January, 2 April 1815.

[26] McClure, R. K. (1981), *Coram's Children: The London Foundling Hospital in the Eighteenth Century*, New Haven; Owen, English Philanthropy, pp. 53-57.

[27] Andrew, D.T. (1989), Philanthropy and Police: London Charity in the Eighteenth Century, Princeton, p. 65.

[28] Andrew, *Philanthropy and Police*, pp. 105-7.

[29] Pye, C. (1818), Description of Modern Birmingham cited in L. Davidoff and C. Hall (1987), Family Fortunes: Men and Women of the English Middle Class, 1780–1850, London, p. 434.

[30] Birmingham City Archives (hereafter B.C.A.) MS 954, Minutes of the Society for Administering Relief to Poor Lying-in Women, 1813-1828.

of the Duchess of Gloucester and the Earl and Countess of Aylesford.[31] The rules of this society, which was part-benefit club and part-charity, as many lying-in charities were, stipulated that 'no person unmarried, or of bad character, or residing more than five miles from Coleshill, be admitted into this society'. If the applicant was 'a proper person to be admitted' they were enrolled by the Steward upon payment of 2s. 6d., and then 6d. on the first Wednesday of every month thereafter. The benefits of membership included attendance by a surgeon during illness or confinement, the loan of baby-linen and a payment of 4s. upon her delivery, and a further 1s. when she returned the linen 'clean ... otherwise she forfeits the one shilling'. She was also entitled to a payment of 4s a week during illness rendering her incapable of work, for up to one year, 1s a week thereafter, upon production of a doctor's certificate.[32] When founded in 1813, the Birmingham society called itself 'A Society for Administering Comfort to Poor Lying-in Women', but by the annual meeting the following year it made it clear that it was a 'Society for Providing Nurses for Poor Married Lying-in Women', living within the area covered by the Birmingham Dispensary. Unlike the Coleshill society this was entirely charitable and did not include an element of self-help. Those women seeking the services of a nurse had to apply to one of the subscribers (at 10s. 6d. a year), who would issue them with a ticket if they were deemed suitable. The society employed nurses who would attend a woman during her confinement and, at the discretion of the visitor, a payment of up to 2s. 6d. might be made to the new mother.[33]

The situation of the unmarried mother was even more precarious. As well as the dangers of childbirth and the economic consequences attendant on the care of a baby, she had to face the opprobrium of society. She received no medical help from the lying-in charities and little indeed was done to care for her and her child. The 'seduced maiden' of popular literature may well have had to resort to prostitution to survive. If she suffered from venereal disease she might be treated in a Lock Hospital, the first one founded in London in 1746.[34] More emphasis was placed on reforming her moral turpitude and returning her to society in some useful capacity – often as a domestic servant. The Magdalen Hospital was initiated in London in 1758 by Robert Dingley, with the publication of his pamphlet, *Proposals for Establishing a Public Place of Reception for Penitent Prostitutes.* This voluntarily funded establishment sought to reform the women through a mixture of religious and moral instruction and training in a useful trade or craft, such as spinning, knitting or fancy manufactures.[35] Once again Birmingham was slow to adopt this type of organisation. It was not until 1828 that a Magdalen Asylum was established, acquiring premises in the Islington area of the town in

---

[31] The Earl of Aylesford's seat is a few miles outside Coleshill.

[32] W.C.R.O. DRB/100/162, Regulations of the Society, in the Coleshill Lying-in Charity Minutes, 1832-1861.

[33] B.C.A. MS 954, Minutes of the Society for Administering Relief to Poor Lying-in Women, 22 September 1813, 21 September 1814.

[34] Owen, *English Philanthropy*, pp. 52-3.

[35] Lloyd, "Pleasures Golden Bait"; Nash, 'Prostitution and Charity'; Owen, *English Philanthropy*, pp. 57-58.

1829. It was 'to be a temporary asylum for women, fallen into vice, who profess themselves penitent' and survived, in modified form, into the twentieth century.[36]

Women Alone

Women could find themselves alone, and therefore dependent upon their own resources, for a number of reasons. The deserted wife, the widowed, and the never wed might face similar practical problems of survival, but society viewed them in different ways, and the means open to them for support were varied. Whatever the cause, it has been estimated that during the eighteenth century between 9 per cent and 14 per cent of all households were headed by women. As might be expected, the majority were mature or elderly women.[37] While the fact of being a woman alone did not necessarily mean poverty, nevertheless research has shown that during the early modern period 80 per cent of those classed as poor were women.[38] The situation of all women without a male 'head' was exacerbated if they had dependent children. The deserted wife was probably in the worst plight, of poverty, uncertainty and social contempt. Although the records of the poor law show payments to such women (or efforts to remove them to their disappeared husband's parish of settlement), there is no clear evidence of organised charitable relief for this category. Such charitable help as there was must have been on the personal level of neighbourliness. Indeed, this informal help by family and neighbours must have supported the elderly, too, for as Pat Thane wrote, 'it is inconceivable that they could have survived on the amount of poor relief they received and other known resources'.[39] The spinster, too, faced an uncertain future, once her parents were dead. The role of domestic servant was the most common employment of single females, but few could hope to emulate the career of Maria Home, who entered the employ of the Earl of Warwick in 1776 and died in 1834 at the age of 93, leaving a fortune amounting to £20,000 amassed during her years in service.[40] Most faced a bleak future once too old to work. Even for those above the servant class, the life of a dependent spinster could be grim, 'unable to work, ashamed to beg', as Mary Wollstonecraft put it in 1792.[41] The widow, of whatever age, was the

---

[36] *V.C.H.*, VII, p. 565.

[37] Wall, R. (1981), 'Women Alone in English Society', *Annales de Demographie Historique*, 16, pp. 303–17, p. 303.

[38] Connors, R. (1997), 'Poor Women, the Parish and the Politics of Poverty' in H. Barker and E. Chalus (eds), *Gender in Eighteenth-Century England: Roles, Representations and Responsibilities*, London, p. 127.

[39] Thane, P. (1996), 'Old People and their Families in the Past' in M. Daunton (ed.), *Charity, Self-Interest and Welfare in the English Past*, London, p. 123.

[40] P.R.O. PROB 11/1832, Will of Maria Home, proved 21 June 1834, *Annual Register* (1834), p. 233.

[41] Quoted in Hill, B. (1989), *Women, Work and Sexual Politics in Eighteenth-Century England*, Oxford, p. 229.

type of female most likely to elicit pity, although there were various stereotypes including the pious widow and the merry widow, as well as the poor widow.[42]

While many of these poor women could, and did, benefit from charities for the poor generally, there were certain charities in Birmingham which aimed specifically to help women. Of nine charities endowed between 1680 and 1831 for the benefit of women, four, ranging in date from 1690 to 1829, were for widows. Two, endowed in 1716 and 1719, were for 'poor women', and two specified a certain number of men and women. Only one, endowed in 1826, was for 'old maidens or single women of virtuous character'. Those for both men and women were the charities of Joseph Hopkins, endowed in 1691, and Elizabeth Hollier, endowed in 1789. Hopkins left £200 to provide coats and gowns for four poor men and four poor women of Birmingham. The money was invested in land and by 1827 the income of £37 was spent on some sixty gowns for women each year. Hollier left land in Aston to provide coats and gowns for twelve poor men and women of Birmingham and eight of Aston. By 1827 her charity, too, was making more gifts to women than to men – in the previous four years it had dispensed only sixteen coats but forty gowns and forty shifts. Neither of these two charities seems to have made additional stipulations for qualification other than poverty. However, in 1716 Samuel Banner, adding to the six coats for men left by his brother Richard, made it clear that the two poor women of Birmingham who were to receive his gowns and petticoats (bearing the letters 'S. B.') were not to be in receipt of parish relief. By 1827 the number of recipients had increased to between six and sixteen men for Richard's coats and between thirty and forty widows for Samuel's gowns, 'given to the most deserving not in receipt of ordinary parish relief'. Mary Sheldon left £1,000 in 1821 to provide an income for 'ten old maidens, or single women of virtuous character, parishioners of Birmingham', although a Charity Commission Scheme of 1860 determined that widows were also eligible. Of the charities for widows, three merely stressed their poverty and residence in Birmingham (within 200 yards of the Bull Ring in the case of George Fentham in 1690), but Anne Wilkinson left £142 in 1829 to benefit twelve poor widows 'who usually attended service at St. Philip's church'.[43]

The selection of residents of almshouse was even more strict than of recipients of doles, and the regulation of their lives consequently more restricting. Although not the most common form of relief, almshouses were one of the most visible aspects of charity to the poor and were almost always found in an urban location. They have tended to be dismissed by historians of welfare as being insignificant in their impact on poverty, although Alannah Tomkins has recently suggested that their contribution on a nationwide scale needs to be reassessed and that where they did exist they would have had made a significant difference to the circumstances of the poor, particularly those on the margins of parochial relief. However, she also pointed out that almshouses were very unevenly distributed around the country and often had very few places available compared with the size of the population. In the

---

[42] Cavallo, S. and Warner, L. (1999), 'Introduction' in S. Cavallo and L. Warner (eds), *Widowhood in Early Modern Europe*, Harlow, pp. 6-9.

[43] *Brougham*, pp. 403-10, 445-7, 448-52, 458, *V.C.H.*, VII, p. 566.

mid-eighteenth century York was unusual in having 147 almshouse places, which gave a ratio of one to seventy-five inhabitants. More usual were the cases of Salisbury, Shrewsbury and Gloucester, with ratios of one to nearly 200 inhabitants.[44] In Birmingham itself there was only one almshouse charity. This was Lench's Trust, a collection of charitable trusts administered by one set of trustees, originating with a trust deed of William Lench in 1526, endowing a charity to keep the streets in repair. The subsequent trusts administered by the trustees included those for many purposes, and it appears that the almshouse for women at Digbeth came into their keeping in 1628. A second set of almshouses was built by them in Steelhouse Lane in 1688. Both of these were replaced by a new almshouse, also in Steelhouse Lane, in 1764. A new house was built in Dudley Street in 1801. The gifts of Ann Scott in 1808, Sarah Glover and Elizabeth Mansfield in 1824 and Judith, Sarah and Mary Mansell in 1829 for the benefit of the almswomen enabled the building of more houses in Park Street in 1815 and 1820, and in Hospital Street, completed in 1829. By 1827 the trust had 112 places for women in three houses in Birmingham – still very few in comparison to the size of the population. The almswomen were 'poor aged females, inhabitants of Birmingham, who ... are allowed to retain their places for life, if they conduct themselves with propriety.[45]

Although almshouses were one of the oldest forms of charitable institution, their foundation had 'gone out of fashion' in the eighteenth century. There seems to have been a revival of interest in this form of charity at the turn of the nineteenth century. This is evidenced by the endowments for the benefit to Lench's almshouses mentioned above (paralleled by similar gifts to Greyfriars Hospital, Coventry) and the foundation of a new almshouse in Warner's Lane, Bordesley, by James Dowell in the late 1820s, and endowed by his widow Elizabeth in1831.[46] How much of this revival was a serious re-assessment of the value of almshouses, and how much part of a vague gothic revival is difficult to tell.[47] Certainly Dowell's

[44] Tomkins, A., 'Traditional Forms of Voluntary Charity: Oxford Almshouses in the Mid-Eighteenth Century', unpublished paper. I am grateful to Dr. Tomkins for sending me a copy of this paper.

[45] *Brougham*, pp. 418–41; *V.C.H.*, VII, pp. 563-64; B.C.A. MS 660542–46 Lench's Trust Minutes, 1771–1920, Bailiff's Accounts, 1630–89, 1785–1944. There was also an almshouse for five men and five women in the adjacent parish of Aston, endowed by Thomas Holte in 1650 and enhanced by W.H. Bracebridge in 1860. *Brougham*, 127-8; B.C.A. MS 1514/6/1-11, minutes, accounts and plans, 1866-1980. In 1824 Sarah Glover and Elizabeth Mansfield gave property for a Birmingham Orphans School Association if such should be founded, and in default of that, an almshouse for women. The latter was built in Steelhouse Lane in the 1830s. *V.C.H.*, VII, p. 559.

[46] Greyfriars Hospital, Coventry, benefited from bequests of William Edwards in 1790 and Mary Picken in 1797, *Brougham,* pp. 921-2; Lichfield Joint Record Office, Will of William Edwards, proved 9 April 1790. B.C.A. MS 1125, Dowell's Retreat, epitome of deeds, rules, regulations etc., 1831–90.

[47] Although not published until 1836, Pugin's *Contrasts* reflected this spirit, and made explicit comparisons in one of its illustrations between a grim 'modern poor house' and an 'antient [*sic*] poor house' of gabled cottages around a cathedral cloister. Pugin, A.W.N. (1836; 1841 edn republished 1969), *Contrasts*, Leicester.

Retreat, as it was called, seemed to reflect a certain medievalism in both its physical as well as its spiritual forms; the residents were even known as 'sisters'. All that was missing was a quaint uniform, as still worn by many other almspeople in the nineteenth century. The cottages were set about a courtyard, with a house at the end for the Superintendent, with a chapel above it. The chapel was decorated with painted glass, depicting English Cathedrals and old Birmingham buildings. Above each cottage door was an ogee-shaped cast iron panel depicting alternately symbols of 'Faith' and 'Hope' – 'Charity' was represented by the almshouses themselves.[48]

'Dowell's Retreat' had particularly strict regulations for the choice of resident and her future conduct. It was 'for the benefit and comfort of such poor women as having lived respectably and seen good days are reduced by misfortune to want', twenty of whom, being widows or spinsters, should occupy houses 1-20, and 'a single woman of capacity and respectability and of Rule do occupy House no 21 as superintendent'. The area of benefit was very limited: 'all proper objects shall be selected from the Liberty of Bordesley and Hamlet of Deritend', failing which from the parish of Aston generally. The women were to be between the ages of 55 and 70 'free from disease, of good disposition and conversation, capable of reading the Holy Scriptures, sound members of the Church of England and partakers of its sacraments and of good character for honesty, sobriety and chastity and that they must bring written recommendations from two respectable Housekeepers of the Parish'. The Superintendent should be between the ages of 40 and 55, a widow or daughter of a clergyman and an Annuitant of the Society for the Benefit of the Widows and Orphans of Clergymen in the Archdeaconry of Coventry, or a widow of a parishioner of Birmingham'. Each person had to make good her title to parochial aid before entering the retreat, and she would then receive an additional 1s. 6d. subsistence allowance from the fund. Habits of industry were encouraged by permitting 'knitting, spinning, quilting, sewing and work … for private friends or for sale but not work for a manufactory, no bench vice or any fixture or noisy work shall be permitted'. Religious observance was to be strict, with attendance in chapel at 9 a.m. and 2p.m. on each weekday to hear a portion of the Book of Common Prayer read, and on Sundays to attend Holy Trinity Chapel in Bordesley in the morning and Saint John's Chapel, Deritend in the afternoons. They were not to have visitors to stay or to keep a pet bird or animal 'as quietness, peace and cleanliness must always be maintained in the Retreat'. The Sister must leave if she married or inherited £20 a year.[49]

Whatever the precise criteria for female 'objects of charity', whether by residence, religious affiliation or personal attributes of integrity and sobriety, the most common causes of poverty to be relieved were age and infirmity. This was reflected in the title of the voluntary society established in 1825, The Society for the Relief of Poor Infirm Aged Women (hereafter Aged Women's Society). As

---

[48] Walker, B. (1944), 'Note re Dowell's Retreat, Warner Street, Birmingham', *Transactions of the Birmingham Archaeological Society*, 65, p. 142.

[49] B.C.A. MS 1125 epitome of the deeds, rules, regulations etc of Dowell's retreat, 1831–90.

their first advertisement, pasted from *Aris's Birmingham Gazette* into the minute book, proclaimed, 'The state of extreme wretchedness and destitution in which great numbers of WOMEN pass the latter term of their existence, after the season for active exertion is gone by, will be allowed to give them a powerful claim to assistance'. Rule Two stated that 'widows and single women of good character, infirm and of the age of 65 years and upwards, not having an income of 4/- per week, shall be deemed proper objects for relief by this charity'. By the end of the first year there were '224 objects' on the books, of whom seventy-three were between 65 and 70 years of age, 112 between 70 and 80, thirty-four between 80 and 90 and five between 90 and 100. Between them they had received £124 16s. 6d in relief (£37 18s. 10d. worth in clothing) and the committee were 'convinced that even greater advantage is afforded to the objects of this Charity by the kindly intercourse which is opened to them with their more wealthy neighbours'. Although ten of the women had died, the committee recorded that 'it is gratifying to know, that through the means of the Society a gleam of comfort has been shed upon the last days of some of the destitute and afflicted'. Unfortunately the visiting books which were kept with details of the women visited have not survived. Only the removal of women from the care of the society was recorded in the minute books – usually by death, but in May 1828 it was recorded that Ann Brown had been removed to the Workhouse, and, on a more cheerful note, in October 1828 Mrs. Gillman had got married.[50]

Women as Agents of Charity

Endowed Charities

The device of the charitable trust, which provides an income for some specified purpose in perpetuity, has medieval origins. Its social usefulness was confirmed by the 1601 Statute of Charitable Uses, which provided the framework for the redress of abuses until the establishment of the permanent Charity Commission in 1853. Only charities as defined by the preamble to that act were charities in law, capable of protection and eligible for tax exemptions.[51] Charitable trusts could be established by a variety of devices: a will, a deed of gift or trust, or an Act of Parliament. A will was the most common form; an analysis of the 758 charities in the Gilbert Returns for Warwickshire which made their origins clear shows that 86 per cent had been established by will.[52]

The founders of endowed charities were a very varied group of men and women. For the majority we know nothing more than their names and how much they gave for a particular purpose. Of the 1184 charities recorded in the Gilbert

[50] B.C.A. MS 886/1, Minute Book of the Aged Women's Society, 1825–1847.

[51] Pinches, S.M. (2001), 'Charities in Warwickshire in the Eighteenth and Nineteenth Centuries', unpublished University of Leicester, PhD thesis, pp. 29–30, 46–48, 50-73.

[52] Pinches, 'Charities in Warwickshire' pp.100-109.

Returns for Warwickshire it is possible to identify the gender and status of 876 donors, representing 74 per cent of all cases. Of these, 80.7 per cent were established by men. This reflects the legal difficulties which prevented married women from disposing of property.[53] Only thirteen women have been identified as endowing charities during the period of this study in Birmingham, Aston, Handsworth and Harborne parishes.[54] Nine of these endowments occurred during the first thirty years of the nineteenth century. As already mentioned, Ann Scott endowed two separate charities during her lifetime, one to enhance Mrs. Crowley's School in 1804, and one in 1808 to provide an income for Lench's almswomen. In 1824 Sarah Glover and Elizabeth Mansfield jointly established almshouses for women in Steelhouse Lane, although, as this was 'in accordance with the wishes of Charles Glover' it is not clear whether this can really be counted as a female foundation. The endowment of Dowell's Retreat by Elizabeth Dowell has been mentioned above. The other endowments were in 1820, when Sarah Dallaway left the income of her pew rents in Deritend Chapel to provide gowns for poor widows; in 1826 Mary Sheldon left money for 'ten old maidens' in Birmingham; also in 1826 Ann Boulton left property to the poor of Handsworth; and in 1829 Ann Wilkinson left money to '12 poor widows'. It will be seen that all but one of these donatrices specified female beneficiaries. The five eighteenth-century donatrices also favoured women. In 1719 Dorothy Parkes founded a distribution of bread to twelve poor people, but also gowns for three women; in 1723 Elizabeth White benefited the Blue Coat School, which included female children; in 1733 Ann Crowley established a school for girls, as well as a gift for the Protestant Dissenting minister; in 1789 Elizabeth Hollier set up a clothing charity for both men and women; Dorothy Huxley in 1797 was the only one not to specifically mention females, leaving money to the choristers and the poor of Handsworth.[55]

Donors chose their trustees with care, with a view to the long-term survival of their endowment and strict adherence to their wishes. Their choice of trustees was often influenced by their own circumstances. A calculation from the Gilbert Returns suggests that 52.7 per cent had private trustees, 36.1 per cent chose some combination of the minister and parish officers, and 11.2 per cent chose corporate trustees. Testators often nominated their executors as trustees. The wealthier, landed sort usually favoured private trustees, as this group in society were used to acting as trustees for each other in family and marriage settlement. Citizens of boroughs often chose the corporation as being a body which could not die and which, in theory at least, consisted of the most worthy citizens, well versed in administration and money matters. As Birmingham was not incorporated until 1838 this was not an option here, and so donors sometimes nominated the trustees of the

---

[53] Staves, S. (1990), *Married Women's Separate Property in England, 1660–1833*, Cambridge, Mass.

[54] Other women left money as one-off gifts to existing charities, voluntary societies, and for immediate distribution to the poor. A thorough search of all the wills of the period would be necessary to bring these to light.

[55] *Brougham,* pp. 396, 414-15, 450-52, 458; *V.C.H.,* VII, pp. 560, 561, 567, 568; W.C.R.O. QS 69/1, ff. 20-21.

Grammar School or of Lench's Trust to oversee new trusts for other purposes. Lesser folk frequently chose some combination of their minister and parish officers.

In theory single women and widows could act as trustees, though there is little evidence of them acting as other than executrices to a will which founded a charity. The Gilbert Returns for Warwickshire suggested that the property of 25 charities was vested in women and none of them were in Birmingham.[56] William Hutton, in discussing the Protestant Dissenting School, said that 'Ann Crowley bequeathed, by her last will, in 1733, six houses in Steelhouse-lane, amounting to eighteen pounds per annum, for the purpose of supporting a school, consisting of ten children. From an attachment to her own sex, she constituted over this infant colony of letters a female teacher: Perhaps we should have seen a female trust, had they been equally capable of defending the property.'[57] Nearly eighty years later when Mrs. Scott made a donation of £100 to provide extra income for the use of the children and mistress of this school it was invested in 3 per cent consols which had to be held in the name of three male trustees (Thomas Lee, Samuel Ryland and John Towers Lawrence). However, Mrs. Scott herself controlled the distribution of the income, and after her death two other women, Mrs. Mansell and Mrs. Lee took over the administration of the charity.[58] Other than these no examples have yet been found of female trustees in Birmingham.

Voluntary Societies

Although voluntary associations for political, recreational and benevolent purposes were not an invention of the eighteenth century, their numbers increased dramatically during the century.[59] A very conservative estimate made forty years ago by Ford K. Brown suggested that between 1700 and 1830 some 160 religious, moral, educational and philanthropic organisations were founded in England.[60] In 1974 Frank Prochaska suggested that about 130 of these were set up in the years 1790–1830.[61] A thorough search of provincial sources would no doubt disclose far more, especially as many societies were of very local operation and some quite short-lived. Voluntary associations also set up institutions such as hospitals, asylums, dispensaries, schools and training colleges. When these, too, are considered, the amount of voluntary activity is truly remarkable. The scope for female involvement with voluntary societies was great, although, as Clark pointed out, there were genuine legal problems: 'the inability of married women to sign legal documents in their own right or to be held responsible for financial accounts was a major obstacle to their participation in associations'.[62] While Fissel

[56] Pinches, 'Charities in Warwickshire', pp.133-5.

[57] Hutton, *History of Birmingham*, p. 201.

[58] *Brougham*, p. 415.

[59] Clark, P. (2000), *British Clubs and Societies, 1580–1800: The Origins of an Associational World*, Oxford.

[60] Brown, F.K. (1961), *Fathers of the Victorians*, Cambridge, pp. 333-40.

[61] Prochaska, 'Women in English Philanthropy', p. 426.

[62] Clark, *British Clubs and Societies*, p. 202.

concluded that these new forms of charity 'denied women any active role in benefaction', Amanda Vickery has argued that the institutionalisation of 'fashionable benevolence' actually allowed for what she terms, 'new arenas for the expression of female conviviality and officiousness'. Thus, rather than being pushed back into the privacy of the domestic sphere 'the public profile of privileged, provincial women had never been higher'.[63]

One of the first, and most important, voluntary initiatives in Birmingham was the establishment of a General Hospital.[64] The initial appeal to raise money in 1765 elicited a good response from Birmingham and the surrounding area, but only 44 of the 413 benefactors (10.7 per cent) were women, who contributed £283 (11 per cent) of the total £2,578. Although none of the women gave more than £31 10s. (the Countess of Cardigan), whereas six men gave over £50, the average given by women was slightly higher than the men, being £6 8s compared with the men's £6 5s. When husbands and wives both gave, the wife's contribution was usually considerably less than that of her husband: The Earl of Dartmouth gave £31 10s., his wife £21; Sir Henry Bridgeman gave £21, his wife £10; Mr. Carles gave £10, his wife £5 5s. The Hospital needed a regular income as well, and 358 people undertook to become annual subscribers. Here the women were less well represented, only 24 (6.7 per cent) subscribing, at an average of £2 2s. rather than the £2 14s. of the men. When the project got under way once more in 1778 similar proportions of female subscribers were recorded in the annual reports printed regularly, but no females appeared in any capacity on the committee or staff of the hospital, except the matron. These lists of subscribers published by so many societies, apart from their later use to historians, served the function of encouraging further donations and satisfying the donors' desire to be acknowledged. William Hutton tartly observed that 'perhaps ostentation has brought forth more acts of beneficence than charity herself' and went on to observe that 'charity and self-interest, like the apple and the rind, are closely connected, and, like them, we cannot separate one without trespassing on the other.'[65]

Frank Prochaska has identified a noticeable increase in female subscribers to a number of societies in the early years of the nineteenth century, although this general trend was tempered by women's tendency to favour certain types of charity over others.[66] Certainly the explosion of auxiliary branches to some of the larger national societies encouraged the participation of women in their fund- raising, not only by becoming subscribers themselves but by organising collections and money-

---

[63] Fissel, M. (1991), *Patients, Power and the Poor in Eighteenth-Century Bristol*, Cambridge, p. 90; Vickery, A. (1998), The Gentleman's Daughter: Women's Lives in Georgian England, Princeton, p. 10.

[64] Although first proposed in 1765 the Hospital was not properly established until 1779. A. Wilson has suggested that the delay may have connections with the political situation in Birmingham. Wilson, A. (1996), 'Conflict, Consensus and Charity: Politics and the Provincial Voluntary Hospitals in the Eighteenth Century', *English Historical Review*, 13, pp. 599-619, especially pp. 615, 617-8.

[65] Hutton, *History of Birmingham*, pp. 250-51.

[66] Prochaska, 'Women in English Philanthropy', pp. 428-31.

making events in their own localities. Particularly active in this field were the various missionary societies which burgeoned under the evangelical zeal of the late eighteenth and early nineteenth centuries. Even the Society for the Propagation of Christian Knowledge, founded in 1698 and initially dependent on corresponding members in the provinces, developed a system of local branches.[67] The British and Foreign Bible Society, which was founded in 1804, had 859 auxiliary branches by 1825, with over 10,000 agents, mostly women organised in Ladies' Associations.[68]

However, it was not just branches of national societies which attracted the support of women. They increasingly established their own local societies, particularly lying-in charities and visiting societies. Although these adopted a modern structure with subscribers and a committee, they were in many ways merely a formalisation of the traditional female activity of visiting the aged, sick and lying-in. Davidoff and Hall have suggested that 'they were modest ventures in which men had little or no part ... lying-in charities and blanket clubs were a favourite focus for women, since modesty precluded male involvement.[69] However, subscriptions and financial support would be sought from men, even when they were not involved with the running of the society. The initial subscriptions, amounting to £43 19s. 6d., for the Aged Women's Society, came from 28 men and 24 women.[70]

A comparison of the committee minutes of the Aged Women's Society with those of the Birmingham and Coleshill Lying-in Charities offers some interesting similarities and contrasts with regard to committee members and officers. The Coleshill Lying-in Charity was run by a committee of ladies, which included the Countess of Bradford, who was a regular attender at meetings. Although Mr. Dale offered to 'officiate for his mother as Bookeeper', the first treasurer was Miss Woods, and the only male involvement, apart from financial contributions, seems to have been the preaching of an annual sermon by 'the clergyman of the parish'. Committee meetings were held in private houses.[71] The Birmingham Lying-in Charity was also run by an all female committee, meeting in private homes, always recorded as the husband's home in the minutes. The general meetings were held at the Birmingham Dispensary. The secretary and treasurer were both women, and at the general meeting on 21 September 1825 it was agreed to pay the secretary £4 a year for her trouble. Unlike the Coleshill society, which had operated under aristocratic patronage from the outset, the Birmingham society was much more bourgeois. It was only in October 1830 that the Duchess of Kent agreed to be patroness, and sent a £10 donation. This had been effected by a particularly active new member of the committee, Mrs. Sophia Hancock. Three years later she organised a 'Grand Concert' which raised 100 guineas for the society. For this she

---

[67] Reports of Warwickshire branch meetings and committees, *Warwick Advertiser* 14 March 1814, 26 February, 15 April 1820.

[68] Owen (1965), p. 128; Prochaska, F.K. (1980), *Women and Philanthropy in Nineteenth-Century England*, Oxford, p. 27; Prochaska, F.K. (1988), *The Voluntary Impulse*, London, p. 60.

[69] Davidoff and Hall, *Family Fortunes*, p. 434.

[70] B.C.A. MS 8861, Minutes of the Society for the Relief of Aged Infirm Women.

[71] W.C.R.O. DRB 100/162 Minutes of Coleshill Lying-in Charity, 1832-1861.

had obtained the patronage not only of the Duchess of Kent, but also of Princess Victoria, five earls and their countesses, and numerous other worthies. On 28 May 1833 the committee recorded its gratitude to Mrs. Hancock, but also noted that 'a few individuals of this committee disapproving of the means by which the above sum was obtained have determined not to avail themselves of the benefits resulting from this additional revenue.' It is difficult to decide whether they disapproved of the entertainment (a number of the committee names belonged to Quaker and Dissenting families in the town), or whether they disliked the seeking of aristocratic patronage, and the particularly sycophantic ode written for the occasion by Charles Hancock. Whatever the reason, for all her obvious energies and abilities, Mrs. Hancock's name soon disappeared from the minutes.[72]

The Committee of the Aged Women's Society operated slightly differently, although in the period 1825-30 some women served on both committees.[73] The Aged Women's Society was inaugurated at a public meeting at the Blue Coat School on 28 January 1825, attended by both 'ladies and gentlemen'. It was chaired by the Rev. Edward Burn. Once established, the chair was taken by the Low Bailiff, John Ryland, and the Rev. J. Moore and Mr. Thomas Beilby agreed to act as joint Secretary, though in January 1826 Mrs. Southall became assistant secretary. Mr. John Pearson became treasurer. However, it would appear from the fact that the secretary's name was only occasionally included in the list of those present at committee meetings, and the treasurer's even less frequently, that the ladies got on and ran the society themselves, including taking the minutes, the official secretary and treasurer only appearing at the general meetings.[74] They divided the town into eighteen districts, appointing a 'visitor' and an 'auxiliary' for each district. These ladies collected money in their district, bringing it to the monthly committee meetings. They were also responsible for visiting the 'objects' and paying the relief.

As well as involvement on committees for middle-class women, these societies offered some employment to women, mainly as nurses. The matron of the General Hospital has already been mentioned. Such institutions employed a number of nurses, cooks and laundry workers. The Lying-in charities employed nurses and paid fees to surgeons. The Birmingham Lying-in charity took on Mrs. Potter as their first nurse in 1813, paying her 8s, for her first week's attendance at a confinement, 1s. a day thereafter. When not attending a case the nurse was paid 4s. a week retainer. Two new nurses were taken on in January 1814, and by 1818 six were employed. Complaints about the conduct or cleanliness of the nurses were

[72] B.C.A. MS 954, Minutes of the Society for Administering Relief to Poor Lying-in Women, 1813-28; Birmingham Local Studies Library 663720, Minutes of the Institution for Providing Nurses for Poor Married Lying-in Women, 1828-1847; 202327 Programme of the Grand Concert, 1833.

[73] Mrs. Shorthouse, Mrs. Lloyd, Mrs. P. M. James, Mrs. Conquest, Mrs. Southall, Mrs. Freeth and Mrs. Neville.

[74] This is comparable with Mary Martin's findings for Walthamstow, where she found that at the annual meetings men made the speeches and the women were silent, 'yet the meetings were formalities; the real business occurred elsewhere'. Martin (1994), p. 131.

dealt with from time to time by the committee. No doubt ladies with servants were used to such disciplinary procedures; sometimes the nurse's explanation was accepted and her services retained, on other occasions she was dismissed. There was also a handful of female schoolmistresses. The honorarium paid to Miss Blyth as secretary is the only example so far found for payment for administrative work for a voluntary society.[75]

Conclusion

This study of the female experience of charity in Birmingham has found similarities with other cities and large towns, but there are differences with regard to the chronology and intensity of activity. These differences may be explained in part by the particular economic and social structure of Birmingham. Its wealth derived from many trades in metalware and arms production, and the increased output towards the end of the eighteenth century was not based upon large manufactories (apart from a few exceptions such as Matthew Boulton's Soho Works in Handsworth), but on an explosive growth in the number of small workshops. It was not an ancient city with a corporation, but was governed by overstretched parochial institutions until 1838. Nor did it serve as an administrative or social regional centre, with local gentry and aristocracy having town houses or regular seasons of visit. All these factors meant that there were few 'natural leaders' of local society and no *cursus honorum* in which involvement in charitable work could play a part. There were few endowed charities, and their income was low in comparison with that in other cities, and Birmingham lacked the longstanding traditions of civic charity to be found in incorporated towns such as Bristol or York.[76] The comparative lack of aristocratic involvement with the town may have contributed to the tardiness in establishing such institutions as a General Hospital; the contacts and influence of aristocrats were often instrumental in smoothing the way of such undertakings, even where the chief impetus came from large employers concerned about keeping a healthy workforce. Although the development of voluntary activity generally in Birmingham was somewhat slower than in other parts of the country, the rise of female-run societies seems to conform more closely with the pattern identified nationally by Frank Prochaska and in Bristol by Martin Gorsky, of increased female involvement in the first thirty years of the nineteenth century.[77] There is evidence of women in Birmingham corresponding with those in other towns about the establishment of voluntary societies. For example, the Aged Women's Society corresponded with the Sheffield Female Friendly Society for the

---

[75] B.C.A. MS 954, Minutes of the Society for Administering Relief to Poor Lying-in Women, 1813-28.

[76] Gorsky, M. (1999), *Patterns of Philanthropy: Charity and Society in Nineteenth-Century Bristol*, Woodbridge, p. 17.

[77] Prochaska, 'Women in English Philanthropy'; Gorsky, *Patterns of Philanthropy*, pp. 164-70.

Relief of Aged Women, asked for copies of the forms they used, and one of their meetings was attended by Miss Smith of the Sheffield Society.[78]

The experience of women as objects of charity in Birmingham was probably typical (and most women's experience of charity would have been as recipients). As already stated, in the early modern period 80 per cent of those classed as poor were women, and as such would have had access to both poor relief and charitable help. There was some slight acknowledgement of the particular situation of women alone in the number of charities for widows, but only one charity was for the benefit of old maids. The almshouse places were for single women, too, whether widows or spinsters, and one of the new voluntary societies also recognised the 'extreme wretchedness and destitution' faced by many aged women. It was only in the early years of the nineteenth century that a society was established to support women in childbed. There may have been some difference between rural and urban experience, with the 'face to face' nature of charity persisting in rural areas, whereas it had been displaced by more institutional forms of relief in urban centres. Even the rise of visiting charities such as the Aged Women's Society in the towns in the early nineteenth century only provided a limited contact between donor and recipient, and a formalised one at that. As the nineteenth century wore on more emphasis was placed upon the benefits of friendly association between the donor and recipient. In 1847 in Bradford it was recorded that, in a campaign for improved lodgings for mill girls, the wives and daughters of the committee '"mingled familiarly with the humble mill girls as sisters with sisters" for "the purpose of raising them up to a higher and happier region of life"'.[79] The recipients of these various forms of charity had to display qualities of respectability as well as fulfil requirements of residence in order to benefit. They were also expected to display suitable humbleness and gratitude. The Aged Women's Society recorded in its second report in 1826 that their assistance 'has, in most cases, been justly appreciated by the objects of this bounty, and received and acknowledged with thankfulness.' However, in November 1828 it was suggested that the visitors 'recommend to the poor objects to call upon their respective friends and thank them for their kindness'. Unfortunately, it was not recorded whether such visits were made, nor what happened in the cases where gratitude was not displayed.[80]

The gratification of the subscriber by suitably appreciative thanks was but one satisfaction for women involved with philanthropic work. For many women the regular distribution of alms, the visiting of the sick and old, perhaps being able to endow a charity at one's death, were all ways of fulfilling a religious duty. For others, these activities were an expression of their feminine and maternal character,

---

[78] B.C.A. MS 886/1, Minute Book of the Aged Women's Society, 1825–1847, 5 April, 1 Dec. 1825. The Sheffield Society had been founded in 1810, and its *Reports* 1815-19 are in the Sheffield Local studies Library. I am grateful to Alison Twells for this information.

[79] Bradford Observer, 24 June 1847, quoted in Koditschek, T. (1990), Class Formation and Urban-Industrial Society Bradford, 1750–1850, Cambridge, p. 550.

[80] B.C.A. MS 8861, Minutes of the Society for the Relief of Aged Infirm Women, 6 November 1828.

a view of women reflected by Thomas Gisborne's opinion that 'in the exercise of charitable and friendly regard to the neighbouring poor, women in general are exemplary'.[81] The development of voluntary societies of all sorts gave women greater scope for such activities, and larger possibilities for recognition. Although women's involvement in major undertakings like the Birmingham General Hospital were confined to the role of subscriber and audience at the music festival, there grew up a range of smaller local undertakings, utilising what Gisborne called the female's 'habitual insight into the local events and local necessities, and her acquaintance with the character and situations of individuals' which 'enable her to adapt the relief she affords to the merits and to the distress of the person assessed'.[82] These societies, with their committees and officers, rule books and annual reports (often including subscription lists) gave a sense of importance to their participants, over and above the satisfaction of 'doing good' and allowed women to enjoy the satisfaction of feeling that they were making a contribution to the good of the local community or town to which they belonged. As one woman wrote of another in 1820, 'Mary likes occupation only in her own way – it gives a little consequence and will employ her mind as she has nothing to do but for herself, and may be of service'.[83] In all these activities, women took a particular but not an exclusive interest in the plight of women. Some historians have seen in these experiences an embryonic feminism, whereby certain women forged a consciousness of their own condition and began to develop the tools with which to campaign for its betterment.[84] This was really a development of the later nineteenth century. During the long eighteenth century bourgeois women, circumscribed by law and convention, often treated as objects by their men folk, could only express agency in relation to objects more powerless than themselves.

---

[81] Gisborne, T. (1797), *An Inquiry into the Duties of the Female Sex*, London, quoted in Andrew, 'Female Charity', (1995), p. 284, n. 36.

[82] Gisborne, *An Inquiry*, p. 291, in Andrew, 'Female Charity', p. 286.

[83] Vickery, *The Gentleman's Daughter*, p. 2.

[84] Martin Gorsky discusses the historiography of this topic, and agrees that 'most would accept that philanthropy was one strand of female activity from which organised feminism was to emerge', but he goes on to point out that 'it is also possible that the satisfaction which partial empowerment offered may have prevented the shared recognition of subordinate status'. Gorsky, *Patterns of Philanthropy*, pp. 162-3, 172.

Chapter 5

Urban Businesswomen in Eighteenth-Century England

Christine Wiskin

Findings from London and English provincial towns in the eighteenth century indicate that women who were economically active were more likely to be found in a limited range of occupations, principally the provision of food and drink, textile and clothing production, shopkeeping and domestic service. To these may be added accounts which highlight the dichotomy between elite, leisured women and poor townswomen whose economic activity was characterised by insecurity, seasonality, low status and poor remuneration. Together, these produce a dispiriting picture that emphasises the poverty, lack of opportunity and agency, and absence of change which were the destiny of the majority. It is also one that fails to address those women of the 'middling sort' who were the owners of businesses in their own right. Economic and business histories have been impoverished by attachment to the belief that women's economic activity was only to be found in employment by others. We need to acknowledge, describe and evaluate the female business owner. For too long it has been assumed that phrases such as 'the female labour market', 'women's work', and 'women's employment opportunities' summed up what was involved in being economically active in industrialising Britain, but they should not be deemed as inclusive of all women for there were many female members of the 'middling sort' who, by their own efforts, provided for themselves and their families. I have been inexorably drawn to this conclusion during my research into urban businesswomen's enterprises in the eighteenth-century West Midlands.[1] Focusing on the commercial aspects of their independent economic activities has forced me to look critically at what running a business in industrialising England meant to the women who did so. I believe that insufficient attention has been paid to the complexities of their enterprises, the management skills required to run them successfully, and the need to examine critically the sources that are available to the historian. As a result, this chapter addresses issues of methodology, as well as discussing empirical evidence and reviewing secondary literature. It will be argued that it is only by asking commercially-oriented questions of what is now a

1 Wiskin, C. (2000), 'Women, Credit and Finance in England, c. 1780-1826', unpublished University of Warwick PhD thesis. (Funded by studentship no. ROO429634128 from the Economic and Social Research Council.)

substantial corpus of evidence on this subject that our understanding will be advanced.

The Urban Setting

English towns, both large and small, experienced a revival in prosperity, which was atypical of Europe in the period. Towns were important as places where supply and demand met. They were hubs in networks of production and distribution where products made in rural hinterlands could be traded. In towns, businesspeople could expect to find skilled workers, to assist them in running their enterprises, and young women to act as domestic servants, permitting their mistresses to devote themselves to business. Urban businesspeople could draw on a much wider customer base than rural ones. As well as dealing with local residents, they could expect trade from temporary visitors drawn in by markets and fairs and, from the mid-century onwards, by the lure of commercially-organised social life. Townsfolk and visitors from the countryside went to town in the expectation of finding there the consumer goods and services which they read about in novels and newspapers and whose merits they discussed with their neighbours.[2]

This volume, and many others, show that town life was important to eighteenth-century women, providing them with a public arena in which to participate. A rapid growth in commercialised polite leisure in towns was new in the eighteenth century. The lead may have been set by London and grand resorts, such as Bath, but, by the mid-century, provincial towns too had developed their own social calendars. The urban round of polite, organised entertainments was to be found nationwide, drawing in participants from town and country alike. Whether they were scions of the landed elite or members of the rapidly-expanding 'middle ranks', towns were places where respectable women could see and be seen. Here they could visit organised entertainments and attend the theatre, balls, race meetings, walk in public parks and gardens, shop in smart emporia. Critics depicted 'the season' as shallow, pernicious, encouraging false values and sexual immorality but circumspect women enjoyed what urban life had to offer, distinguishing between the meretricious and what was within the bounds of acceptable society. Aristocratic and gentry women presided over metropolitan assemblies, such as Almacks, and provincial polite public gatherings. Committees of ladies, deciding who should be admitted and who excluded, were recognised as powerful in decision making about taste and conduct. Thus, provided that they conducted themselves in a modest and genteel manner, respectable women from the affluent classes could engage with urban society without damage to their good reputations.[3]

---

[2] Borsay, P. (1989), *The English Urban Renaissance: Culture and Society in the Provincial Town*, Oxford, pp. 199-212; Corfield, P.J. (1982), The Impact of English Towns 1700-1800, Oxford, pp. 83, 96-7.

[3] Borsay, *English Urban Renaissance*, pp. 267-83; Brewer, J. (1997), The Pleasures of the Imagination: English Culture in the Eighteenth Century, London, pp. 56-98; Vickery,

There was an important economic side to the growth of organised sociability. Enterprising individuals, often from modest backgrounds, recognised that catering to the wishes of those with time and money on their hands presented chances for self-advancement and enrichment, marketing the trappings of politesse. They provided, and charged for, a catholic range of services to satisfy body and mind, becoming adept in facilities management, arranging for premises (sometimes erecting purpose-built ones) where assemblies, balls, concerts, race meetings, could take place. Dancing masters taught etiquette and deportment, as well as the correct steps, appropriate in such venues. Other businesspeople catered for the growing demand for all types of print culture by founding newspapers, particularly in the provinces, opening bookshops and setting up circulating libraries.[4]

Like their male counterparts, urban businesswomen benefited from the larger customer bases and greater availability of staff which town life offered. There were other advantages. In incorporated towns, there were traditions of allowing women to work in certain trades, to belong to guilds and generally be economically independent of men. By the eighteenth century, however, guild or borough ordinances and customs might work in favour of businesswomen or against them. Where they were favourable, married women could trade as though single, widows could continue their late husbands' trades, and daughters of freemen those of their deceased fathers. In some towns, widows or unmarried women in business were tolerated provided they did not encroach on male occupations. In others, if guild strength and influence was on the wane, ordinances might be invoked against women in an attempt to re-assert the power of the particular institution in its neighbourhood.[5] It is difficult to arrive at a satisfactorily inclusive conclusion because of such conflicting evidence. The use of customary protections or sanctions was uneven, seeming to be as much concerned with local political and economic factors as issues of gender or fears of independent, 'masterless' women with the potential to disturb the stability of society.

What we can say, however, is that the growth in the size of towns and the nature of the goods and services available in them were significant to the urban businesswoman. Urban expansion was accompanied by the growth of urban service

---

A. (1998), The Gentleman's Daughter: Women's Lives in Georgian England, London, pp. 225-71.

[4] Borsay, *English Urban Renaissance,* pp. 213-4; Barker, H. (1996), 'Catering for Provincial Tastes: Newspapers, Readership and Profit in Late Eighteenth-Century England', *Historical Research*, 69, pp. 42-61.

[5] Pinchbeck, I. (1930 reprinted 1969), *Women Workers and the Industrial Revolution,1750-1850,* London, pp. 284-85; Prior, M. (1985), 'Women and the Urban Economy: Oxford 1500-1800' in M. Prior (ed), *Women in English Society, 1500-1800*, London, pp. 93-117; Earle, P. (1989), *The Making of the English Middle Class: Business, Society and Family Life in London 1660-1730*, London, pp. 159-60; Wright, S. (1989), 'Holding Up Half the Sky: Women and Their Occupations in Eighteenth-Century Ludlow', *Midland History*, 14, pp. 53-74; Laurence, A. (1994), *Women in England 1500-1760: A Social History,* London, pp. 125-29; Sanderson, E.C. (1996), *Women and Work in Eighteenth-Century Edinburgh*, London, p. 39; Hufton, O. (1997), *The Prospect Before Her: A History of Women in Western Europe, Volume 1, 1500-1800,* London, pp. 239-45.

sector trades. It became increasingly easy to purchase all sorts of food, drink, and clothing which traditionally had been produced at home. Did the proliferation of prepared foods, pie shops, ready-made clothing, and the availability of lodgings at all prices and levels of salubriousness affect the urban businesswoman? Dorothy George thought so, pointing out that, in London, the highly-developed service industries in the capital meant that working women could avoid the 'double bind' of housework and cooking after a day spent in the counting house or workshop.[6] Her expression of what has been conceptualised more recently as 'the industrious revolution' has much to recommend it.[7] It suggests how women could utilise the opportunities presented by the development of urban service industries. It may explain why Hester Pinney, a successful early eighteenth-century London businesswoman, lived in lodgings.[8] Boarding in other people's homes, or in taverns, she had, by purchasing services as she needed them, found a way round the domestic side of life and was in a better position to devote the majority of her time to business. Connections between the service providers and the businesswomen who used them were mutually advantageous. Women who prepared food and drink or made and sold dresses and millinery had a ready market amongst other businesswomen too busy to make them and with sufficient money to buy what they needed.

Nationwide, businesswomen who aspired to make their livings from the demand for commercial entertainment in towns marketed a wide choice of items to all levels of polite society. They organised and sold tickets for concerts, assemblies and balls, presented exhibitions, made and marketed the new clothes which were worn at these events, and sold the china ware on which elegant suppers were served. In London, Mrs Cornelys was an entertainer and impresario who presented lavish spectacles to audiences drawn principally from high society, albeit frequently its more raffish members. Anticipating patronage from a more circumspect clientele, Mary Linwood and Eleanor Coade were amongst many women who organised commercial exhibitions of artistic craft work intended to educate and enlighten their visitors.[9] Women were also to be found making money, and in some cases their fortunes, from the quieter, more reflective side of polite entertainments. 'Middling sort' women, with some education as well as natural aptitude and considerable application, helped to meet the demands of their contemporaries for reading matter. Writing novels, histories, essays, poetry, and conduct books was a business in which professional female authors engaged. However, women's connections with print culture went further than the writing and reading of texts.

---

[6] George, M.D. (1925), *London Life in the Eighteenth Century*, London, p. 169.

[7] De Vries, J. (1993), 'Between Purchasing Power and the World of Goods: Understanding the Household Economy in Early Modern Europe', in J. Brewer and R. Porter (eds), *Consumption and the World of Goods,* London, pp. 85-132.

[8] Sharpe, P. (1999), 'Dealing with Love: The Ambiguous Independence of the Single Woman in Early Modern England', *Gender & History*, 11, pp. 209-32.

[9] Altick, D. (1978), *The Shows of London: A Panoramic History of Exhibitions,* 1600-1862, London, pp. 400-40; Kelly, A. (1990), Mrs Coade's Stone, Upton-upon-Severn, pp. 65-72; Brewer, The Pleasures of the Imagination, pp. 397-98.

Recent research has revealed women's involvement in printing, publishing, selling books, periodicals and newspapers, and the ownership of circulating libraries. This offers more than another way of interpreting women's engagement with urban commercialised leisure and entertainment. Many were extensive, prosperous undertakings which provided good livings for their female owners.[10]

Acknowledging the Urban Businesswoman

Arguments based on individual case studies, however encouraging or inspiring they may be, are vulnerable to criticism that they are only examples and, because they do not address the aggregate, fail to carry the discussion further. Yet contemporary newspapers, urban directories and fire insurance policy registers show that many female business proprietors were to be found in eighteenth-century England. Each of these sources has its shortcomings. None can be assumed to be comprehensive. Provincial businesspeople were less likely to insure against fire than metropolitan ones and the uneven penetration of fire insurance outside London means that policy registers are of limited use beyond the capital. All were essentially self-referential; individuals were recorded because of their ability to pay the fees required for entry, thereby excluding the lower levels of the business community. Yet, despite their shortcomings, we can use them to put forward some conclusions.

We can say that women were to be found in the business community nationwide. Their presence was, however, variable. Women were a small minority, whether we are talking about London or the provinces. In some areas they appear well-represented, in others they were only a handful. In all cases, these are minimum numbers and probably constitute an under-estimate. Fragmentary and biased though the sources may be, assessing the extent of 'middling sort' women's participation in the business community is not a completely fruitless task. As far as urban directories are concerned, because the poorer types of trades- and businesspeople were unlikely to have been able to afford to advertise, the self-referential entry may be a useful signpost to the social and economic status of those who did. What we may be witnessing in the urban directory, therefore, is the recording of a discrete, 'middling sort' commercial community.

Collating and comparing data from these different sources for different towns reveals similarities and suggests that we can put forward some tentative estimates. When we are talking about urban areas, approximately 5 per cent of businesses may have been female owned and run. Interpolation of the findings of Peter Earle and L.D. Schwarz on fire insurance policies issued to London businesswomen shows that, in the capital, they constituted at least 5.3 per cent of the policy holders in 1726-9 and that for the period 1775-87, 6.7 per cent of policy holders in more prosperous occupations were women. There are similar results from English

---

[10] Barker, H. (1997), 'Women, Work and the Industrial Revolution: Female Involvement in the English Printing Trades, c.1700-1840' in H. Barker and E. Chalus (eds), *Gender in Eighteenth-Century England: Roles, Representations and Responsibilities*, Harlow, pp. 81-100.

provincial towns. Margaret Hunt demonstrated that at least 6 per cent of the advertisers in the *Manchester Directory* of 1772 were women. Moreover, findings for eighteenth-century Colchester and early nineteenth-century Bath suggest that, in some towns, women's participation in the business community was much higher, reaching at least 20 per cent. Bath and Colchester were regional centres with attendant high demand for luxury goods or services. These were at the top end of occupations seen as typically 'feminine' ones and it is plausible that there were high percentages of these types of businesswomen in such towns.[11] Surveying urban directories for Birmingham during the half-century from 1774 to 1825, I found that, although their participation rates fluctuated, approximately 5 per cent of the advertisers were women.[12]

Whatever their shortcomings, eighteenth- and early nineteenth-century directories are probably the best guide to the proportions of 'middling sort' men and women in business in towns but the information in them can be refined further. The essential information about each advertiser included name, occupation and address. This enables the historian to identify the settlement patterns of businesspeople and to relate them to town centres, dock areas or landmarks with particular local significance. Plotting the addresses of women's businesses produces interesting results. 'Middling sort' businesswomen may have been found clustered in occupations traditionally seen as feminine ones: the provision of food, drink, clothing, the education of the young, and certain trades and crafts specific to particular English regions. The apparently lowly nature of these trades might encourage us to assume that their participants would be found on the margins of town settlements, or confined to specific quarters. Aggregating research from various towns in the eighteenth century suggests the contrary. It was common in medieval and early modern English towns for women to trade from their own areas, described as the 'women's market', but by the eighteenth century businesswomen were not restricted to a specific quarter in the towns in which they lived and worked. Furthermore, 'middling sort' businesswomen were unlikely to be banished to the periphery of towns and cities. 'Middling sort' women who engaged in trade or business did not automatically put themselves beyond the pale of polite society. They were not poor women who peddled goods at street corners or from doorways.[13] Shani D'Cruze, for example, notes that women retailers were located

---

[11] Earle, *Making of the English Middle Class,* pp. 168-69; D'Cruze, S. (1986), 'To Acquaint the Ladies: Women Traders in Colchester 1750-1850', *Local Historian,* 17:3, pp. 158-61; Schwarz, L.D. (1992), *London in the Age of Industrialisation: Entrepreneurs, Labour Force and Living Conditions, 1700-1850,* Cambridge, pp. 20-21; Finn, M. (1994), 'Debts and Credit in Bath's Court of Requests, 1829-39', *Urban History,* 21, pp. 211-236; Hunt, M.R. (1996), *The Middling Sort: Commerce, Gender, and the Family in England 1680-1780,* Berkeley and London, CA, pp. 129-32.

[12] Findings based on *New Birmingham Directory,* (1774), Birmingham; *Pearson & Rollason's Birmingham Directory,* (1780), Birmingham; *Pye's Birmingham Directory (1785-1797),* Birmingham; Wrightson's Triennial Directory of Birmingham (1805-1833) Birmingham.

[13] Lemire, B. (1997), *Dress, Culture and Commerce: The English Clothing Trade*

in the principal shopping streets in the town centre of late eighteenth-century Colchester.[14] For the same period in Birmingham, when I plotted businesswomen's addresses, listed in the town's directories, against a contemporary map I found that the largest concentrations of businesswomen were in the town centre.[15] The mantra of the modern estate agent - 'location, location, location' - was equally applicable in the recent past. Participators in local, national, and even international, business networks, women had to locate themselves where they could be easily found by their connections. Women retailers needed premises accessible to both their suppliers and their customers. It was no use to manufacturers if their goods were sold by shopkeepers in out of the way locations. Genteel customers were unlikely to venture into streets away from the town centre. Address details from directories also show that widowhood did not mean that women were forced to the edge of urban life. Those who continued their late husbands' enterprises did so from the same premises. Others relocated but their actions do not appear to have been the result of exclusionary tactics by men. Rather, businesswomen widows who moved their business premises were motivated by commercial needs. Ambitious women sought to upgrade premises or site themselves in more advantageous locations.

Urban directories also permit us to establish how and when those engaged in particular occupations relocated. Continuing to compare the addresses of businesswomen with a contemporary map of Birmingham, I discovered that, by 1825, their settlement patterns had changed. The majority were now to be found in the streets north of the centre but, because nearly a quarter remained in the town centre, it does not seem that they were being forced out of the main trading streets. Nonetheless, the difference is striking and can be explained by changes in their occupations. By 1825, most of the businesswomen in the area north of the centre of Birmingham were school proprietresses. Their choice of location was deliberate. Until the 1840s, this area was inhabited principally by middle-class families with children to educate. Most of the housing stock was relatively new and located at a distance from, and on higher ground than, the original town settlement and cleaner air and more space were important to the successful marketing of schools.

On the basis of these sources, the existence of urban 'middling sort' businesswomen in the eighteenth century cannot be denied, even though their numbers may not have been large. Fire insurance records also suggest that women's businesses tended to be the smaller, less capitalised ones; Eleanor Coade's Artificial Stone Manufactory, insured for £1000, being exceptional.[16] However, there is still debate on how findings should be interpreted. Directories provide us with some indication of aggregate figures for both sexes but some aspects of urban life were deeply gendered. Women were excluded from office-holding and its accompanying perquisites, which carried an increasing commercial value as the

---

Before the Factory, London, pp. 96-104.

[14] D'Cruze, 'To Acquaint the Ladies', pp. 158-61.

[15] Name, address and occupation details as in note 12 above were compared with C. Pye (1795), *Plan of Birmingham Survey'd in the Year 1795.*

[16] Kelly, *Mrs Coade's Stone*, p. 29.

national economy became more sophisticated.[17] Yet these developments, constituted on gendered lines, may not have had the totally negative effect frequently argued for. When we are considering the eighteenth and early nineteenth centuries, women's businesses did not necessarily suffer because their owners were physically excluded from urban institutions. It is possible to advance an alternative thesis. Announcements in contemporary newspapers, entries in urban directories and references in wills indicate that businesswomen conducted their enterprises in whole worlds, made up of men and women traders. Many had sons, or male employees or business partners who could participate in the new types of urban institution. These male connections brought back information which female proprietors could act upon, enabling them to make informed decisions about the conduct of their enterprises.[18]

Family, Life Cycle and Life Style

Family and life cycle were central to a woman's economic activity, whether she was one of the labouring poor or came from the 'middling sort'. A woman's presence in business was contingent on factors of family and life stages but we need to go further and stress that they had a particular significance for the 'middling sort'. Discussed, debated, and fraught with problems, 'middling sort' as a social category is a hostage to historiographical fortune. It does not lend itself to precise or easy definition. Increasing numbers of people in the eighteenth century claimed this status but how far their assertions reflected reality, rather than their dreams, remains uncertain. However, contemporary commentators based their definitions on a combination of economic and social values, including living standards, occupational categories and working conditions.[19] On this basis, 'middling sort' status can be attributed to individuals who were proprietors of their own enterprises, owned personal and/or real property, were likely to be literate (inasmuch as they could write their names), and bequeathed their property by testamentary dispositions. Self-perception also has to be factored in. If we examine the ways in which 'middling sort' people saw themselves, it is evident that pride in one's occupation and the expertise which was deemed to accompany it were important, yet these were also attributes of the industrious independent artisan. If we are to distinguish the 'middling sort' from artisans, we must look further at questions of loyalty and affiliation. The artisan expressed his in terms of the protection of his trade or craft, frequently described as a 'mystery', with its attendant meanings of exclusivity and skill, the acquisition of which was complex and restricted to a few with special personal qualities. He was anxious to protect his

[17] Hunt, *The Middling Sort*, pp. 129-32.

[18] Discussed in detail in Wiskin, 'Women, Credit and Finance in England', pp. 93-97, pp. 189-90.

[19] Corfield, P.J. (1991), 'Class by Name and Number in Eighteenth-Century Britain' in P.J. Corfield (ed), *Language, History and Class*, Oxford, pp. 101-32.

craft and the interests of his guild or trade association against competition from those without formal training.

Family loyalty, however, was the hallmark of the 'middling sort'. The family, both immediate and extended, was the bedrock of 'middling sort' status and stability. In the pursuit of their business interests, connections, capital and credit were crucial to the 'middle ranks' of eighteenth-century commercial society. Family money and influence helped to set up sons, nephews and cousins in their own enterprises or in the expansion and diversification of existing ones.[20] Wealthy kin, worldly-wise through a lifetime's experience of business, were in demand to fill formal roles with legal status, such as executors or sureties. Informally, their advice was sought on financial and personal matters of all sorts. Conversely, less fortunate relatives looked to their prosperous ones for help. These were life-long responsibilities and were often summed up in their wills. In their lifetimes, 'middling sort' businesspeople, who were successful, acquired business assets and quality consumer items. Items acquired through hard work and thrift, cared for and valued during an individual's lifetime, were not to be treated in a cavalier fashion after death. They were to be transferred to specific beneficiaries. Possessions were described, categorised and bequeathed by 'middling sort' people in their wills. Will making offered the chance to confirm existing loyalties and obligations. Precise testamentary dispositions of business and personal assets were a medium by which testators might fulfil those obligations and re-reinforce their 'middling sort' status. Conversely, will making was a way to settle old scores and punish by a derisory bequest, such as the infamous 'shilling', or by no bequest at all.[21] This combination of the personal and the pecuniary fits well with accounts of male economic advancement from the traditional, such as Dick Whittington, to examples of the modern entrepreneur but, above all, it is deeply gendered. Women were either excluded or marginalised; their roles being limited to marriage partners, who consolidated commercial connections, or as helpmeets who provided unpaid labour to the enterprise.

Historians of women's work have had few problems with female involvement in business, seeing it as part of a feminist trajectory of women's history as the history of their life cycles, embedded in a matrix of familial relationships of daughter, wife, mother, and widow. Locating women's business activities in the context of their life cycles has benefits. It reminds us that the independent businesswoman was unlikely to be a friendless individual abandoned in a world of competitive market forces; she had family and kin on whom she might call for assistance. Life cycle explains why 'middling sort' women were in business. Differences in life expectancies between men and women meant that, provided they survived the dangers of childbirth, wives were likely to outlive their husbands and that, unless their

---

[20] Mathias, P. (1979), 'Capital, Credit and Enterprise in the Industrial Revolution', in P. Mathias (ed), *The Transformation of England: Essays in the Economic and Social History of England in the Eighteenth Century,* London, pp. 88-111.

[21] Davidoff, L. and Hall, C. (1987), *Family Fortunes: Men and Women of the English Middle Class 1780-1850,* London, pp. 206-207, pp. 215-19; Hunt, *The Middling Sort*, pp. 49-53.

husbands had been farsighted and provident, widows would have to support themselves and, possibly, their dependent children.[22]

As well as widows, never-married women were to be found in business in the eighteenth century. Unmarried 'middling sort' women in the past have been depicted as poor, powerless and put upon.[23] Case studies, such as those outlined in this essay, indicate that this was not necessarily always the case, but how might we explain the contradiction? There were historically-determined factors. In this period, many families still expected their young female relatives to become self-supporting. Notwithstanding the preponderance of conduct books which advised 'middling sort' women and girls how to be dependent wives and mothers, rather than economically active, women's participation in business was debated by some eighteenth-century writers. Joseph Collyer, for example, recognised that there were young women who would have to provide for themselves despite the fact that they came from prosperous families.[24] Demographic contingency also played an important part. Many parents wanted their enterprises to continue after their deaths but, in some families, there were no male heirs; in others, only daughters grew into adults. Parents and kin without sons or nephews looked to daughters or nieces to take on new enterprises in the same town or to develop new trading connections in more distant ones. Spinster businesswomen were survivors, who might not have been in business had there been male kin capable of inheriting and continuing the family enterprise. Thus they appear to have been fulfilling the role of surrogate sons. Hester Pinney, an early eighteenth-century spinster, became a successful businesswoman in London. Pinney's elder brothers died young and her father needed a representative in the capital to sell the high-quality lace which he manufactured in the West Country.[25] Pinney's situation was not unique; other eighteenth-century businesswomen, such as Eleanor Coade or Sarah Florry, who both lived until their eighties, were the unmarried daughters of 'middling sort' businessmen without sons.[26]

The connections in 'middling sort' families between life cycle and life style explain how women were able to operate in business and how they acquired the monetary and social capital to do so. Linkage of the pecuniary and the personal was not restricted to 'middling sort' men but applied also to women. Her connections, acquired during her life, were part of the construction of a woman's business persona. She relied on others for the assets of her business, by earning, borrowing, being given or bequeathed, the wherewithal to set up on her own. It is a feature of

---

[22] Pinchbeck, *Women Workers*, pp. 2, 282, 284-85; Hufton, *The Prospect Before Her*, pp. 217-32, 235-50.

[23] Hufton, O. (1984), 'Women without Men: Widows and Spinsters in Britain and France in the Eighteenth Century', *Journal of Family History*, 9, pp. 355-76; Davidoff and Hall, *Family Fortunes*, pp. 346-50.

[24] Quoted in Snell, K.D.M. (1985), *Annals of the Labouring Poor: Social Change and Agrarian England 1660-1900*, Cambridge, pp. 293-94.

[25] Sharpe, 'Dealing with Love', p. 210, pp. 225-27.

[26] Kelly, *Mrs Coade's Stone*, pp. 21-3; Wiskin, 'Women, Credit and Finance', pp. 213-16.

the historiography of women in business that their ownership of business assets was predicated on inheritance, that particular aspect of family relations which was the hallmark of the 'middling sort' life style. This involved a transmission of property from a husband, father, mother, aunt, sister, with transfer from husband to wife being the most common. The business assets she was likely to receive included the ownership or tenancy of premises, tools, a stock of raw materials and finished goods, unfinished or incomplete orders awaiting her attention, debts due to the deceased and which she would have to collect. She would also be responsible for settling the debts which the deceased had not paid when alive.[27]

These made up the monetary capital of the enterprise but social capital was important too. Her business reputation, which was essential for her to participate in networks of credit and commercial information, depended not only on how well she treated customers and how promptly she paid creditors, but on who she was and whom she knew, or to whom she was related. Businesswomen were likely to have acquired much of this whilst looking after the commercial side of the enterprise during the lifetime of male kin. In the counting house, or behind the shop counter, wives and daughters learned more than book-keeping, essential though this was. They also learned who paid promptly, who were good credit risks, whose word could be trusted. Social capital became more important as customary norms of reciprocity declined in the face of market-oriented imperatives. It was this intimate knowledge of business which, by their control of its commercial side, enabled widows and daughters of business- and tradesmen to continue family firms. Daniel Defoe, writing his textbook for the 'middling sort' urban businessman, recognised that bereaved wives might find themselves with a business to run and children to rear. His account is typical of the combination of life cycle and life style which characterised 'middling sort' behaviour in the eighteenth century. Spurning her father's advice to sell up, invest the proceeds and live on the income so generated, the widow set out her plan for continuing the business to provide for herself and her family. She would turn herself from widow, with its implications of powerlessness and dependence, into businesswoman, with authority, agency and independence. She intended to employ a journeyman to do the routine or heavy work whilst she supervised the counting house and raised her children.[28]

Spinster businesswomen appear to have been surrogate sons and businesswomen widows stand-ins for deceased husbands. It could be argued that there was a

---

[27] Clark, A. (1919 reprinted 1982), *Working Life of Women in the Seventeenth Century,* London, pp. 150-54; Pinchbeck, *Women Workers,* pp. 282-86, p. 302; Todd, B. J. (1985), 'The Remarrying Widow: A Stereotype Reconsidered', in M. Prior (ed), *Women in English Society 1500-1800*, London, pp. 54-92; Berg, M. (1993), 'Women's Property and the Industrial Revolution', *Journal of Interdisciplinary History*, 24, pp. 233-50; Prior, 'Women and the Urban Economy', pp. 93-117; Hufton, *Prospect Before Her,* pp. 235-39; Barker, 'Women, Work and the Industrial Revolution', pp. 90-96; Churches, C. (1998), 'Women and Property in Early Modern England: A Case Study', *Social History*, 23, pp. 165-180.

[28] Defoe, D. (1726 reprinted 1987), *The Complete English Tradesman* (London and Stroud, pp. 206-208.

measure of 'Buggin's Turn' about their economic independence, permitted by other family members in the absence of suitable male candidates and, in the case of widows, until their sons were old enough to take over. Are we doing them less than justice by classifying them as second-best alternatives who made good despite the odds? Individual case studies suggest that we are. Many became skilled businesswomen who, by deployment of opportunities and connections, enriched themselves despite operating in commercial circles dominated by men. Hester Pinney, Eleanor Coade, and Sarah Florry acquired wealth and status from their businesses. This was recognised in their family circles, where their influence and advice was sought by friends and relations. In the wider, commercial world, these life-long spinsters became known as 'Madam' or 'Mrs', honorary titles awarded in recognition of their importance in their respective business communities.[29] As far as businesswomen widows were concerned, some retired when their sons were old enough to take over. Others did not, so that the business style of 'Mrs X & Son' meant what it said; Mrs X remained in control of the enterprise, with her son as a junior partner. Only after Mrs X's death would her son come into his own.

Like their male counterparts, 'middling sort' businesswomen exercised power and fulfilled family obligations by their will making. The legal nature of testamentary dispositions meant that their wording was formulaic as well as formal. Stock phrases appeared regularly, and the wording was as likely to have been the work of the attorney's clerk as the testatrix herself. Nonetheless, as Maxine Berg has argued, the wills of eighteenth-century women engaged in trade or business indicated knowledge and understanding of basic legal precepts and the desire to ensure that, on their deaths, their property passed to specific beneficiaries. They wanted daughters or nieces, as much as sons or nephews, to inherit the assets which would enable them to continue family enterprises, should they wish to do so.[30] Female life cycles explain why urban women had to provide for themselves; family circumstances were a form of empowerment, providing monetary and social capital for the widows and daughters of businessmen. We must now turn to evaluating how they ran their enterprises.

Managing the Business

Situated in locations favourable to their businesses and willing to relocate if it were likely to be in their interests, urban businesswomen displayed shrewdness not altogether in keeping with their presence in typically 'feminine' trades, associated with nurturing and homemaking. Was there a paradox, some sort of conflict between reality and society's ideas of womanhood? It might have been that individual businesswomen, even if engaged in women's trades, did not possess

---

[29] Kelly, *Mrs Coade's Stone,* p. 23; Sharpe, 'Dealing with Love', pp. 222-24; Wiskin, 'Women, Credit and Finance', p. 140.

[30] Berg, 'Women's Property and the Industrial Revolution', pp. 245-50.

what contemporaries deemed an essentially 'feminine' outlook on life or business. Alternatively, it may be that historical perspectives on women's work have concentrated too closely on stereotypes of womanhood, of woman as homemaker and nurturer, instead of addressing what was involved in running service sector enterprises. There has been a tendency to depict women's activities in the service sector as an extension of what women did best - activities which were domestic, small-scale, requiring personal skills, often involving manual dexterity, with little need for, or evidence of, their intellectual input. This was undoubtedly the case for the majority of working women but 'middling sort' businesswomen were not the majority of the female population. In the case of 'middling sort' businesswomen, their ownership of the means of subsistence put them in a different economic and social category from the labouring poor. Attributing the high incidence of women in the service sector to homemaking and nurturing which were somehow 'natural' to women ignores the range of management and inter-personal skills needed to operate successfully in this sector.

Histories of businesses run by men have been based on books of accounts and correspondence. The archives have been extensive enough to provide historians with sufficient data from which to write studies plentiful in quantitative analysis, which could be supported by reference to quotations in business correspondence, and then placed within specific economic contexts, such as corporatism. Reconstructing histories of women's businesses is a very different matter. Corporatism is not a suitable model of analysis for women's businesses in this period. Large-scale, highly-capitalised concerns were exceptional; most enterprises were small- or medium-sized and run to answer family needs, rather than the demands of shareholders. In addition, researchers are likely to find only small amounts of primary material, distributed amongst various types of sources and archives. For example, only occasionally are women's approaches to business revealed in their correspondence or other writings. This is because few business records have survived from the eighteenth century and the majority are those of large enterprises, rather than the more modest ones which women generally owned and operated. Writing of the seventeenth century, Amy Erickson has regretted that the paucity of their personal writings means that information on the daily lives of ordinary women is negligible.[31] Nonetheless, a picture of the lives of businesswomen in eighteenth-century England is retrievable but this is a lengthy and laborious process requiring the linkage of material from many sources. The development of sophisticated database packages has speeded up its processing but the collection of data remains time-consuming. Nonetheless, although the picture of urban businesswomen's lives that may be derived from such sources has blank spaces and indistinct outlines, it is by no means as incomplete as we might expect, given the fragmented nature of the sources. Indeed, much can be learned of how women ran their businesses by linking together information from very different types of records. As we have already seen, urban directories demonstrate the public

---

[31] Erickson, A.L. (1993), *Women and Property in Early Modern England*, London, p. 223.

presence of businesswomen. Despite their shortcomings, fire insurance records can be an indicator of the capital that women employed in their businesses. Although the detail recorded in policy registers varies, the figures point to the order of magnitude involved: whether thousands, hundreds, or tens of pounds were laid out in property, stocks of goods and raw materials, utensils and tools. Newspaper advertisements can show business connections, such as agencies, and the composition of individual enterprises - whether it was a partnership, and whether men, as well as women, were employed in it. Wills also can provide details to flesh out the historian's understanding of the lives of businesswomen. In addition to information on property holding and its disposition amongst family and kin, one finds, from time to time, references to male employees or business partners.

Such findings are interesting in themselves and they help to sustain arguments for women's independent economic activity. This is data which is commercial and managerial in its nature and it becomes more difficult to see women's involvement in business as principally an extension of their domestic roles but should historians of women's work be satisfied with this? Specific details of the activities of urban businesswomen gathered from disparate sources are like the peaks of icebergs: indicators that much remains concealed below the surface. Details of women's presence in business, likely capital employed, business connections and networking and the structures of individual enterprises suggest that further interrogation of the sources is called for.

Given a reasonable run of urban directories, supplemented by local newspapers, it is possible to establish the duration of many businesses. Most businesses were short-lived and so, where it can be established that they had existed for five years, we can assume that suppliers and customers alike had confidence in the proprietor. She was likely to be running a concern which was commercially viable, even if it is uncertain whether it was particularly profitable. If it can be established that the enterprise ran for ten years or more, we can be reasonably confident that it was, that its proprietor was active in developing new lines of production, stock, or services offered to the public, improving existing premises or moving to new ones, and developing its standing in the locality. She had built up a strong reputation for good business practice in her relations with suppliers and in her responsiveness to the demands of customers. Eleanor Barford, for example, ran a confectionary business in late eighteenth- and early nineteenth-century Birmingham. Its duration from 1795 to 1825 can be established from town directories and the local newspaper, *Aris's Birmingham Gazette*.[32]

We can, however, look more critically at advertisements in provincial newspapers. Let us a take a common example: an urban businesswoman becomes an agent for goods produced or services supplied from a source located in another part of the kingdom. This is what we would expect given our understanding of the 'consumer revolution' of the eighteenth century. That luxury or semi-luxury goods were being sold by a woman trader would be consonant with our knowledge of

[32] *Wrightson's Triennial Directory of Birmingham (Birmingham 1805-1833)*; Aris's Birmingham Gazette, 5 October 1795.

women's traditional involvement in marketing. Eleanor Barford announced in the local press that she had obtained the sole agency for prepared foods marketed by a London businessman. Selling Burgess's 'sauces, spices and gravies'[33] would have fitted well with her business as a purveyor of speciality foods. The announcement could also be interpreted as an example of how a traditional type of 'women's work' was reformulated in the commercial market economy of the eighteenth century. So far so good yet, if we look more closely at what lay beneath the surface of this and hundreds of similar announcements in the provincial press, a more complicated picture comes to light.

Agencies and connections depended on networks of credit and business intelligence. To establish them, often with distant businesses, urban businesswomen had to prove the viability and creditworthiness of their own enterprises to the satisfaction of potential connections. Manufacturers and suppliers took these matters seriously, seeking detailed assurances before they would take on new stockists.[34] The most usual way of doing so was to obtain references from other members of the urban commercial community. This required some sort of engagement with that community, which was a predominantly male one. Widows and daughters of deceased businessmen appear to have confirmed connections made by their husbands or fathers and to have taken over their networks but making new connections may have raised new issues. If businesswomen were excluded from the new institutions of urban life, how did they find out about new business opportunities? If they heard of them from male employees or business partners, how did they acquire the references that suppliers demanded? Businesswomen took on new lines and agencies and we have to assume that they were able to provide credit references that were acceptable to their new connections but we know very little of the ways in which references were solicited and provided between members of different sexes. It would be reasonable to ask whether proprieties were subverted if a businesswoman requested, and received, recommendations from businessmen. Were businessmen able to provide references without harming their own reputations and were businesswomen able to request them without endangering theirs? Was it so commonplace that it occurred without adverse comment or was it vulnerable to the suspicion of the trading of sexual favours? It has not proved possible to establish how Eleanor Barford obtained her agency. She had been employed by a Birmingham baker.[35] We can speculate that she had had the opportunity to build up a network of connections so that she was aware of the best suppliers in her trade and that she was also known to local businesspeople who would be in a position to vouch for her craft skills, personal reputation, and aptitude for business when she set up on her own. Personal reputation was a vital component of a businessperson's creditworthiness but creditworthiness did not depend on personal qualities alone. It rested on a subtle and complex meshing of

[33] Aris's *Birmingham Gazette*, 5 October 1795.

[34] Harte, N.B. (1977), 'The Growth and Decay of a Hosiery Firm in the Nineteenth Century', *Textile History*, 8, pp. 7-55.

[35] Lichfield Joint Record Office (LJRO) B/C/5/1792/34-35, Inventory of John Griffin, baker, Birmingham.

personal and commercial factors. Substance mattered: well-appointed premises in a good location were persuasive in the formation of creditworthiness, and Barford's shop was in one of the principal shopping streets in the town centre.[36] Suppliers doing business with her could, therefore, be confident that their goods would be marketed from a prominent location, rather than a back street, and by the type of proprietor likely to attract an affluent 'middling sort' clientele, interested in novelty items and with sufficient disposable income to purchase non-essential goods.

More or often than not, it is difficult to give full or conclusive answers to these types of questions but that does not mean that we should not ask them. On the contrary, if scholars wish to take forward the study of women's business activity in the historical past, they ought to consider them. Business is not a static activity, and it never was, but the pro-active stance of 'middling sort' women engaged in it in the historical past is only now receiving attention. In the eighteenth century, 'middling sort' businesswomen worked from fixed premises, delegating to men tasks which required constant travelling. We are not talking of women like Joan Dant, a seventeenth-century widow, who trudged the streets of London as she peddled haberdashery nor of those eighteenth-century chapwomen of dubious reputation who were examined for vagrancy.[37] Nonetheless, 'middling sort' businesswomen confirmed connections made by their predecessors and made new ones. In doing so, we have to assume that their participation in their business communities of their towns was more public and extensive than we might have expected. We can speculate that businesswomen were not confined all day behind the counter or in the counting house; that we might find them sometimes in their business premises and on other occasions, beyond them, travelling to business meetings in the same town, or further afield. Travel for business was expected of elite women, such as Elizabeth Montagu, who crisscrossed the country overseeing the management of her estates and industrial enterprises but the likelihood that the female proprietors of more modest undertakings might have done so has not been widely discussed. The blame for this lies in the dominance of domestic ideology, because of its assumptions that middle-class women were cloistered in the seclusion of the home, venturing out only to shop or pay calls. These assumptions are restrictive, particularly as women undertook their business activities in mixed-sex commercial communities, quite different from the 'feminised' world of the home.

Engagement in business in the eighteenth century was a perilous affair. Many small-scale or medium-sized family firms run by 'middling sort' people lurched from financial crisis to financial crisis, sometimes eventually failing. On the other hand, others survived, some achieving modest levels of success. Being successful in business was about multi-tasking, managing ranges of demands and needs. It was far more complicated than occupational designations might suggest. We find a complex, ambiguous picture if we investigate below the surface of the printed page or manuscript source. Occupational designations tended to hide as much as they

---

[36] *Wrightson's Triennial Directory of Birmingham* (Birmingham, 1805-1833).

[37] Clark, *Working Life of Women*, pp. 32-3; Spufford, M. (1984), *The Great Reclothing of Rural England: Petty Chapmen and Their Wares in the Seventeenth Century*, London, pp. 23-5.

revealed. Multiple economic activities were concealed behind simple, single-word descriptions. The uncertainties of commercial life and the fact that eighteenth-century England was, to all intents and purposes, what we would recognise as an 'emerging market' meant that the majority of those in business had multiple occupations. The same person might engage simultaneously in several trades, or deal in different lines within the same trade. Victuallers owned and ran inns, providing food, drink and accommodation to townspeople and travellers. The inability, or reluctance, of some customers to pay for this meant that innkeepers might become informal pawnbrokers. Victuallers were often engaged in transport, as proprietors of stagecoach services or hiring out horses and wheeled vehicles. As the owners of properties with large public rooms, they were important figures in commercial, political and social urban life. Such rooms were hired for auctions, petty and quarter sessions, the meetings of local learned societies, and all manner of balls, concerts and celebratory feasts, particularly in the first half of the century when there were few purpose-built premises.[38]

Retailing took all sorts of forms and covered a wider range of activities than we might expect. General descriptions of 'shopkeeper' or 'salesman/woman', and more specific ones, such as 'bookseller', 'tailor', 'mantua maker' require amplification. It is now common ground amongst historians that booksellers, for example, did more than sell books. Because bookselling usually provided only a meagre living, almost all booksellers took on additional lines, wholesaling to smaller shops in outlying areas, and retailing the new goods of the consumer revolution which made eighteenth-century private life more comfortable. Other shopkeepers in provincial towns were also wholesalers, supplying stock, such as non-perishable foodstuffs or clothing, to retailers in the smaller towns and villages of the surrounding countryside. In the clothing trades, salesmen and saleswomen sold clothing, new and second-hand, which was ready-made for mass markets. Mantua makers, milliners, tailors, shoemakers, staymakers probably sold a mixture of ready-made clothing and bespoke items. Provincial sellers of ready-made clothing might be involved additionally in small-scale production of garments.[39]

The uncertainty of trade and the ramifications which lay behind apparently straightforward occupational descriptions meant that running a business in eighteenth-century England was considerably more complicated than was immediately apparent. If they were to survive, let alone achieve success, proprietors needed to use complex methods of time management, delegating some tasks to staff whilst dealing with the more important ones themselves. Those in business, whether male or female, had to manage staff, stock, premises, money and credit. Many female proprietors were engaged in the service sector but too frequently the

---

[38] Borsay, *The English Urban Renaissance*, pp. 144-45, pp. 210-11; Clark, P. (1983), *The English Alehouse: A Social History 1200-1830*, London, pp. 7-9.

[39] Alexander, D. (1970), *Retailing in England during the Industrial Revolution,* London, pp. 96, 100-104, 110-58; Mui, H-C. and Mui, L.H. (1989), *Shops and Shopkeeping in Eighteenth-Century England,* London, pp. 47-48, pp. 231-32; Lemire, *Dress, Culture and Commerce*, pp. 57-62.

capacity to care, nurture and provide for others has been treated as gendered and unproblematic. Historians should read women's occupational descriptions more critically, asking themselves what was really involved, remembering how apparently unambiguous occupational designations may well hide complex businesses, which carried many lines and sold to retail and wholesale customers. For too long, it has been too easy to dismiss the female victualler, the schoolmistress, the milliner, the china dealer as not being engaged in genuine occupations. When considering eighteenth-century 'middling sort' businesswomen, it is imperative that their activities be examined in terms of business, rather than as extensions of their domestic life. Doing so may require a major shift in thinking but it is now time to recognise that 'middling sort' women's businesses were run on a commercial basis. Anything less would be to ignore the economic evidence and diminish the achievements of female proprietors.

Let us begin with education. Davidoff and Hall stressed the gentility of school keeping and its links with women's natural role as carers of children. Teaching may have been the best option, or the last resort, of a genteel, educated young woman but running a successful school meant more than that. Susan Skedd has provided an alternative reading of women in education. Whilst she accepts that, because it resembled managing a large household, running a boarding establishment had its domestic aspects, she stresses that this was only part of what was involved in good school keeping. She is conscious of the sexual division of labour within many mid-eighteenth-century girls' schools, but points out that the practicalities of school life were not gendered. The school owner, whether male or female, had to find suitable premises, equip them and engage staff. These were business matters, to be addressed in a business-like way. She emphasises that the schools which women opened were businesses, run on commercial lines. Their owners actively sought out suitable premises at economical prices in desirable locations in order to draw in pupils from the best families, whilst keeping their fees competitive.[40]

The male victualler has been described in terms of a businessman or entrepreneur whereas the female victualler has been depicted as caring and cooking in an environment only slightly removed from the domestic. The majority of victuallers were men but, in some towns, sizeable minorities were female. In late eighteenth-century Birmingham and Liverpool, nearly 30 per cent of victuallers were women. In the case of women victuallers, however, it is time to put aside homemaking connections and look more closely at what was involved in running this type of business. As we have already seen, there was more to running an inn than the sale of drink and food. Discipline was an issue. Large inns in prominent positions had to attract a large and varied clientele if they were to be successful. Victuallers had to balance the likelihood of this clientele manifesting an equally varied range of behaviour against their need to maintain high standards. Good order mattered, both for the comfort of guests and to present a positive image to local

[40] Skedd, S. (1997), 'Women Teachers and the Expansion of Girls' Schooling in England, c. 1760-1820', in H. Barker and E. Chalus (eds), *Gender in Eighteenth-Century England: Roles, Representations and Responsibilities,* London, pp. 101-25.

legal authorities. Women innkeepers had to be particularly careful to avoid slurs on their reputations and they could not afford to be seen to be running inefficient enterprises. There was, after all, only a fine line between a disorganised inn and a disorderly one. Yet, as Peter Clark points out, division of labour within innkeeping families meant that the innkeeper's wife increasingly became responsible for good order. She was expected to greet, and assess, customers, refusing admittance to the impecunious or disreputable, becoming practised in doing so without giving offence.[41] This was yet another way in which wives might acquire that social capital which would serve them well in their widowhood.

These victualling widows would have become accustomed to the delegation of specific tasks to family and staff and, on the death of the landlord, sufficiently familiar with the organisation of the inn to step into his shoes quickly and efficiently. Ann Dunn was the mistress of the George Inn, Digbeth, in Birmingham. The inn, in a prominent position where the main road from London entered the town, was a local landmark, a place where auctions and public meetings were held, and an important centre in transport networks. Dunn became mistress on the death of the master, her husband William, in 1774.[42] For twenty-two years, she managed what was, in reality, a diverse, capitalised service sector business. She was a good landlady. If she had not been, the business would have failed. In the absence of specific detail, we will have to assume that she supervised the domestic side of innkeeping, caring for the comfort of her guests and customers and for the good order and reputation of her premises. Dunn, however, was also a businesswoman, intent on building up the enterprise so that, when she died, she could hand on an improved and more valuable property to her children. Some ten years after her husband's death, she recruited other innkeepers, in towns from Wolverhampton to London, to form a consortium, styled 'Ann Dunn & Co', running stagecoaches to London.[43] This venture required a willingness to take risks and high levels of inter-personal skills. As far as the uncertainties of the new venture were concerned, Mrs Dunn was in a position to take informed decisions. The years she had spent at the George Inn would have given her plenty of chances to observe, assess and evaluate customers' needs for transport, to familiarise herself with the reputations and creditworthiness of other innkeepers on the route between Wolverhampton and London, and to estimate how much money might be needed to set up such a venture. Having done so, Dunn had to employ inter-personal skills in its management. She had to trust the honesty and efficiency of her partners and to make arrangements with them to ensure that the service was a reliable one. The consortium's advertisements promised punctuality: a meal in Digbeth at 3 p.m. followed by arrival at Wolverhampton the same evening. Failure to reach this performance target would have endangered the partnership's reputation and undermined the likelihood of its success. All the foregoing is a far cry from the

---

[41] Clark, *English Alehouse*, pp. 287-89, p. 302, n.46; *Pye's Birmingham Directory* (1785).

[42] *Aris's Birmingham Gazette*, 7 February 1774.

[43] *Aris's Birmingham Gazette*, 12 January 1784.

domestic world of cooking, cleaning and caring. Ann Dunn ran the George Inn as a business, delegating some tasks, keeping others under close personal control and, in the end, bequeathing a flourishing undertaking to two of her five daughters.[44]

Historical perspectives on women's occupations have emphasised lack of change. Peter Earle, for instance, has argued that women were to be found in the same poorly paid, low status, predominantly temporary occupations in 1850 as they had been a century or more earlier. There was, he concluded, no 'golden age' of women's work.[45] It is not the intention of this essay to suggest that there was but it is possible to discern how social and economic change in the eighteenth century might have affected the likelihood of 'middling sort' women achieving economic independence. Susan Skedd's work recognises this. A new and widespread interest amongst thinkers and writers in the education of women was translated into an expansion in demand for it. The desire of parents for good-quality day and boarding establishments, in turn, presented 'middling sort' educated women with opportunities of economic independence, for here was a ready-made market ripe for development. Changes in retailing practices and the appearance of new consumer goods provide explanations for the new opportunities available for female shopkeepers in the eighteenth century. Historical perspectives on women's buying and selling have conceptualised it as part of their domestic roles, finding and paying for the provisions needed to nurture a family. From there, it was only a short step to buying and selling goods for profit. Since medieval times, there had been urban 'women's markets' but it was a feature of eighteenth-century retailing that consumers were less likely to buy at markets and fairs. They made more and more of their purchases from permanent shops. It might be expected that this would result in fewer retailing opportunities for women. The old transparency had been lost; businesswomen no longer heard rumours about where new openings in trade might be profitably found or whose credit looked shaky, as they had done when business was conducted and information exchanged in the public arena of the town market.[46] The absence of reliable data makes it impossible to quantify the effects of this change but, as directories show, women continued in retailing, operating from fixed premises frequently in prominent positions in town centres. The move to fixed premises did not affect their capacity to conduct business. Transparency was reformulated in different ways. Agents and travellers visited them in their shops and counting houses, offering them new lines and confiding business news. Fixed premises might be the lock-up booths in purpose-built Exchanges, such as the Royal Exchange in London, where Hester Pinney sold lace produced in the West Country.[47] Probably more commonly, buildings were converted to retail use - shops were to be found on the ground floor, with the shopkeeper living above.

---

[44] LJRO, will of Ann Dunn, 1796; *Aris's Birmingham Gazette*, 29 February 1796.

[45] Earle, P. (1989), 'The Female Labour Market in London in the Late Seventeenth and Early Eighteenth Centuries', *Economic History Review*, 2nd series, 42:3 pp. 328-53.

[46] Thwaites, W. (1984), 'Women in the Market Place: Oxfordshire, c. 1690-1800', *Midland History*, 9, pp. 23-42.

[47] Sharpe, 'Dealing with Love', p. 212.

The ownership of fixed premises entailed on-going financial and managerial responsibilities quite different from possession of the hawker's pack or trestle stall. Management skills were needed if retailers were to prosper. Retailing required knowledge, an eye for detail and the ability to organise. Organisational skills were necessary for the stock, however fashionable or fine, did not sell itself. Order and regularity were essential if businesses were to flourish in the eighteenth century. This required adequate book-keeping, prompt payments and a general regime of tight managerial control.[48] The application of reason to the business process runs counter to many contemporary literary accounts of women's intellectual capacity. New notions of the masculine and the feminine equated the latter with sensitivity and sensibility rather than double entry book-keeping or stock control, yet the successful businesswoman had to manage these issues. We would have no difficulty in ascribing commercial values to successful male shopkeepers but there has been reluctance to accept that women needed them too, and possessed them. Stock had to be kept and displayed in an orderly way, and contemporary engravings, advertisements and trade cards confirms that it was. This was very different from the piles of goods heaped on her stall by a market trader or samples carried round by a chapwoman. The tasteful arrangement of stock in ways which would invite customers to buy was an issue for all retailers. To be shown at its best, it had to be arranged with care, generally on purpose-built furniture, which, in turn, meant that thought had to be given and money expended in its acquisition and siting within the shop. Women retailers, as much as men, attended to these matters.[49]

Shopkeepers also needed good observation skills. First, to counteract shop-lifting, because theft from shops supported a thriving trade in stolen goods.[50] Second, because the shopkeeper's success depended on combining awareness of customers' preferences with an appreciation of new fashions or designs and their marketability. This was the case whether we are talking of clothing, books or luxury furnishings, such as china and glassware. Women shopkeepers who sold clothing travelled to London to buy the latest styles. They needed a practised eye to observe subtle changes of cut and colour from season to season and to transmit them to a provincial clientele. By the early nineteenth century, shrewd retailers were developing the connections between the gentility and refinement of their stock and the calendar of polite entertainments in the locality. The arrival of new stock was linked to important functions, for example, the Birmingham Music Festival, and women retailers advertised that they had ordered new lines expressly to coincide with it.[51] The Festival was an event of irreproachable respectability, patronised by the leading lights of local society, and, women retailers had linked their stock, their business and themselves to that refined and exclusive world. This combination of

[48] Pollard, S. (1965), *The Genesis of Modern Management: A Study of the Industrial Revolution in Great Britain*, London, pp. 261-5.

[49] Walsh, C. (1995), 'Shop Design and the Display of Goods in Eighteenth-Century London', *Journal of Design History*, 8, pp. 157-76.

[50] Lemire, Dress, *Culture and Commerce*, pp. 135-45.

[51] For example, an announcement by Mrs Allen, a Birmingham milliner, in *Aris's Birmingham Gazette*, 25 September 1804.

snobbery and selling was a conscious business ploy. The enterprising woman retailer had observed social change and used the new medium of newspapers to reach polite society.

Neil McKendrick and John Brewer have argued for a 'revolution' in English purchasing habits during the eighteenth century. Possessed of greater disposable income than in earlier times, men and women spent it on semi-luxury goods for self adornment, comfort and status.[52] Many of these goods were purchased by women, and scholarship has focused on their buying habits and the meanings with which they endowed their purchases.[53] These readings emphasise shopping as a leisure occupation for dependent women and have reinforced the concept of a specifically 'feminine' retail sector. Insufficient attention has been paid to the implications of these goods for the 'middling sort' women who sold them. Developments in production meant that large quantities of items which previously only the rich could afford were now much cheaper and widely available. The significance of these changes in supply and demand should not be under-estimated as far as urban female shopkeepers were concerned. They were important as intermediaries aiding the dissemination of the new goods. Claire Walsh's discussion of the importance of London retailers as mediators of taste and style between producers and consumers may be applied to the provinces.[54] Many producers had London showrooms but they relied on a multitude of local retailers to reach customers throughout the kingdom. Women retailers made an important, though unquantifiable, contribution to the supply side of production by selling, in regional towns and cities, books, sheet music, china wares, patent medicines, high-quality candles, as well as 'Brummagem' wares - steel buttons, buckles, painted or enamelled trinkets.[55] Thus they could offer their customers wider ranges of merchandise. There would be novel or entertaining goods to be inspected; those who intended only to browse might be tempted to buy. The availability of manufactured goods meant women were able to sell items which they had not made themselves. That rendered irrelevant women's limited access to apprenticeships, lack of craft skills or physical strength (if indeed they lacked them). Selling goods made by others required transferable, inter-personal aptitude, which was not restricted by gender. Indeed, it could be argued that the culture of politesse with which the selling of these goods

---

[52] McKendrick, N., Brewer, J. and Plumb, J.H. (1982), *The Birth of a Consumer Society: The Commercialization of Eighteenth-Century England*, London.

[53] McKendrick, N. (1974), 'Home Demand and Economic Growth: A New View of the Role of Women and Children in the Industrial Revolution', in N. McKendrick (ed), *Historical Perspectives: Studies in English Thought and Society in Honour of J.H. Plumb*, London, pp. 152-210; Nenadic, S. (1994), 'Middle Rank Consumers and Domestic Culture in Edinburgh and Glasgow, 1720-1840', *Past and Present*, 145, pp. 122-56.

[54] Walsh, 'Shop Design and the Display of Goods', p. 174.

[55] Amongst the many examples of provincial urban women retailers selling these goods, the following may be cited: *Aris's Birmingham Gazette*, 20 December 1813 (Mary Rollason), *Coventry Mercury*, 18 October 1779 (Hannah Downes), ibid. 2 February 1804, 3 July 1809 (Elizabeth and Jane Parker), *Wolverhampton Chronicle*, 16 December 1789 (Ann Cresswell).

was associated was suited to what contemporaries perceived as ideals of womanhood - polite manners, good taste and genuine refinement. In the well-fitted premises of the urban woman retailer, there was no room for hoydenish behaviour which might dislodge displays and damage stock.

Conclusion

Urban life had plenty to entertain leisured women of the social elite and historians have paid much attention to it. The activities of urban 'middling sort' businesswomen have received much less notice yet, despite the polemical writings of contemporary commentators, respectable women were economically independent as proprietresses of their own enterprises. Widows or daughters came into their own when they inherited the business. They were now in a position to choose whether to wind it up and live on the proceeds, or to continue it. Many took the former route but a sizeable minority did not. The minority who chose the latter course experienced lives very different from the marginalisation so often associated with women's work. Many businesswomen may have engaged in typically 'feminine' trades, although not all did. Dismissing those who did as merely exploiting women's domestic expertise is too simplistic. Occupational designations frequently hid complex, prosperous businesses, requiring the proprietress's skilful management of resources and staff, rather than a kind heart or manual dexterity. Previously left to mind the shop when husbands or fathers went out to pursue orders, female proprietors had now to take the initiative if they were to stay in business or expand it further. When we look carefully at the albeit fragmentary evidence of women's businesses, we discover their urban visibility and activity which models of domestic ideology would have denied us. It can no longer be assumed that 'middling sort' businesswomen played little part in economic life in the eighteenth century. Despite their being a small percentage of the business community, their presence in a wide range of distributive businesses meant they were ideal intermediaries between the producers of new goods and services and the consumer. Women were in the mainstream of urban commercial life, running their enterprises from prime locations, selling the new consumer goods and marketing the trappings of polite sociability. Thus, we find them talking, listening, and watching, as well as working in the counting house or in the shop. They sent staff to run errands, they attended meetings with other businesspeople, made deals, collected debts and paid creditors, visited their suppliers, ordered goods, displayed them, conversed with callers and customers. Their recognition as independent 'middling sort' businesspeople in the eighteenth-century urban economy is long overdue.

Chapter 6

Women Entrepreneurs and Urban Expansion: Manchester 1760-1820*

Hannah Barker and Karen Harvey

Like those of other northern towns, traditional accounts of late eighteenth- and early nineteenth-century Manchester focus strongly on industrialisation. In descriptions of Manchester's industrial revolution, changes in the organisational structure of manufacturing loom large, with the move to the factory-system taking centre-stage for both social and economic historians alike. This fascination with the factory echoes the descriptions of numerous nineteenth-century commentators. Writers on Manchester as disparate as Frederick Engels and Benjamin Disraeli were keen to convey the impression of a factory-dominated landscape, and, more misleadingly, a factory-dominated society.[1] This lead is one also followed by historians of women's work in the late eighteenth and early nineteenth centuries. Indeed, for many who have researched this field, the history of female labour during the industrial revolution *was* primarily the history of factory work – not just in Manchester, but for much of the rest of the country. Ivy Pinchbeck was one of the first of many historians who described how women's work was profoundly altered by industrialisation and the associated rise of capitalism, resulting – as it supposedly did – in a large proportion of the population (both male and female) being propelled into the factory.[2]

The potency of this model and its impact on historians of both women and labour mean that when looking at Manchester, perhaps more than any other town, the prominent image of the female factory worker – in the specific guise of the cotton operative – is hard to ignore. This is true for those who, like Pinchbeck, celebrated her newly found independence as a wage earner free from the clutches

* Research for this article was funded by the ESRC. We are also grateful for the generous help we received from the following: Ann Brooks, Sarah Davnall, Bryan Haworth, Peter Kirby, Colin Phillips and Michael Powell.

[1] Kidd, A. (1993), *Manchester*, 2nd edn, Keele, p. 26.

[2] Pinchbeck, I. (1930), *Women Workers and the Industrial Revolution, 1750-1850*, London; Hill, B. (1989), *Women, Work and Sexual Politics in Eighteenth-Century England*, Oxford; Richards, E. (1974), 'Women in the British Economy Since About 1700: an Interpretation', *History*, 59, pp. 337-57. Although for more complex interpretations see Rendall, J. (1990), *Women in an Industrializing Society*, Oxford; Valenze, D. (1995), *The First Industrial Woman*, Oxford; and Sharpe, P. (1996), *Adapting to Capitalism: Working Women in the English Economy, 1700-1850*, Basingstoke.

of familial control and destined to embark on a series of political campaigns and trade union activism.[3] But it holds equally for those who, conversely, mourn the female factory worker's imprisonment within a poorly paid job with long hours and dangerous conditions, where gender determined both status and pay to the detriment of women.[4] More recently, the factory girl has also been cast as part of a workforce that pioneered the use of new technologies and modes of production, thus playing a vital role in the kinds of innovation which have been traditionally associated with the industrial revolution.[5]

Clearly the history of women's involvement in factory-based work and in innovative methods of industrial production is important. Indeed, as Maxine Berg has suggested, examining the role of female labour in newer progressive manufacturing sectors is probably crucial to a fuller understanding of industrial development in Britain.[6] Yet reassessments of the nature of industrialisation in recent years mean we can no longer assume that the 'factory girl' was representative of women workers in this period,[7] even in places like Manchester.

---

[3] Pinchbeck, *Women Workers*. See also Morgan, C.E. (1992), 'Women, Work and Consciousness in the Mid-Nineteenth-Century Cotton Industry', *Social History*, 17, pp. 23-41.

[4] Hill, *Women, Work and Sexual Politics*. See also Lown, J. (1990), *Women and Industrialisation: Gender at Work in Nineteenth-Century England*, Cambridge; Freifield, M. (1986), 'Technological Change and the "Self-Acting" Mule: a Study of Skill and the Sexual Division of Labour', *Social History*, 11:3, pp. 319-43; Huberman, M. (1987), 'The Economic Origins of Paternalism: Lancashire Cotton Spinning in the First Half of the Nineteenth Century', *Social History*, 12:2, pp. 177-92; Humphries, J. (1991), 'Lurking in the Wings ... Women in the Historiography of the Industrial Revolution', *Business and Economic History*, 20, pp. 32-44; Humphries J. and Horrell, S. (1995), 'Women's Labour Force Participation and the Transition to the Male-Breadwinner Family, 1790-1865', *Economic History Review*, 2nd series, 48, 89-117; John, A.V. (ed.) (1986), *Unequal Opportunities: Women's Employment in England, 1800-1918*, Oxford; Jordan, E. (1989), 'The Exclusion of Women From Industry in Nineteenth-Century Britain', *Comparative Studies in Social History*, 31, pp. 309-26; Rose, S. (1988), 'Gender Antagonism and Class Conflict: Exclusionary Strategies of Male Trade Unionists in Nineteenth-Century Britain', *Social History*, 13, pp. 191-208.

[5] Berg, M. (1988), 'Women's Work, Mechanization and the Early Phases of Industrialization in England', in R.E. Pahl (ed.), *On Work: Historical, Comparative and Theoretical Approaches*, Oxford; Berg, M. (1993), 'What Difference Did Women's Work Make to the Industrial Revolution?', *History Workshop Journal*, 35, pp. 22-44; Berg, M. (1994), *The Age of Manufactures, 1700-1820,* 2nd edn, London.

[6] Berg, 'Women's Work'; Berg, 'What Difference Did Women's Work Make'; Berg, *The Age of Manufactures.*

[7] See, for example, Vickery, A. (1993), 'Golden Age to Separate Spheres? A Review of the Categories and Chronology of English Women's History', *Historical Journal,* 36:2, pp. 383-414; Sharpe, P. (1995), 'Continuity and Change: Women's History and Economic History in Britain', *Economic History Review,* 2nd series, 48:2, pp. 353-69; Crafts, N.F.R. (1985, *British Industrial Growth During the Industrial Revolution*, Oxford; Wrigley, E.A. (1989), *Continuity, Chance and Change: The Character of the Industrial Revolution in England*, Cambridge; Hudson, P. (1992), *The Industrial Revolution*, London; O'Brien, P. and Quinault, R. (eds) (1993), *The Industrial Revolution and British Society*, Cambridge; Berg, *The Age of Manufactures*.

Indeed, it is now clear that Manchester was never merely a mill town in the way that places like Oldham and Blackburn were.[8] There are other stories to be told of women's economic activity – and of the economic landscape as a whole – that an exclusive focus on factory workers obscures. For whilst we know a fair amount about some trades in eighteenth- and early nineteenth-century Manchester – particularly cotton and other textiles, but also silk throwing, silk weaving and paper and hat making, which also flourished – very little else is known about the town's economic life. Yet there was a rich world of economic activity which a restricted focus on the 'cottonopolis' of large-scale, factory-based manufacturing obscures. In particular, we know surprisingly little about service, retailing and small-scale manufacturing industries. All of these undoubtedly developed, and generally prospered, alongside the more well-charted sectors of the town's economy, but its small-scale economic activity has, perhaps not surprisingly, been ignored by historians eager to study the rise of textiles and tell the story of the 'industrial revolution proper'.[9]

Concentrating on trade and service industries, and on small-scale manufacturing firms, reveals a world of economic activity in which women played prominent roles, and where women of the middling sort – who often laboured as hard as those below them on the social scale, but whose efforts are generally overlooked or undervalued by historians – were particularly important. Women's involvement in such arenas has been explored, but this work has focused on the roles women played as consumers.[10] Yet, as Manchester grew in size and wealth, women traders sought to cash in on developments, and in so doing, helped to increase the town's prosperity. Rather than retreat into domestic indolence or, like more elevated

[8] Here cotton manufacturing employed at least 40 per cent of population in the early nineteenth century. Yet according to the 1841 census, in Manchester cotton employed no more than 18 per cent of the Manchester labour force: Kidd, *Manchester*, p. 25.

[9] Wilson makes a similar point concerning Leeds: Wilson, R.G. (1980), 'Georgian Leeds', in D. Fraser (ed.), *A History of Modern Leeds*, Manchester, p. 33.

[10] On women, consumption and the industrial revolution see McKendrick, N. (1975), 'Home Demand and Economic Growth: a New View of the Role of Women and Children in the Industrial Revolution', in N. McKendrick (ed.), *Historical Perspectives: Studies in English Thought and Society in Honour of J.H. Plumb* (eds), Cambridge, pp. 152-210; N. McKendrick (1982), 'Introduction' and 'The Consumer Revolution of Eighteenth-Century England' in N. McKendrick, J. Brewer, and J.H. Plumb (eds), *The Birth of a Consumer Society: The Commercialization of Eighteenth-Century England*, Bloomington. On women and consumption more generally see Barker Benfield, G.J. (1992), 'Women and Eighteenth-Century Consumerism', in G.J. Benfield (ed.), *The Culture of Sensibility: Sex and Society in Eighteenth-Century Britain*, Chicago, pp. 154-214; Vickery, A. (1993), 'Women and the World of Goods: a Lancashire Consumer and Her Possessions, 1751-81', in J. Brewer and R. Porter (eds), *Consumption and the World of Goods: Consumption and Society in the Seventeenth and Eighteenth Centuries*, London, pp. 274-301; and Weatherill, L. (1986), 'A Possession of One's Own: Women and Consumer Behaviour in England, 1660-1740', *Journal of British Studies*, 25, pp. 131-56.

middle-class women, remain uninvolved in business, trade and production,[11] it seems likely that the increasing pressures and opportunities resulting from economic change produced quite a different response amongst the female members of Manchester's 'petite bourgeoisie'. Apparently free from the sort of customary restrictions that women in trade (and married women in particular) were subject to in other English towns,[12] Mancunian women appear to have involved themselves in a great variety of business ventures.

The Range of Female Economic Activity

There is evidence of widespread female economic activity in late eighteenth- and early nineteenth-century Manchester, although the sources available to historians to trace the lives of women in trade, service industry and small-scale manufacturing are neither plentiful nor full. Even when a variety of disparate pieces of information are gathered together, the resultant picture is usually sketchy at best. In part this is a result of the peculiarities of the evidence. Trade and commercial directories did not claim to be censuses and are notoriously incomplete.[13] Similarly, newspaper advertising was undertaken by only a fraction of the trading community. Such difficulties are compounded by the factor of gender. The economic activity of individual women was often hidden behind that of male relatives in official sources such as rate books, tax and insurance records and legal documents. Such problems are not, of course, restricted to historians working in this particular field; nor are they insuperable. In spite of such drawbacks, information which is both quantitatively and qualitatively significant can be found and used to produce a revealing picture of female economic activity. Trade directories still provide us with the best overall view of non-factory-based economic life, while newspaper advertisements open rare windows onto women's trading histories and the languages through which they presented their working lives. This material can be married with local histories, memoirs and household accounts, which provide more detailed descriptions of women's work.

---

[11] Alice Clark (1919) noted this development in the seventeenth century: *Working Life of Women in the Seventeenth Century*, London. For the eighteenth century, see Davidoff, L. and Hall, C. (1987), *Family Fortunes: Men and Women of the English Middle Class 1780-1850*, London; Hill, *Women, Work and Sexual Politics*; Prior, M. (1985), 'Women in the Urban Economy: Oxford 1500-1800', in M. Prior (ed.), *Women in English Society, 1500-1800*, London. See also Vickery, 'Golden Age to Separate Spheres?'.

[12] Bateson, M. (ed.) (1904-6), *Borough Customs,* 2 vols, London; Prior, M. 'Women and the Urban Economy'; Bennett, J. (1992), 'Medieval Women, Modern Women: Across the Great Divide', in D. Aers (ed.), *Culture and History 1350-1600: Essays in English Communities, Identities and Writing*, Hemel Hempstead; Barker, H. (1997), 'Women, Work and the Industrial Revolution: Female Involvement in the English Printing Trades, c. 1700-1840', in H. Barker and E. Chalus, (eds), *Gender in Eighteenth-Century England: Roles, Representations and Responsibilities*, Harlow, pp. 81-100, pp. 98-9.

[13] Corfield, P.J. with Kelly, S. (1984), '"Giving Directions to the Town": the Early Town Directories', *Urban History Yearbook*, pp. 22-35.

When combined, this material reveals the sheer diversity of female trading interests. There were women pawnbrokers, drapers, booksellers, seedswomen, hosiers, tallow chandlers, farriers, victuallers, printers, tobacconists, auctioneers, circulating library owners, milliners, linen drapers, staymakers and haberdashers. Women sold timber, earthenware, medicines, ran servants register offices and lodging houses, were coffee house owners and appeared as inn-keepers in great numbers. R.J. Richardson's manuscript notes for a history of late eighteenth- and early nineteenth-century Manchester (a work almost entirely devoted, it seems from his initial scribblings, to public houses) lists thirty female publicans (of a total of 200) in 1794.[14] The household records of Dunham Massey Hall, the home of the Grey family near Manchester, show the widespread use of women traders in the 1820s, with Mary and Sarah Dean receiving payment for the supply of clothing, bedding, fabrics and paper, Ann Sykes being paid for chimney pots, Sarah Southern for leather skins and Mary Allen for the repair of a thermometer, plus the supply of tobacco water and silver paper.[15]

Manchester trade directories for the years 1773, 1788, 1804 and 1817 are suggestive of the extent of female economic activity.[16] The number of entries of trading women listed rose from fifty-six in 1773, to 160 in 1788, 392 in 1804, and 615 in 1817, although these figures represented a fairly consistent proportion of the total number of trading individuals.[17] In addition to the considerable numbers of women offering services and engaged in trade and manufacturing, the quantitative evidence yielded from trade directories confirms the variety of women's trading interests. The range of trade labels ascribed to women grew from thirty-eight in 1773, to eighty-five in 1788, 127 in 1804, and 173 in 1817.[18] It is important to note that the growth in the number of trades was outstripped by the increase in the numbers of women given trade labels: between 1773 and 1817, the numbers of

---

[14] Chetham's Library, A.0.12, Richardson MS [1808-61]. Similar figures are given for female victuallers in the *Manchester Directories* for 1788 and 1804.

[15] John Rylands Library, Papers of the Grey family, EGR7/12/1-12.

[16] These statistics derived from analysis of the following directories: Raffald, E. (1773), *The Manchester Directory; containing, ... The Names of the Merchants, Traders and Principal Inhabitants in the Town of Manchester*, Manchester; Holme, E. (1788), *A Directory for the Towns of Manchester and Salford, For the Year 1788*, Manchester; (1804) *Deans & Co.'s Manchester & Salford Directory; or, an Alphabetical List of the Merchants, Manufacturers, and Inhabitants in General*, Manchester; and (1817) *Pigot and Deans' Manchester and Salford Directory, for 1817; Containing an Alphabetical List of the Merchants, Manufacturers, and Inhabitants in General*, Manchester.

[17] These figures represented 4.7 per cent, 8 per cent, 6 per cent and 6 per cent respectively of the total entries (men and women) with trades.

[18] These totals represent the actual number of trade labels with no standardisation. Thus 'milliner', 'mantua-maker and milliner', 'fustian cutter' and 'fustian-cutter' are counted as four trade labels. Note that the discussion in this paragraph does not incorporate the women whose addresses were inns or taverns and who may well have been victuallers. Counting such entries would amend the totals to fifty in 1773, and ninety-nine in 1788.

women listed with trade labels rose by 998 per cent, but the range of trade labels rose by only 355 per cent. Whereas in the directory of 1773 each trade label was used to refer to 1.47 women, this rose to 1.88 in 1788, 3.09 in 1804, and 3.56 in 1817. Like much evidence of women's work, these figures are important but partial. To some extent they may chart the development of the genre of directories and linguistic trends which bear a debatable relationship to actual work organization. They may also reflect the limits of general economic diversification as much as the clustering of women in a relatively smaller range of trades. Most importantly, specialized trade labels can obscure significant diversification of women's work in terms of broad occupational categories or economic sector. For example, while retailing and service activities, particularly in the sectors of textiles, food and drink, were consistently well-represented amongst women's work, the nineteenth-century directories included women dealers and manufacturers in heavier sectors. In contrast to arguments that the range of trades available to women contracted over the eighteenth century,[19] it appears that there was a significant expansion in the range of trading opportunities for women. An increase in the number of trade labels of 355 per cent is substantial.

Family Businesses

In histories of women's work, questions of sheer numbers and range of occupations are generally aligned with those focussing on the qualitative aspects of women's working experiences. Much work has explored the determining role of a woman's marital status and the trade of her male relations.[20] Such factors were crucial to women's trading activities in late eighteenth- and early nineteenth-century Manchester. For many women, widowhood marked the point at which they assumed formal responsibility for a business. Indeed, many women who traded under their own names were widows who had inherited businesses from their husbands. Phoebe Fletcher, for example, took over the Old Iron Foundry in Red

---

[19] Hill, *Women, Work and Sexual Politics*, p. 260.

[20] On women without men, see Clarkson, L.A. and Crawford, M. (1991), 'Life After Death: Widows in Carrick-on-Suir, 1799', in M. MacCurtain and M. O'Dowd (eds), *Women in Early Modern Ireland*, Edinburgh, pp. 236-54; Davies, N.Z. (1982), 'Women in the Crafts in Sixteenth-Century Lyon', *Feminist Studies*, 8:1, pp. 47-80; Brodsky Elliot, V. (1981), 'Single Women in the London Marriage Market: Age, Status and Mobility, 1598-1619', in R.B. Outhwaite (ed.), *Marriage and Society: Studies in the Social History of Marriage*, London, pp. 81-100; Erickson, E. (1993), 'How Lone Women Lived', in her *Women and Property in Early Modern England*, London, pp. 187-203; Hill, *Women, Work and Sexual Politics*, pp. 153, 240-8; Wall, R. (1981), 'Women Alone in English Society', *Annales de Démographie Historique*, 16, pp. 303-117; and Hufton, O. (1981), 'Women, Work and Marriage in Eighteenth-Century France' in R.B. Outhwaite (ed.), *Marriage and Society: Studies in the Social History of Marriage*, London, pp. 186-203; Hufton, O. (1984), 'Women Without Men: Widows and Spinsters in Britain and France in the Eighteenth Century', *Journal of Family History*, 9, pp. 355-76; Hufton, O. (1995), *The Prospect Before Her: A History of Women in Western Europe*, Volume One: 1500-1800, London; Prior, 'Women in the Urban Economy'; Rendall, *Women in an Industrialising Society*, pp. 27-30.

Bank after the death of John Fletcher in 1785 and managed it successfully.[21] Similarly, Sarah Willet or Willatt, listed in the Manchester directories of 1773 and 1788 as 'mistress' and 'keeper' of the post office in St. Ann's Square, assumed control when her husband died and clearly continued the business for many years.[22] Business acumen was suggested in the way women used newspaper advertisements to publicise the fact that they were continuing the businesses of deceased husbands. In 1804, M. Bancks announced that she had taken charge of her late husband's printing business:

> M.BANCKS, No. 10, Exchange-street,
> GRATEFUL for the many favours conferred on her late Husband, respectfully informs her Friends and the Public, that the *Business of Stationary, Letter-press Printing, and Book-binding*, will be carried on as usual, for the benefit of herself and her family; and hopes by strict attention and punctuality to merit their future favours.[23]

In the same year, Elizabeth Baron similarly gave notice that she would take over her husband's cabinet-making business:

> *Cabinet-Maker, Upholsterer, Auctioneer & Sworn Appraiser, No. 35, Smithy-Door.*
> ELIZABETH BARON
> EMBRACES the present opportunity of returning her most sincere Thanks to her Friends and the Public for the very liberal encouragement she has experienced since the death of her late husband, in the *Cabinet* and *Upholstery* business; and likewise, with the assistance of her son, as auctioneer, sworn appraiser, &c.

As the advert went on to explain, Elizabeth's new business of cabinet-maker did not mark the beginning of her trading career, rather it was an addition to a business she had run with her son for some time:

> The business of auctioneer, sworn appraiser, and commission brokers, will be carried on as usual by E. BARON, and her son THOMAS BARON, who has been in the auction business for several years past, at their old established shop, No. 35, Smithy Door, where all orders for either of the above concerns will be gratefully received and punctually attended to, on the shortest notice, in town and country.[24]

---

21 Wright Proctor, R. (1874), *Memorials of Manchester Streets*, Manchester, p. 44.

22 See also Roeder, C. (1905), *Beginnings of the Manchester Post-Office* Manchester, pp. 40-2.

23 *Manchester Mercury*, 4 December 1804.

24 *Manchester Mercury*, 31 July 1804.

Widowhood constituted an important moment in a woman's trading career. For both Bancks and Baron, a newspaper advertisement was used to mark the change, as well as providing an opportunity to publicise their businesses. Whilst widowhood increased women's prominence, however, it is evident that for some this moment merely rendered their involvement in trade visible following an often lengthy and active involvement in a marital economic venture.

While accounts of women's work often focus on widows or spinsters when highlighting female economic independence, a good many women traders in Manchester proved in other ways that female economic power was not always subservient to male interests. In some cases, a woman might run a business under her husband's name. This was clearly true of the wife of James Hopps. In James Weatherley's unpublished manuscript, 'Recollections of Manchester and Manchester characters' written in 1860 and detailing his life as a travelling (and generally penniless) bookseller, he describes how James Hopps, returning home in 1815 after fighting on the continent, bought a book shop, but thereafter left the management entirely to his wife. She was, according to Weatherley, 'a very good and kind and civil woman and very attentive to the business for her Husband would not take any Interest in the Shop but left it entirely for her to manage ...', choosing instead to spend his pension on gin. Not surprisingly, Weatherley notes that 'Mrs. H. survived him for many years'.[25]

Other families ran businesses in ways that appear to have presumed a significant degree of female independence. Josiah Slugg's *Reminiscences of Manchester* outlines the history of the Thorps, who ran a druggists in Oldham Street and whose story reveals a complex picture of gender and familial relations. During much of the 1790s, Ann Thorp managed the shop alone, whilst her son, Issachar, 'acquired a knowledge of the business when a young man' from his mother, but on coming of age began work as a calico printer. When his mother died, he took on her shop and 'for a few years he had both businesses on his hands'. 'I doubt not', Slugg remarked, 'that his wife Ellen assisted him at this time in the shop, and was so enabled to follow them up after his death'.[26] The Thorp's story suggests that age, as well as gender, was a precondition of economic power in family businesses. Although Ann Thorp may well have been a widow who had inherited her shop from her husband, she did not relinquish control to her son once he had come of age nor did she retreat into 'idle' domesticity or a minor role in the family business. She had presumably trained Issachar to take over once she had become unable to work, due to illness, infirmity or death, rather than for reasons of social propriety.

Complex familial relationships furnished women with the space in which to conduct businesses related to other family ventures but nonetheless considered distinct and legitimate. This was evidently the case for the Binyon family in the closing decade of the eighteenth century. Whilst brothers, Thomas, Edward and

---

[25] Chetham's Library, Weatherley, J. (1860), 'Recollections of Manchester and Manchester characters and anecdotes relating to Manchester and Lancashire Generally from the year 1800 to 1860', p. 21.

[26] Slugg, J.T. (1881), *Reminiscences of Manchester Fifty Years Ago*, Manchester, p. 69.

Benjamin, worked as twine manufacturers and calico printers and ran shops in St. Ann's Square and Oldham Street, their sisters, Deborah, Hannah and Ann ran a linen shop in Piccadilly and operated as tea dealers in Portland Street.[27] In other cases, wives appear to have been involved in family businesses in their own right. In the early nineteenth century, Sarah Broadhurst was a partner in a linen drapers and hosiers business with her husband John Broadhurst, and Michael Peacock. An announcement in the *Manchester Mercury* showed that the business was conducted in her previous name (Weaver), rather than her husband's (Broadhurst), and the *Manchester Directory* of 1817 listed the business of 'Weaver and Peacock, wholesale and retail linen drapers and hosiers'.[28]

Other married couples ran parallel but apparently separate businesses. As a single woman, Susanna Franks advertised her 'new and elegant assortment of MILLINERY and DRESSES' available at her shop on Exchange Street. Months later, on 20 October 1804, she married John Taylor.[29] Within a few weeks, John began to place adverts for the new linen drapery business he had established at the same address, but noted that 'The Millinery and Dress making business will be carried on as usual by Mrs. T. late S. Franks'.[30] While John may have worked in the linen-drapery line prior to his marriage, his marriage to a milliner appears to have given him the opportunity to establish a new business at Susanna's address. At the same time, Susanna's trade endured. Living in Manchester at the same time, the Styarts also ran related but distinct businesses. The *Manchester Directory* of 1804 mentioned Charles Styart's 'French, commercial and literary academy, 94 Oldham-Street', before listing Mrs Styart's 'Boarding school for young ladies' at the same address. Adverts placed by this couple reinforced the sense that these businesses were distinct:

> Manchester - Oldham-street, No.94, July 6th, 1804.
> MRS. STYART.
> IN returning her sincere acknowledgements for the liberal patronage of her friends, informs them and the public in general, that her School, which closed for the Midsummer vacation, on the 23d of June last, will open again on Monday the 23d inst. And that such of Mrs. STYART'S Pupils, either Boarders or day-Scholars, who wish to be instructed in the *French Language*, will be taught it grammatically by Mr. STYART, at the additional terms of 10s. 6d. per quarter.
> *Drawing*, and likewise *Painting upon Velvet* will also be taught at the usual terms, by a Lady of superior abilities, engaged by Mrs. S. as her teacher.[31]

---

[27] Slugg, *Reminiscences of Manchester*, p. 93-4.

[28] *Manchester Mercury*, 23 December 1817; *Pigot and Deans' Manchester and Salford Directory, for 1817.*

[29] *Manchester Mercury*, 15 May 1804; 23 October 1804.

[30] *Manchester Mercury*, 6 November 1804.

[31] *Manchester Mercury*, 17 July 1804.

As Susan Skedd has shown, the occupation of schoolmistress was not limited to spinsters, and men did assist in their wives' schools.[32] Certainly, while Mr. Styart's services were available as an additional service, it was clear that Mrs. Styart took responsibility for her own pupils and employed her own staff.

Polite Spaces

Women's experiences of work were therefore moulded by a range of factors such as marital status, age, gender and familial relations. Experiences were also shaped, of course, by location, and the preceding discussion of women's trade and business suggests that female ventures were particularly associated with the growth of 'polite' society in Manchester. The development of a more sophisticated and diverse social scene was something which the town's historian, John Aikin, linked to the strong continental trading links which Manchester formed from around 1770:

> Within the last twenty or thirty years the vast increase of foreign trade has caused many of the Manchester manufacturers to travel abroad, and agents or partners to be fixed for a considerable time on the Continent, as well as foreigners to reside in Manchester. And the town has now in every respect assumed the style and manners of one of the commercial capitals of Europe.[33]

Whilst this description was something which many visitors to Manchester would have baulked at (particularly the individual who described the town as a 'dog hole' in 1792),[34] local commentators were less critical and strove to paint a picture of polite sociability, cosmopolitan tastes and cultured amenities. In many of these descriptions, female traders and services provided by women featured prominently. Recalling Manchester in the early nineteenth century, Hayes noted that the Star Hotel (which ran from Deansgate into Lower King Street):

> was a house which for generations had occupied a very high position with the country gentry and carriage folk … It was kept at one time by a Miss Yates, a lady who was highly respected, and occupied a somewhat unique position amongst hotel proprietors. Here you would see some of the best saddle and carriage horses being put up and stabled, and their well-to-do owners alighting on their arrival in town.[35]

---

[32] Skedd, S. (1997), 'Women Teachers and the Expansion of Girls' Schooling in England, c.1760-1820', in H. Barker and E. Chalus, (eds), *Gender in Eighteenth-Century England: Roles, Representations and Responsibilities*, London, pp. 117-18.

[33] Aikin, J. (1795), *A Description of the Country from Thirty to Forty Miles Round Manchester*, London, p. 184.

[34] Andrews, C.B. (ed.) (1934-8), *The Torrington Diaries*, 4 vols, London, iii, p. 116. See also White, J.E. (1815), *Letters on England*, 2 vols, Philadelphia, i, pp. 46-9.

[35] Hayes, *Reminiscences of Manchester*, p. 131.

Women provided some of the spaces for polite culture; they also enabled the growth in literacy and an expansion in the reading public which were integral to the spread of politeness in eighteenth-century English towns. Developments in print culture and polite sociability were intricately linked. For example, Hayes also described how one of the occupants of the Manchester Arcade, which had sat on the site of what became the Manchester Exchange, was a Miss Richardson:

> who kept a library, and whose shop was a great place of meeting for ladies, who made this their rendezvous for social chat. My recollection of the shop is that it was dark and gloomy-looking, but Miss Richardson possessed large treasures in the shape of the writings of Fernimore Cooper, Captain Marryat, Harrison Ainsworth, and G.P.R. Jones.[36]

In 1816, Joseph Aston's *Picture of Manchester* noted that the present librarian of the Manchester Circulating Library in King Street, which boasted 370 subscribers, was a Miss Blinkhorn 'who, for correctness and attentions to the subscribers, deserves much praise'.[37] By the Summer of 1817, Miss Blinkhorn was hunting for 'A LARGE ROOM in a Good Situation, for the use of the King-street Library'.[38] Frequented by the commercial, professional and mercantile groups, circulating libraries expressed and maintained the confidence of the booming eighteenth-century town.[39]

Women were prominent in Manchester's polite society, and this prominence is particularly marked when focusing on the central fashionable, trading area of Manchester. Newspapers were instrumental in promoting the idea of the polite and fashionable areas of a town. James Harrop's *Manchester Mercury* marketed its own address – Market Place – as the centre of Manchester. But despite the particular motivations of the proprietor, Market Place was undoubtedly an important site for trade and commerce. Centrally placed in the town, Market Place was just off one of Manchester's two main thoroughfares – Market Street Lane, leading to London – and was very close to the two bridges connecting Manchester and Salford. By 1788, Market Place was clearly a prime spot for trade. One collection of buildings, including a dwelling house, warehouse, and stables, situated in Deansgate and Red-Lion-Street, near St. Ann's Square, was advertised as 'most advantageously situated, very substantial for carrying on an extensive Business, being in the Centre of the Town of Manchester, and very near the Market-place'.[40] When Mrs. Gregson left the Coach and Horses Inn in Deansgate, the advert described the location as 'extremely convenient', being 'in the direct

[36] Hayes, *Reminiscences of Manchester*, p. 159.

[37] Aston, J. (1816), *A Picture of Manchester*, Manchester, p. 175.

[38] *Manchester Mercury*, 22 July 1817.

[39] Brewer, J. (1997), *The Pleasures of the Imagination: English Culture in the Eighteenth Century*, London, pp. 176-83.

[40] *Manchester Mercury*, 26 August 1788.

Road from the Market-place, in Manchester, to the new Stone Bridge, which leads to Warrington, Liverpool, Chester'.[41] Despite the establishment of other markets at the turn of the century, Market Place retained this status as a central reference point and a location of some status. Houses and shops for sale were described as 'being very near the Market-place', and even 'Country Lodgings to Let' were measured as 'not two miles and a half from the Marketplace, Manchester'.[42]

Prior to 1800, Market Place accommodated varieties of economic activity. Specialisation emerged only in the early nineteenth century as new markets were established away from the centre of town. Potatoes were to be sold in St. John's Market in Camp Field not on Shude Hill, while hay, straw, clover and cattle fodder were removed from Market Street Lane to a market in Bridgewater Street, Deansgate.[43] Increasingly, Market Place saw a narrowing of types of trade. By 1804 the status of Market Place as a fashionable trading centre was established. In October of that year, a meeting of the inhabitants of Manchester and Salford decided 'that the erection of a handsome building, in the Market-place, for the purpose of a COMMERCIAL COFFEE ROOM and TAVERN, is highly desirable, and would afford great accommodation to the merchants and manufacturers of this town and neighbourhood'.[44] Yet even by the early 1770s, Market Place was undeniably a place where fashionable businesses could thrive. The hairdresser Philip Worrall, who specialised in head-dresses of 'Ease and Elegance, according to the newest Taste now used in LONDON', was based there.[45] Worrall's hair-dressing business remained in Market Place for many years, and by 1788 he had been accompanied by a female relative, Mary, who operated there as a clear-starcher.[46] Although it accommodated the Shambles, at the centre of Market Place was the classically-pillared Exchange: a building which expressed something of the confidence Mancunians felt for their town.

In this vibrant place of trade and business, women were conspicuous. Market Place was home to many of those businesswomen who helped to promote Manchester's polite and consumerist credentials through trade, and who were instrumental in the growth of Manchester in the late eighteenth century. The *Manchester Mercury* yields a vision of Market Place in which two enterprises were particularly important: Mary Berry's grocers and auction house and Mary Crompton's Coffee House. John Berry, printer, grocer and auctioneer, died in 1765, and his wife Mary and sons Joseph and Peter took over the business. The firm of 'MARY BERRY and SONS, And THOMAS BERRY' operated at Hanging-Bridge until April 1773. The business then diversified, as Mary Berry and Sons moved to Market Place, leaving Thomas on the other side of the Collegiate

---

41 *Manchester Mercury*, 4 November 1788.

42 *Manchester Mercury*, 14 February and 27 March 1804.

43 *Manchester Mercury*, 24 January and 14 February 1804. On changes in market provision, see Scola, R. (1992), *Feeding the Victorian City: The Food Supply of Manchester, 1770-1870*, in W.A. Armstrong and P. Scola (eds), Manchester, pp. 150-57.

44 *Manchester Mercury*, 9 October 1804.

45 *Manchester Mercury*, 4 May 1773.

46 Holme, E., (1788) *A Directory for the Towns of Manchester and Salford for the Year 1788*.

Church.[47] The business activity which took place at Mary Berry and Sons' premises at Market Place was varied. The property incorporated a grocers' shop and what came to be known as 'the Old Auction-Room', as well as the house, and by 1775 adverts referred to 'Berry's Lottery-Office'.[48] Mary Berry was quickly and firmly integrated into the world of Manchester small businesses. In December 1773, she was the sole female name amongst 32 other grocers, tea-dealers and tobacconists who announced their decision 'to abolish the oppressive Custom of bestowing Cards, Boxes, Tea, Spice, Tobacco, Snuff, or any other Gratuity whatsoever, upon Customers or their Servants, under the Denomination of *Christmas-Boxes*, or *New-Year's Gifts*', due to which fellow traders had suffered 'many recent and melancholy Instances'.[49] The Berry business at Market Place seems to have been growing and occupied as important a place in Manchester's trading world as many other male-run operations. The variety of activities undertaken by Berry was echoed in the business life of Mary Crompton. Crompton's Coffee House, at 29 Market Place, hosted card assemblies, commissions of bankrupts, meetings, and auctions of property and business goods, in addition to selling tickets for theatrical performances. Mary Crompton's coffee house also served as a site for sessions of the Court Leet between the years 1768 and 1775.[50] Like the other inns, taverns and coffee-houses in Manchester – many of them run by women – Crompton's establishment provided a space in which both the leisure and commerce of the burgeoning English provincial towns could thrive.

Indeed, both Crompton and Berry were part of a community of traders and businessmen and women who were emblematic of Manchester's small-scale economic activity. There existed a small network of individuals facilitating and exploiting the growth in Manchester's trade in which women were prominent. The sheer visibility of these women was illustrated through the attempts of the hairdresser, John Pollitt, to establish a new business in Market Place. On moving from 'the Country', Pollitt attempted to sell his house at Thomas Vaux's Dog and Partridge in Market Place opposite the Exchange.[51] By July, however, the house was being auctioned in Berry's Auction Room.[52] It appears that some commercial deal was struck between Pollitt and Berry, because by August of 1773 readers of the *Manchester Mercury* were invited to apply to Pollitt in order to get details of

[47] An advert in the *Manchester Mercury* on 13 April 1773 noted 'Mary Berry and Sons, in the Market-Place' and 'MARY BERRY and SONS, And THOMAS BERRY in HANGING-BRIDGE'. From 27 April, only Thomas Berry was given an address at Hanging-Bridge.

[48] *Manchester Mercury*, 1 January 1788; 14 November 1775. Mary died in 1787, and by the following year adverts in the *Manchester Mercury* referred to the business as 'Peter Berry and Co', 'Berry & Co', or 'Mess. Berry and Co. grocers'.

[49] *Manchester Mercury*, 21 December 1773.

[50] *The Court Leet Records of the Manor of Manchester,* 11 vols, Manchester, viii, p. 117ff.

[51] *Manchester Mercury*, 23 February 1773.

[52] *Manchester Mercury*, 20 July 1773.

houses being sold by auction at Berry's auction room.[53] Early in 1773, Pollitt set up a fashionable hair and wig shop. Not only was he originally from London – regarded as an indicator of his fashionable credentials – but he had 'newly fitted up his Shop … in a neat, genteel, and handsome manner'.[54] Pollitt was part of the rise of fashion, and was keen to tell potential customers that he 'dresses in the highest Taste, after the *English* and *French* Fashion; he likewise has the Fashion, each Spring'.[55] Significantly, the marker Pollitt chose to give his readers as a guide to his shop was the business of Mary Crompton: his shop was 'next door to *Crompton's* Coffee-House, near the *Exchange*'. Interestingly, though Pollitt clearly relied to varying extents on businesswomen in Manchester, the business venture of his wife was apparently short-lived. On opening his shop in February 1773, Pollitt announced that his wife intended to keep a register office at the same address, 'at which place, Ladies and Gentlemen may meet with good Servants, in the different Departments of Household Business, whose characters will be particularly enquired into before they are registered, and none recommended but those of Credit and Ability'.[56] By May, however, the name of the business had changed to 'J. Pollitt's REGISTER OFFICE'.[57]

Elizabeth Raffald

Another important family of traders with links to Market Place were the Raffalds. Elizabeth Raffald opened a grocery shop there in 1766, her brothers and husband ran a stall in the vicinity and there is a suggestion that she and her husband ran the Bull's Head Inn in Market Place a short time later.[58] Although the details of most women's traders' careers remain largely unknown, and what evidence can be gleaned from directories and newspapers provides only snapshots of their lives, Elizabeth Raffald is a noticeable and important exception. In comparison to most of her contemporaries, the life of the grocer, confectioner, cookery book writer and compiler of trade directories was exceptionally well recorded. Raffald's life is not only accessible to the historian, but provides a perfect example of the way in which women involved in Manchester's trades could – acting in their own right – benefit from the developments, and in particular, the growing prosperity, which was taking place all around them, at the same time that they themselves acted to push those changes forward. Indeed, Raffald's working life illustrates many of the points already made. Over her lifetime she was engaged in a wide range of activities; her marriage may have conditioned the nature of her work somewhat, but it did not eliminate her independent ventures; and finally, she not only benefited from urban

[53] *Manchester Mercury*, 10 August 1773.

[54] *Manchester Mercury*, 2 March 1773.

[55] *Manchester Mercury*, 16 March 1773.

[56] *Manchester Mercury*, 23 February 1773.

[57] *Manchester Mercury*, 11 May 1773.

[58] Raffald, E. (1889), *The Manchester Directory for the Year 1773*, reprint with prefatory memoir, Manchester, 'Preface', pp. vi, viii.

growth and prosperity, but played a highly visible and facilitative role in these developments.

Elizabeth Raffald was born Elizabeth Whitaker in 1733. She spent her early adult life in domestic service before landing the job of housekeeper at Arley Hall in Cheshire, home of the Warburton family, in 1760. Here she met and married the head gardener, John Raffald. In 1763 the pair left to start a new life in Manchester. Whilst her husband ran a market gardening business with his brother, managing plots in both Manchester and Stockport, Elizabeth took up retailing.[59] Within a short time she began to advertise her shop in Fennel Street, near Apple Market, in the *Manchester Mercury*. Here she sold Yorkshire hams, tongues, Newcastle salmon, potted meats, portable soups (glue-like tablets to which one added hot water), sweetmeats, lemon preserve and mushroom ketchup. Her business grew quickly. By 1764 she began to advertise a register office for servants at her Fennel Street premises. At the same time her grocery business had expanded, and now promised customers 'Cold Entertainments, Hot French Dinners, Confectionery &c, and still continues to serve Her Friends with everything in that way in the genteelest Taste and on the easiest terms'.[60]

In August 1766 the Raffalds moved to new premises at 12 Market Place. Elizabeth had her first child in this year (at least five more daughters were to follow over the next seven years).[61] She continued to advertise frequently, and soon expanded her stock even further to include confectionery goods such as creams, possetts, jellies, flummery, lemon cheese cakes and even grander productions. In 1770 she announced 'Mrs Raffald returns thanks for the great encouragement she meets with in making Bride and Christening Cakes, and those who are pleased to favour her with their commands, may depend on being served with such cakes as shall not be exceeded'. By May 1771 she had also turned her hand to the supply of cosmetics, and now sold perfumed waters, French and Hungary doubled distilled lavender water, shaving powder, violet powder for the hair, swan-down puffs, lip salve and six varieties of wash balls.[62] In addition she rented 'genteel lodgings' and storage space, took on 'the daughters of the principal local families' as cookery students,[63] and sold an increasingly exotic array of foods, including anchovies, isinglass, vermicelli, macaroni, truffles, hartshorn shavings, and drops flavoured with peppermint, lemon, ginger, cinnamon, clove,

[59] Harland, J. (ed.) (1866-7), *Collectanea Relating to Manchester and its Neighbourhood, at Various Periods*, 2 vols, Manchester, ii, 144-6; Raffald, *The Manchester Directory for the Year 1773*, p. vi; Shipperbottom, R. (1997) 'Introduction' to Elizabeth Raffald, *The Experienced English Housekeeper*, Lewes, pp. vii-ix.

[60] *Manchester Mercury*, 22 November 1764.

[61] Harland, *Collectanea Relating to Manchester*, ii pp. 149-50; Grindon, L.P. (1877), *Manchester Banks and Bankers*, Manchester, p. 37; Shipperbottom, 'Introduction', p. xiii.

[62] *Manchester Mercury*, 28 May 1771.

[63] *Manchester Guardian*, 19 May 1852.

saffron, barbery and currant.[64] In June of that year she published a cookery book, *The Experienced English Housekeeper* by subscription (raising more than £800). The book contained 'over 800 Original recipes' and included advice on spinning sugar and how to select the best wine. Within a short time the London publisher, Richard Baldwin, bought the copyright of her book for £1,400.[65] At least 25 editions were produced by various printers over the years, and it was published regularly in both England and America until 1834. The popularity of Raffald's recipes was such that they even found their way into Princess (later Queen) Victoria's manuscript recipe book, where she copied several pieces, including the one for King Solomon's Temple in Flummery.[66]

In the following year, 1772, the Raffalds moved to the King's Head in Salford, just over the river from Manchester. In August, an advertisement appeared in the *Mercury* which declared that the Raffalds had fitted up their inn 'in the neatest and most elegant manner for the reception and accommodation of the Nobility, Gentry, Merchants and Tradesmen who shall be pleased to honour them with their company where they may be assured of the utmost civility and good treatment.'[67] A card assembly was to be conducted every Thursday evening during the winter season, and they arranged the annual meeting and dinner of the Beefsteak Club.[68] In addition, like many inns, the King's Head served as a site for the auctions of property[69] and horses,[70] plant sales,[71] and flower competitions.[72] The world John and Elizabeth inhabited at the King's Head Inn was clearly busy with Manchester's burgeoning trade and commerce as well as being a place of leisure. Victuallers and innkeepers represented a considerable proportion of women traders during these years: twelve in 1773, seventeen in 1788, thirty in 1804, and thirty-four in 1817.[73] Like these women, Elizabeth provided space for the trading and social activities so crucial to burgeoning provincial towns.

The same year that the Raffalds moved to the King's Head, Elizabeth Raffald also produced Manchester's first trade directory, noting that 'The want of a DIRECTORY for the large and commercial Town of MANCHESTER, having been frequently complained of, ... I have taken upon me the arduous Task of compiling a *Complete Guide*, for the easy finding out of every Inhabitant of the least Consequence.'[74] A second edition appeared less than a year later, and on

---

[64] *Manchester Mercury*, 12 November 1771.

[65] Harland, *Collectanea Relating to Manchester*, ii p. 147.

[66] Shipperbottom, 'Introduction', p. xvi.

[67] *Manchester Mercury*, 25 August 1772.

[68] *Manchester Mercury*, 23 August 1773.

[69] *Manchester Mercury*, 2 and 16 March 1773.

[70] *Manchester Mercury*, 7 August 1773.

[71] *Manchester Mercury*, 5 January 1773.

[72] *Manchester Mercury*, 10 August 1773.

[73] Note that these figures include those directory entries without a trade label but with an address of an inn. Victualler was the most common trade for women in the directory of 1773, the second most common trade for women in the directories of 1788 and 1804, and the third most popular trade for women in the directory of 1817.

[74] Raffald, E. (1772), *The Manchester Directory for the Year 1772 ...*, London, p. ii.

Tuesday, 16 March 1773, an advertisement for it appeared in the *Manchester Mercury*:

> To the Inhabitants of MANCHESTER.
> A New Edition of the MANCHESTER DIRECTORY being intended to be published with all convenient speed; it is proposed, in order to make such an useful Work as correct as possible, to send proper and intelligent Persons round the Town, to take down the Name, Business, and Place of Abode of every Gentleman, Tradesman, and Shop-keeper, as well as of others whose Business or Employment has any tendency to public Notice; the Proprietor therefore humbly requests, that every one will please to give the necessary Information to the Persons appointed, that she may be enabled to give an accurate Edition of a Work so advantageous to such a large, populous, and trading Town as this is; in the Completion of which, she can assure the Public, that no Labour or Expence shall be spared to make it worthy of their Approbation, as an easy and sufficient Directory, not only to Strangers, but likewise to the Inhabitants of this Town. [75]

Elizabeth Raffald's notice stressed the utilitarian nature of her directory. It placed the work in the context of a bustling town, replete with gentlemen, traders and retailers; a town that required a directory in order to facilitate efficient exchange.

By June 1773, Raffald was giving advance notice of the publication of the new edition, noting her previous work on housekeeping, and thus drawing on her established reputation in the publicity for her newest ventures.[76] Yet as a married woman, Raffald did not present herself as a *femme sole*. She did not include herself in her trade directory of 1773: her husband was entered as 'Raffald John, Inn-holder, King's-Head, Salford'. Indeed, in adverts for the third edition of *The Experienced House-keeper*, Elizabeth stressed the business partnership she shared with her husband. After giving her address as the King's Head Inn and detailing the third edition, she declared, 'It will be needless to say any Thing in praise of this valuable Work, as its own Merit has proved it by the Sale of two large Impressions in less than four Years.' The advert continued:

> … JOHN and ELIZABETH RAFFALD beg Leave to return their most sincere Thanks to their Friends and the Public for all their past Favours; and also to inform them, that by Additions and Improvements, they have fitted up the aforesaid large and well-accustomed Inn for the Reception of Ladies, Gentlemen, Travellers, &c. in the most Elegant Manner; have laid in a large Stock of the best Wines, Brandy, &c. and are determined to use every Means in their Power to merit the future Favours conferred upon them.[77]

[75] *Manchester Mercury*, 16 March 1773.
[76] *Manchester Mercury*, 29 June 1773.
[77] *Manchester Mercury*, 12 October 1773.

Though the advert began as publicity for her own venture, by the close Elizabeth and John were reestablished as a partnership, inviting locals and those passing through to frequent their genteel inn.

Within four years of the move to the King's Head, Elizabeth's sister, Mary Whitaker, had opened a shop opposite the inn, which sold confectionery, pickles and also operated as a servants' register office.[78] Elizabeth's family concerns appeared to be thriving, but there were evidently problems hidden from the public gaze. In 1780 John went bankrupt and the Raffalds had to leave the King's Head. John Raffald had become a heavy drinker and was said to have been deeply depressed, even suicidal.[79] Whether this was the cause, or the result, of the couple's money problems is unclear. It is certainly possible that they had over-stretched themselves financially. Despite falling on hard times, Elizabeth remained irrepressible. During the Manchester race season she ran a refreshment stall selling strawberries near the Ladies stand on Kersal Moor.[80] When John was appointed master of the Exchange coffee house, Elizabeth began to sell soup there, even though it had not formerly been an eating place.[81] She also compiled and published the third edition of her Manchester directory. Yet her frantic activity was cut short on 19 April 1781, when, aged just 48, she died of what appears to have been a stroke.[82] Within a week John Raffald's creditors, now lacking, it would seem, the security of Elizabeth's industry, took steps to remove him from the coffee house. The Raffald's minor business empire was at an end.[83]

Elizabeth Raffald's career in Manchester was short-lived but prolific. She arrived just as the town was beginning to expand rapidly, and quickly latched on to the fact that the fast changing economic and social environment in which she found herself provided a wealth of opportunities for the entrepreneurial businesswoman. Seemingly unhindered by her gender, she sought to exploit new and expanding markets by appealing to 'polite', upwardly mobile and most importantly, moneyed, expectations and tastes through her grocery, confectionery, cosmetics, inn-keeping and servant employment businesses. In so-doing, Raffald helped to promote Manchester's economic and cultural development. Not only did Raffald understand fashions in taste, and the aspirations of a developing commercial class, but she also realised the potential of another product of late eighteenth-century urban growth: print culture. She advertised her various business ventures extensively in Manchester's newspapers, as well as producing her own publications. Of these, her trade directories provide the clearest indication of her understanding of, and ability to exploit, the changing Manchester scene. In doing so, she herself became one of the prime movers in that changing environment. When Raffald catalogued the town's merchants and traders, she was listing members of the community that had

[78] *Manchester Mercury*, 27 June 1776. After Elizabeth Raffald's early death, Mary took her daughter, Anna, into business with her. The pair subsequently took on apprentice pastry-cooks: Harland, *Collectanea Relating to Manchester,* ii, pp. 155-6.

[79] Harland, *Collectanea Relating to Manchester,* ii, p. 149.

[80] *The Manchester Directory for the Year 1773*, p. viii.

[81] Shipperbottom, 'Introduction', p. xvi.

[82] Shipperbottom, 'Introduction', p. xvi.

[83] See *Manchester Mercury*, 1 and 22 May 1781.

ensured her success. Although this success was neither spectacular, nor indeed permanent, it did demonstrate the possibilities which industrialisation, urbanisation and commercial growth opened up for women in trade. Her career, like those of the other Mancunian women discussed here, suggests an alternative model for understanding female labour in the late eighteenth and early nineteenth centuries, and for exploring the position of women of the middle classes in particular. It is one in which we see businesswomen not only potentially benefiting from urban growth and commercial development, but in many cases, positively flourishing under capitalism.

Conclusion

Existing work on women and industrialisation tends towards a story of decline and fall. The case of middling-sort women in Manchester – a town at the heart of England's industrial growth – reveals a significantly different picture. First, women in trade and business in late eighteenth- and early nineteenth-century Manchester enjoyed new economic opportunities which they could actively exploit. Arguments about the decline of the family economy and associated reductions in women's work opportunities (particularly in 'domestic industry'), often based on looking lower down the social scale, thus appear partial. A focus on the range of trades open to women, the numbers listed in directories, and the determining role of marital status and household or familial relations reveal some of the limits to, and constraints on, women's working lives. But these limits and constraints can be overstated. The range of trades and businesses open to women were expanding, the proportion of women in this level of the economy seems to have remained consistent, and women operated as reasonably independent economic actors against the backdrop of a variety of familial circumstances. Secondly, while taking advantage of new economic opportunities, these women were not simply parasitic but facilitative. If a 'consumer revolution' is central to a full understanding of industrial growth, then women were indeed at the centre of this – but emphatically not merely as consumers. Women provided spaces – taverns, auction rooms and coffee houses – where merchants and industrialists could engage in the negotiation so crucial to the development of trade and commerce. But more than this, women involved in trading and business activities were themselves key players in the expansion of manufacturing, exchange and the provision of services. In this way, female-run businesses were at the cultural and physical heart of Manchester's expanding economy.

Chapter 7

Prudent Luxury: The Metropolitan Tastes of Judith Baker, Durham Gentlewoman*

Helen Berry

This chapter sets out to provide a case study of the 'shopping' habits of a Durham gentlewoman during a crucial period in the economic expansion of British towns. Shopping was, and is, an activity peculiarly associated with urban life, and is of particular relevance when considering the rise of commercial culture in eighteenth-century England. Making purchases from shops was a key feature of the urban experience of middling and elite women. It is true that 'shops' (often no more than wooden shacks with an opening onto the street) had existed throughout the medieval and early modern period and, strictly speaking, the concept of 'shopping' could be applied to the purchase of any number of items, whether from the marketseller's stall, or from the 'criers and hawkers' who peddled their wares about the streets.[1] But it was during the eighteenth century that retail establishments came to resemble more what we would recognise as shops today: the more expensive ones were fitted out with glass display cabinets, and the number of bow-fronted shop windows increased in every town, featuring enticing window displays.[2] During the eighteenth century, the number of shops increased exponentially both in London and provincial urban centres: the female consumer

* Research for this chapter was originally undertaken as part of the ongoing project at the University of Northumbria, 'Nationalising Taste: National Identity and Cultural Value in Eighteenth-Century Britain'. The author would like to thank Mrs J. Linda Drury, Dr. J.M. Fewster, and Miss Margaret McCollum of Palace Green Library, University of Durham for generously giving of their time and helpful advice. I should also like to thank Jeremy Boulton, Thomas Faulkner, Anthony Fletcher, Elizabeth Foyster, Jeremy Gregory, Lorna Scammell (formerly Weatherill), Roey Sweet and Gill Thompson, for diligently reading and commenting upon earlier drafts.

[1] Street sellers appeared in English art from as early as 1600, and were drawn extensively by Marcellus Laroon in 1687; see Shesgreen, S. (1990), *The Criers and Hawkers of London*, Aldershot. See also Davis, D. (1966), *A History of Shopping*, London, *passim*.

[2] See for example Walsh, C. (1990), 'The Design of London Goldsmiths' Shops in the Early Eighteenth Century', in D. Mitchell (ed.) *Goldsmiths, Silversmiths and Bankers: Innovation and the Transfer of Skill, 1550-1750*, London.

had more places to shop than any of her predecessors, and a wider range of goods from which to choose.[3]

The subject of shopping raises key questions regarding the exercise of female choice in the realm of consumer behaviour. A central premise of this collection is that women had a distinctive contribution to make in the ongoing and accelerating process of eighteenth-century urbanisation, in which the English population doubled, London emerged as the largest European metropolis, and provincial urban centres with more than 20,000 inhabitants proliferated. A picture emerges of an 'upward spiral of economic growth' that was confidently charted by late eighteenth-century writers and political thinkers of the Scottish Enlightenment such as Hume, Steuart and Adam Smith.[4] Their classical (and somewhat Whiggish) account was of an inexorable march towards a 'more splendid way of life' facilitated through the supply of an ever-growing range of domestically manufactured and imported colonial goods. This picture has been modified, but not significantly altered, by the more recent assertion that women played a large part in fuelling consumer demand. Maxine Berg has posited a shift during the eighteenth century from 'relative self-sufficiency to market-oriented production by most household members' that would 'involve a reduction of domestically-produced goods, many of which were formerly produced by the women of the household'.[5] Thus, particularly in a context where more and more women were wage-earners, 'the wife or other female members of the household took a greater part in decision-making over commercially-produced consumer goods'.[6]

Such an account seems highly plausible, focusing as it does upon the growing sector of the middling ranks in the context of the rise of mass consumer markets. Berg's emphasis upon this social group is however in contrast to the contemporaries of Hume, who emphasised aristocratic consumption as the motor of economic growth. John Millar noted in 1787 that 'mutual emulation' was the stimulus for people to earn a 'comfortable subsistence'.[7] The vexed question of the role of emulation in stimulating demand is one which has elicited considerable debate among historians ever since. John Brewer, among others, cites the spirit of emulation – the desire of middling sorts 'on the make' to ape the gentry through

[3] Craig Muldrew (1998) has highlighted the rise in the number of shops by showing that, by the start of the eighteenth century, the total number of places that issued trade tokens was 1,534, which was twice the number of market towns in England, in *The Economy of Obligation: the Culture of Credit and Social Relations in Early Modern England*, London, p. 54. See also Shammas, C. (1990), *The Pre-Industrial Consumer in England and America*, Oxford, pp. 225-6 and *passim*.

[4] Wrightson, K. (2000), *Earthly Necessities: Economic Lives in Early Modern Britain*, New Haven and London, p. 5.

[5] Berg, M. (1994), *The Age of Manufactures, 1700-1820: Industry, Innovation and Work in Britain*, 2nd edn, London and New York, pp. 133-5.

[6] Berg, *The Age of Manufactures*, p. 135.

[7] Wrightson, *Earthly Necessities*, p. 7.

the acquisition of the trappings of a genteel lifestyles, mirrored in the 'improving tale of imitation and emulation' that marked the spread of metropolitan culture to provincial towns.[8] This hypothesis had been dismissed by Lorna Weatherill in her study of eighteenth-century probate inventories up to 1725.[9] The middling sorts, Weatherill argued, established their own pattern of consumption that was highly distinctive from that of the minor gentry, who frequently lagged behind in the consumption of newly-manufactured and/or imported goods such as clocks, china, and silverware. The truth is probably mid-way between Brewer and Weatherill's hypotheses. Doubtless, the purchase of a tea-set by a tradesman's wife could be motivated by a desire to emulate her socially superior neighbour, or because she merely liked the design.[10]

Suffice it to say that, regarding consumer behaviour, gender and status are, as always, inextricably linked. The feminised language of eighteenth-century advertising, and the marketing of goods and services as 'genteel' specifically in order to appeal to women of the middling sort, is just one example.[11] In a recent study by Margot Finn, however, the assumption that it was women who were largely responsible for making decisions regarding household expenditure has itself been challenged.[12] Following an oft-cited study by Neil McKendrick of George Packwood and the commercialisation of the razor, Dr Finn urges us, on the basis of the evidence gained from men's diaries, to remember that Hanoverian society contained 'highly acquisitive men as well as compulsively possessive women'.[13] However, it is an extreme position to endorse, as Finn does, the claim that 'nowhere' is there evidence that eighteenth-century women were the 'primary shoppers' for their families.[14] It is also curious to distil the social processes by which consumption was feminised — in the complexities of consumer choice, the

---

[8] Brewer, J. (1997), *The Pleasures of the Imagination: English Culture in the Eighteenth Century*, London, p. 496.

[9] Weatherill, L. (1996), *Consumer Behaviour and Material Culture in Britain, 1660-1760*, 2nd edn, London, pp. 194-6 and *passim*.

[10] The acquisition of goods in relation to the construction of selfhood and identity is indeed problematic. A case for the 'complex and variable' role of material possessions in the formation of domestic culture is made by Nenadic, S. (1994), 'Middle Rank Consumers and Domestic Culture in Edinburgh and Glasgow, 1720-1840', *Past and Present*, 145, p. 124. An anthropological definition of consumption highlights the complexity of the subject: 'a ritual process whose primary function is to make sense of the incohate flux of events'. See Douglas, M. and Isherwood, B. (1996), *The World of Goods: Towards an Anthropology of Consumption*, 2nd edn, London, p. 43.

[11] See Lemire, B. (1991), *Fashion's Favourite: The Cotton Trade and the Consumer in Britain, 1660-1800*, Oxford, pp. 55-61 and *passim*.

[12] Finn, M. (2000), 'Men's Things: Masculine Possession in the Consumer Revolution', *Social History*, 25:2, p. 135. See also McKendrick, N. (1982), 'George Packwood and the Commercialization of Shaving: the Art of Eighteenth-Century Advertising or "The Way to Get Money and be Happy"', in N. McKendrick, John Brewer, and J.H. Plumb (eds), *The Birth of a Consumer Society: The Commercialisation of Eighteenth Century England*, Bloomington.

[13] Finn, 'Men's Things', p. 135.

[14] Finn, 'Men's Things', p. 134.

language of marketing, and the design and fabric of the products themselves, into the modern term 'primary shopper'.

Another, arguably more productive, route into considering the specific issue of women and consumption in the eighteenth century is to look not only in more detail at how goods were acquired by men and women ('who bought what'), but also more generally at how consumption was framed within a cultural context.[15] Amanda Vickery, for example, has greatly advanced the study of gentlewomen as consumers during this period.[16] Her work has highlighted the way in which English women of gentry status 'turned to personal and household artefacts to create a world of meanings', which she suggests was a response to the fact that they were usually debarred from inheriting real property (land).[17] Certain objects were treasured gifts from loved ones, and prompted recollections of family history; mothers made and mended their sons' shirts long after they had left home. Gifts of second hand goods were made with networks of local patronage in mind: servants were given clothing, and small presents were bestowed upon social inferiors. Solid and respectable furniture and other 'luxury' items for their homes, such as tableware and linen, not only signified the social standing of the gentry, but facilitated sociability amongst their peers, making their homes a fit place to enjoy dinners, tea parties and other entertainment.[18]

Vickery has thus drawn attention not only to the significance of gentry consumption, but also to the subtle variation in the acquisition and use of goods according to gender at this level of society. Relatively speaking, however, the study of the role of the gentry, and of gentlewomen in particular, in the rise of urban commercial culture has been neglected in favour of the middling sort. This is curious given the continuing affluence and power of many provincial gentry families at this time, and the existence of extensive but under-used archives relating to this social group, particularly in the north of England. One such archive relates to the Baker family of county Durham, and is especially important for its collection of papers relating to one particular eighteenth-century gentlewoman, Judith Baker. The survival of hundreds of Judith's receipts, and a near-complete set of personal account books, from the time of her marriage in 1749 to her death in 1810, offers us an insight into the minutiae of consumer choices made by a woman of her status and fortune at this time. What is more, it promises the opportunity to consider in more depth the phenomenon noted but not elaborated by Amanda

[15] A comprehensive case for 'putting the consumer back into consumerism' is made by Sara Pennell (1999) in her historiographical survey, 'Consumption and Consumerism in Early Modern England', *Historical Journal*, 42, pp. 549-64.

[16] Vickery, A. (1998), *The Gentleman's Daughter: Women's Lives in Georgian England*, New Haven and London.

[17] Vickery, A. (1993), 'Women and the World of Goods: a Lancashire Consumer and her Possessions, 1751-81', in J. Brewer and R. Porter (eds), *Consumption and the World of Goods*, London.

[18] Vickery, 'Women and the World of Goods', p. 287.

Vickery — the habitual purchase of goods from London by provincial gentlewomen, in addition to shopping in their regional urban centres.[19] The present study intends to highlight the repetition of this pattern across time and geographical location, suggesting that this was an important feature of consumption among the gentry throughout the early modern period. Considering what we know about the rise of 'national culture' in the eighteenth century, what does the fact that gentlewomen divided their shopping between provincial towns and London tell us about their contribution to the development of urban life in the eighteenth century?

The evidence of Judith Baker's accounts suggests that our subject went to great lengths to overcome the relative disadvantage (to a woman who liked to keep abreast of fashion) of living at a great distance from the metropolis. A long-established characteristic of the English gentry, as Susan Whyman has illustrated in her study of the Verney family, was their adaptability: they had their roots in the land, but spent time in towns; their most consistent source of income was as rentier landlords, but many were also familiar with the urban worlds of commerce and finance.[20] What is instructive about the case of Judith Baker is the speed of communication and exchange of goods that was made possible in the course of her lifetime between her estate in the north-east and London. The itinerant pattern of Judith's shopping trips illustrates the seasonal variation in the urban experiences of eighteenth-century gentlewomen. Whether shopping in person, or through a network of neighbours, friends and relatives, Judith was able to obtain a wide variety of consumer goods in local urban centres, and in the metropolis. The fact that she was able to exercise choice as to whether to shop locally or in London was a mark of her personal status and wealth. As we shall see, this unique brand of 'urban experience' demarcated and fittingly mirrored the prestige and status enjoyed by gentry families in their locality.

Surviving documents allow us to assemble a picture of Judith's personal expenditure in local urban centres and the metropolis over a period of more than half a century. Before we embark upon a closer examination of them, it is necessary to observe that these surviving records are, of course, also fraught with problems. Judith's personal intent, motivation and attitudes towards the items which she purchased must remain largely speculative. Unlike the diligent Lancashire gentlewomen studied by Amanda Vickery, for whom there are a wealth of private records, we are sadly lacking in personal documents such as letters or diaries in which Judith may have given us a deeper insight into her motives and attitudes towards consumption. Even the simple matter of discerning the use to which she put many of the items that she bought is largely impossible. Nevertheless, the detailed documentation and broad time span of this particular archive make it a rare and notable one. What follows is a largely qualitative study of the available sources that addresses the question of how this particular

[19] Vickery, 'Women and the World of Goods', p. 280: 'When parcels and boxes of metropolitan products arrived, Mrs Shackleton listed their contents, registering how well they had survived the journey and whether they suited her taste'.

[20] Whyman, S. (2000), *Sociability and Power in Late-Stuart England: The Cultural World of the Verneys, 1660-1720*, Oxford; see also Wrightson, *Earthly Necessities*, p. 274.

gentlewoman exercised her choices as a consumer.[21] This is considered within the context of the opportunities and constraints afforded to a woman of her status, given the circumstances of her family and their standing in county Durham, as well as the macroeconomic circumstances that afforded her the possibility of close connection with metropolitan, as well as local, urban markets.

Judith's tastes and attitudes towards consumption, I suggest, may be appropriately characterised as 'prudent luxury', a phrase coined in the *Town and Country Magazine* for 1787.[22] 'Prudent luxury' encapsulates the hypothesis presented herein that Judith's expenditure on 'luxury' items, defined here as goods noted for their quality, fashion, rarity and/or expense, was rationalised through the application of strict account-keeping. Through the prudence of good household economy, she succeeded (where her profligate husband and son failed) in living according to her means. Judith's exercise of consumer choice provided a stimulus to the economy, yet exhibited a certain simultaneous restraint that safeguarded the moral and economic health of her family. This was in marked contrast to the prevailing ideas of her day which suggested that women were overly fond of luxury, and morally culpable for ruining their families by their dissipation.[23] Our subject's preference for buying goods, such as expensive foods, silk and other fine clothing in London is powerful evidence of the magnet which the capital held for women of her status. Since at least the sixteenth century, the metropolis had featured large in the life of the country gentry, who by the eighteenth century had formalised a seasonal pattern of 'going up' to London for at least part of the year, and 'going down' to their country estates for more bucolic pleasures.[24] In addition, during the late seventeenth and eighteenth centuries, provincial urban centres expanded and developed cultural lives of their own, 'little Londons' replicated across England, with social seasons that were timed to fill in the long months of country retirement.[25] Yet the lure of the capital persisted — the entrepôt for all manner of leisure and consumption that no provincial centre could rival. Distance thus lent an added dimension of luxury to imported goods that applied not only in the import of rare items from far-off colonial lands, but also to the distinctiveness of London in relation to provincial urban centres. As Marcia Pointon has shown in her study of the letters of Elizabeth Harley, sent from Herefordshire to her husband in London, distance established the conditions for 'fantasy and desire', whether of

---

[21] A more detailed and large-scale quantitative study of this valuable archive is planned by the present author.

[22] *Town and Country Magazine*, September, 1787, pp. 394-6. Quoted in Raven, J. (1995), 'Defending Conduct and Property: the London Press and the Luxury Debate', in J. Brewer and S. Staves (eds), *Early Modern Conceptions of Property*, London and New York, p. 305.

[23] Vickery, 'Women and the World of Goods', p. 277.

[24] Borsay, P. (1989), *The English Urban Renaissance*, Oxford, *passim*.

[25] Ellis, J. (2000), 'Regional and County Centres, 1700-1840', in P. Clark (ed.), *The Cambridge Urban History of Britain, Vol. II, 1540-840*, Cambridge, pp. 673-704.

an absent loved one, or the consumer pleasures that were only available in the capital. Professor Pointon comments 'removal from London may have emphasised rather than diminished the desirability of those things that were only available in London'.[26]

In north-east England, we may observe a similar correlation between distance and desire in the relationship between the northern consumer and the metropolis. Close economic links were forged between the two: the growing exploitation of coal reserves fed domestic fuel demands in London.[27] Indeed, the coastal shipping trade that arose to transport the coal meant that Newcastle developed almost as a 'satellite' town to the capital.[28] Well before the eighteenth century, the stimulation of the local economy, in the form of employment and capital investment in this primary sector brought with it urban growth: the pattern of this growth, however, was determined by the distribution of wealth that resulted from the coal trade in the era of proto-industrialisation.[29] Evidence presented here of a coastal 'export' of luxury items 300 miles from London to Durham via Sunderland confirms the operation of powerful cultural attitudes among the gentry. Preference for London goods among the indigenous gentry of the north-east is indicative of their cultural ambivalence towards the so-called 'Black Indies', the 'barbarian' coal-producing region which was the source of their wealth, but into which 'culture' had to be imported from elsewhere.[30]

Let us start with some rudimentary biographical details. Judith was born in 1725, a 'gentleman's daughter'. Her father was Cuthbert Routh, a respectable landowner, and through her mother (after whom she was named), Judith was related to the powerful family of the Milbankes and through them, the titled nobility (her grandfather was Sir Mark Milbanke). In 1749 she married into an ancient Durham family, the Bakers, who owned estates in Northumberland, Durham, Westmorland, and Yorkshire. They also possessed a principal share in the Boulby alum works, in the North Riding of Yorkshire, as well as interests in coal

---

[26] Pointon, M. (1997), *Strategies for Showing: Women, Possession, and Representation in English Visual Culture, 1665-1800*, Oxford, p. 21. A similar mechanism may be observed in the expanding market for London prints in Scotland during the eighteenth century. See Nenadic, S. (1997), 'Print Collecting and Popular Culture in Eighteenth-Century Scotland', *History*, 82, pp. 203-22.

[27] See Cromar, P. (1978), 'The Coal Industry on Tyneside, 1715-1750', *Northern History*, 14, pp. 193-207.

[28] Wrigley, E.A. (1987), *People, Cities and Wealth: The Transformation of Traditional Society*, Oxford, p. 159.

[29] Ellis, J. (1984), 'A Dynamic Society: Social Relations in Newcastle-upon-Tyne, 1660-1760', in P. Clark (ed.), *The Transformation of English Provincial Towns*, London, pp. 190-227.

[30] Ellis, J. (2001), 'The "Black Indies"': the Economic Development of Newcastle upon Tyne, c. 1700-1840', in R. Colls and W. Lancaster (eds), *Newcastle: A Modern History*, Chichester. Ellis proposes that it was capital-intensive investment by 'local entrepreneurs', rather than aristocratic landowners, that moved coal exports 'sharply upwards' from the 1790s.

and lead mining.[31] Judith's husband, George Baker, was the son of George Baker of Crook Hall, and Elizabeth, only daughter and heir of Thomas Conyers, of Elemore Hall, county Durham.[32] Judith herself was thus of gentry status by birth, and consolidated her connections through marriage: she dined with the most powerful men in the county, including the bishop of Durham and the duke of Northumberland. That the Rt. Hon. John Bowes, earl of Strathmore was executor to George Baker's will was another reflection of the Bakers' local influence.[33]

Piecing together Judith Baker's character as well as her economic and social status is a slow and somewhat ambitious task in the light of the remaining sources, but is illuminated by the occasional fragment of letters from Judith to her married sisters, Dorothy ('Hester') Chapeau and Elizabeth Bland, to whom she was very close. Judith was well liked by contemporaries such as her kinsfolk, the Noels and Milbankes, relatives of Viscount Wentworth, who were otherwise extremely scathing about the lack of 'polite' company in the provinces. Judith Milbanke's exacting sister Sophia wrote on 19 Oct 1781, 'I am of your mind about Mrs Baker, as I think she is one of the best I saw in the North'.[34] The Milbankes' daughter, Ann Isabella, who later became the wife of Lord Byron, was born at Elemore Hall, the Bakers' country seat, in 1792.[35] Judith could clearly create a favourable impression among the best society: she loved fine clothes, fashion and horses. Another of her passions was politics, which shaped her experience of urban life in the north-east. Her father-in-law had been the MP for Durham city between 1713 and 1722,[36] and the Bakers were closely involved with local elections. Although George Baker came from a Tory family, he and his wife's sympathies lay with more radical politicians. They both supported Sir Thomas Clavering, who stood against the bishop of Durham's candidate, Ralph Gowland, in the Durham city by-elections that took place during six days in December 1761, following the sudden

---

[31] Fewster, J.M., 'The Baker Baker Papers', *Durham County Local History Society Bulletin*, 3, p. 13.

[32] Hutchinson, W. (1785), 'Pedigree of Baker of Crook Hall and Elemore', in, Surtees, R. (1820), *History and Antiquities of the County Palatine of Durham*, ii, Newcastle and London, p. 358.

[33] Documents relating to George Baker, mortgages, marriage settlement with Judith Routh, and his will; See Dixon-Johnson Collection, Section II, Palace Green Library (PGL), University of Durham.

[34] Judith Milbanke, related to Judith Baker by marriage through the maternal line, commented on the mayor of Newcastle's wife 'Lady Ridley herself is not the Pink of Gentility but very good humoured, & *takes care* of her Company, which pleases very well in this Country.' Our subject nevertheless escaped such censure. See Elwin, M. (1967), *The Noels and the Milbankes: Their Letters for Twenty-Five Years*, London, p. 181.

[35] Elwin, *The Noels and the Milbankes,* pp. 17-18. PGL/BB17/72 [n.d.] is a note from the Milbankes requesting thanks to be conveyed to the Bakers' servants and for money to be distributed to them for assistance at the time of Ann's birth.

[36] Drury, J.L. (1996), 'The Baker Baker Portfolio of Prints – its Content and Acquisition', *Durham County Local History Society Bulletin*, 56, p. 9.

of the most controversial elections of the eighteenth century.[37] Letters to Judith from fellow supporters of Clavering indicate the active part which she played in the political campaigning on behalf of her candidate in Durham. Her strategy to win over the votes of individual freemen relied upon a parish by parish prediction by the Town Clerk, Robert Robinson, of how the vote would go.[38] Judith also collected a total of twenty four songs and poems that appeared about the election, including a verse in her own handwriting that was composed on the walls of Durham castle — a meditation upon the feudal corruption of past bishops and homage to liberty.[39] Support for Clavering would have secured his victory, had not the corporation of Durham sworn in two hundred and fifteen 'occasional' freemen 'fetched out of Yorkshire, Westmoreland, Cumberland, Northumberland and County Durham' — so-called 'mushroom' freemen — to have his election overturned.[40] This not only succeeded in bankrupting the corporation, but led eventually to a parliamentary act, the Durham Act of 1763, which made it illegal for freemen to vote in elections within one year of their appointment.[41] In the second round of voting, Judith's preferred candidate for Durham city, Major General Lambton, was returned to parliament. Her direct part in securing his victory is confirmed by the presence of an account in Judith's hand which records that she was reimbursed by Lambton for distributing 'treats' to several voters, amounting to nearly £12.[42] The influence of the Bakers in this campaign was reflected in the shower of praise which Judith received when Lambton was elected.[43] A ballad entitled 'The London Voters Ditty Humbly inscribed to Mrs. B-a-k-r' also reflects the strong association between Judith Baker and Lambton's campaign.[44] She later wrote a chronology of 'Memorable Events' between 1746 and 1776, which documented her close involvement with Durham politics and the social dimension of political schism that had divided the city and county for so long. The assemblies in Durham city, she recorded, were divided according to whether or not the party supported the bishop's candidate.[45] Judith's participation

---

[37] Hughes, E. (1952, reprinted 1969), *North Country Life in the Eighteenth Century: The North-East, 1700-1750*, Oxford, pp. 262-3.

[38] Robert Robinson to Judith Baker, Durham, 5 November 1760. PGL/BB11/16-17.

[39] 'Wrote upon the Castle walls: Once in this Pallace Durham Holy Lords did dwell/ But the Anointed's fled, & all's a Hell/Where lurks Corruption with her gaudy Train/And Echo's Shafto, Shafto Echo's Vane.' Robert Shafto, another political opponent of the Bakers, was elected MP for Durham County in 1760. PGL/BB11/29/xxi.

[40] Hutchinson, W. (1785), *History and Antiquities of the County Palatinate of Durham*, ii, Newcastle and London, pp. 45-6.

[41] Durham was by no means unique, nor the last of the smaller counties to experience 'vote rigging' of this nature. The Durham Act failed to eradicate 'mushroom' freemen. In Huntingdonshire, for example, between 1765-7, 154 freeholders were created in anticipation of a general election. See Langford, P. (1991), *Public Life and the Propertied Englishman, 1689-1798*, Oxford, pp. 272-3, 286.

[42] PGL/BB11/45.

[43] PGL/BB11/105. Letter from J. Simpson [in London?] to Judith, 11 May 1762.

[44] PGL/BB/11/78/8.

[45] PGL/BB 14/86a.

in urban political life thus had many dimensions. In Durham, Judith was a considerable figure of local importance, who concentrated her energies on lobbying local freemen and using her network of personal contacts to help combat what she perceived as an outmoded form of feudal power wielded in the constituency by the bishop of Durham. We may surmise from her active distribution of Lambton's bribes and 'treats', that her influence as a patron among local freemen would have been considerable.

In terms of national politics, her role was of the informed observer, gleaning news from the press and via letters from relatives in the metropolis. Judith's important and extensive collection of political prints confirms the significance of national as well as local politics in her life. Between her marriage in 1749 and her death in 1810, she collected a total of nearly 200 prints on a wide variety of themes, such as politics, fashion, horseracing and gambling, an important collection that is the subject of a comprehensive study by J. Linda Drury.[46] Judith's love of collecting news cuttings and ephemera, as well as her extensive print collection amassed over many decades, are indicative of her investment in what Dror Wahrman has called 'national society'.[47] The receipts and vouchers that accompany her account books indicate that she kept abreast of current affairs via local newspapers from Newcastle, and London papers which were sent to her directly via employees, family and friends. The manager of the Bakers' alum business in London, Thomas Core, unabashedly told his mistress 'I have sent your shoes, stockings, silk, magazine[s] and North Britons by the Waggon which set out yesterday.'[48] Judith was clearly well read – her rare surviving letters indicate a familiarity with the latest novels, she loved the theatre, and wrote in a fluent, as well as precise, hand. Her account books indicate that her household subscribed to local newspapers such as the *Newcastle Courant*, and serials emanating from London, such as the *Gentleman's Magazine*. It is highly likely that she read these newspapers herself, from which she compiled political scrapbooks, and even cut out recipes to keep.[49] Scandal as well as politics occupied her attention, particularly if there was a local dimension to the subject. One of the most closely-chronicled events in her collection was the scandalous divorce proceedings initiated by one of her neighbours, Mary Eleanor Bowes (formerly Lady Strathmore) against her husband, Andrew Stoney Bowes.[50] Judith carefully preserved ephemera relating to the couple, such as the following ballad 'A New SONG', set to the tune of 'O London is a fine Town', which satirised Andrew Stoney Bowes's brazen attempt to

---

[46] Drury, 'Baker Baker portfolio', *passim*.

[47] Wahrman, D. (1992), 'National Society, Communal Culture: An Argument About the Recent Historiography of Eighteenth-Century Britain', *Social History*, 17:1, pp. 43-72.

[48] PGL/BB77/35/46, London, 20 June 1769. Thomas Core to Mrs Baker.

[49] PGL/BB86/51a/24 for example, includes a bill from Ann Clifton of Durham for the purchase of the *Courant* and the *Gentleman's Magazine* for 1783.

[50] PGL/BB71/238-248.

stand for parliament in Newcastle, notwithstanding scandalous revelations about his adultery and debts.[51]

Judith also cut out the *English Chronicle*'s satirical accounts of each MP at Westminster and collected them week by week, pasting them carefully into a scrapbook, 'To the Freeholders of England, the following short History of ye Representatives, May 1779'.[52] The care with which she compiled her own scrapbooks from the London papers, suggest that she was well informed about politics and national affairs. It also illustrates her demotion of status on a national level; at home, she was a powerful presence in Durham city; in London, she was a minnow, reduced politically to the rank of spectator. Nevertheless, her enjoyment at participation in urban life in the metropolis was marked by her frequent trips there, and the constant communication she enjoyed with family and friends. In this context, we know that Judith Baker had two children, George and Elizabeth, who survived to adulthood, and that her childbearing had ceased long before the death of her husband, who had been weakened by ill health for some years. Her unusually long widowhood clearly gave her a certain degree of independence and an opportunity to pursue activities that were beyond the usual female sphere. After the death of her husband in May, 1774, she alone was responsible for the management of the family alum business and administration of the Baker estates while her son was in his minority. Even after her son turned 21 in 1775, she continued to keep the Elemore accounts, and provided him with pocket money. It was only after George's marriage in 1787 that she ceased her career in business and removed from Elemore to Tynemouth, near Newcastle. In the twin areas of consumption (hereafter characterised as her appetite for 'luxury') and the exercise of astute financial management (summed up as 'prudence'), this Durham gentlewoman exhibited a degree of agency and broad network of business associates and friends in London.

Luxury

The debate regarding the definition of 'luxury' and its moral dimensions was framed some years ago by John Sekora, who argued that during the eighteenth century, a shift took place, from the classical construction of luxury as a morally culpable impulse which had to be restrained through temperance, to one in which uxury could be construed as a virtuous and beneficial attribute.[53] Luxury

---

[51] 'Newcastle was a canny place, a plain and thriving town/But now 'tis like to rise apace to honour and renown;/For we shall have a member soon, if Faction has its way, /No man can say, he e'er did ill, or ever went astray...'. PGL/BB71/238 enclosure. The details of the divorce proceedings, and Stoney Bowes's extraordinary behaviour, are set out in Sherwen, R. (1989), 'Mary Eleanor Bowes, Countess of Strathmore, John Lyon, 9th Earl of Strathmore, and George Gray', *Durham County Local History Society Bulletin*, 43, pp. 25-34.

[52] PGL/BB15/39.

[53] Sekora, J. (1977), *Luxury: The Concept in Western Thought, Eden to Smollett*, Baltimore.

stimulated demand, and therefore wealth, in the context of a modernising commercial culture and increasing imperial expansion. Sekora's model has attracted criticism, not least from those who highlight his over-reliance on a limited number of literary texts to explain a supposedly widespread attitudinal shift. However, arguments over the luxury debate were undoubtedly 'pressing and influential' for contemporaries of the period, and represented an attempt to document and accommodate the social impact of the transition to a new type of commercial culture.[54] Early in the eighteenth century, Bernard Mandeville's *Fable of the Bees* (1714) had famously advocated enlightened self-interest as the surest way to happiness, facilitated through the acquisition of material goods.[55] It was a theme which was taken up and elaborated by the political economists of the Scottish Enlightenment, from Hume, who praised the 'spirit of avarice and industry' that arose from individual self-interest, to Adam Smith, who perfected what Roy Porter has called 'the science of human appetite'.[56] The moral effects of a descent into 'luxury' also attracted widespread popular debate through the pages of the *Spectator* and *Gentleman's Magazine*, beloved of the literate classes and gentry, including (as we have seen) the Bakers themselves.[57] The *Spectator* explored the paradox that those who profited from the sale of luxury clothing were seldom personally rich, due to the whimsy of fashion. Thus, the trade of lace and fringe-makers, 'being founded upon vanity, keeps them poor by the light inconstancy of its nature'.[58] Anxiety over the moral decline that was thought to follow a descent into luxury was directed in the main towards the middling householder with social ambitions, and the lower sorts, who knew no better. Petty shopkeepers who preferred to dress more finely than was meet for their station and who idled their time away in coffee houses were memorably characterised by Defoe as 'brass washed over with silver'.[59] Likewise, those apprentices who affected to wear long wigs and swords were soon likely to fall into 'wickedness and debauchery', and petty tradesmen were publicly criticised for their love of 'fine wigs, fine holland shirts of six to seven shillings an ell, and perhaps lac'd also'.[60]

---

[54] Pointon, *Strategies for Showing*, p. 4.

[55] de Mandeville, B. (1714), *The Fable of the Bees: or, Private Vices, Publick Benefits*, London. An indication of the influence of this work is that it had run to the sixth edition by 1725.

[56] Wrightson, *Earthly Necessities*, p. 8; Porter, R. (2000), *Enlightenment: Britain and the Creation of the Modern World*, London, p. 389.

[57] Raven, 'Defending Conduct and Property', pp. 301-16, argues that the debate over luxury intensified in the quarter-century *after* 1750, inspired both by 'changes in the literary market and by changing economic conditions, notably in domestic consumption, productivity, and landownership', p. 301.

[58] *Specator*, 478, 8 September 1712.

[59] Defoe, D. (1727), *The Complete English Tradesman*, 2nd edn, London, p. 86.

[60] Defoe, *The Complete English Tradesman*, pp. 106, 118-19.

Defoe's censure of the consumption which he witnessed suggests that men as well as women of all social ranks participated as they were able in the market for luxury during the eighteenth century. On one level, this appears to endorse the case made by Margot Finn for reinstating the male consumer as a significant presence in the eighteenth-century marketplace.[61] However, Robert Jones has argued persuasively that ideas of beauty and taste, which impacted upon the luxury debate at this time, can only be understood as a specifically gendered construct, one which was most often associated with ideals of feminine beauty and feminised aesthetics.[62] The idea that women had a dual position 'as both agents of corruption and idle ornament', was one of the most frequently-repeated ideas in eighteenth-century literature.[63] This observation is an important reminder of the prevailing cultural context within which eighteenth-century women lived, in addition to the normative constraints under which they operated. Thus, we see how, in the conduct of her everyday business, Judith Baker paid lip service to the necessary conventions of her day. Her every decision — how to spend her 'pin money', or how to pay off her husband's considerable debts — was framed by the social expectations of her sex and status. A letter to her neighbour William Lambton, for example, regarding the sale to him of her family's estate at Dinsdale is prefaced in this fashion: 'Dear Sir, I am sorry to trouble you with a Letter on Business w[hi]ch you will think out of a Female Sphere'.[64] Judith then proceeded to complain to Lambton that his lawyer, Mr Burke, has been disrespectful to her sister Mrs Bland, and had sent her what she described (underlined to indicate the irony) a '<u>polite letter</u>' which she forwarded to Lambton so that he could read the offending article for himself. While we do not know the nature of the insult, what is conveyed forcefully in Judith's letter is her own sense of social position as a gentlewoman and the deference which she normally felt was due to her by men of inferior status. She observed of Burke's letter 'it's a Singular stile to write into [unto] a Gentlewoman'.[65] In private correspondence with a close female member of her family, Judith gave a tantalising yet all too brief indication that she was aware of the paradoxical nature of a woman's condition: her responsibilities and labours were many, yet the onus was also upon her to exhibit the necessary female decorum. In hastily-scribbled notes to her sister, she gave advice on a sick cow, and mentioned that she was up to her eyes in 'raking' and 'Business at Home', with visitors arriving, and a servant, Mr Polk, busy 'distillering' under her supervision. Turning from these mundane cares to address her sister directly, she

---

61 Finn, 'Men's Things', *passim.*

62 Jones, R.W. (1998), *Gender and the Formation of Taste in Eighteenth-Century Britain: The Analysis of Beauty*, Cambridge.

63 Jones, *Gender and the Formation of Taste*, p. 6.

64 PGL/BB/128/106g. Copy of a letter from Judith Baker to Mr Lambton, 14 July 1771.

65 PGL/BB/128/106g. Copy of a letter from Judith Baker to Mr Lambton, 14 July 1771.

contrasted her own hectic life with 'you Mrs Chapeau that is at the fountain of Politeness'.[66]

From the evidence of the Baker Baker archive (a nineteenth-century form of the family name), it appears that Judith herself played a primary role in the acquisition of goods from tradespeople and wholesalers ('shopping') and management of household consumption (payment of bills). Even when bills were made out in the name of her husband or son, it was Judith who kept the vouchers neatly in bundles, adding marginal comments, deciding when (and indeed whether) to pay, and balancing debit and credit columns month by month down to the last penny. In doing so, she exemplified the model of an enlightened eighteenth-century consumer, one who was both *acquisitive* and *rational*. In theory, reason was a quality largely meted out to men.[67] In practice, there were many women of Judith's rank who quietly got on with the highly rational business of keeping their families solvent. The vouchers and account books kept by Judith Baker are also powerfully suggestive of the Baker family's investment in the display of luxury goods as a mark of their status. This applied to the 'fixed goods' of their country seat, its fabric and andornment, the 'movable goods' of their personal consumption as individual family members (such as their rich dress and jewellery), and to the 'consumable goods' — the expensive foods and wine which they purchased. Let us consider each of these in turn.

The marriage between George Baker and Judith Routh on 27 May 1749 at Dinsdale church was reported in the *Newcastle Courant*. Judith was conventionally described as a 'beautiful young lady with a handsome fortune'. The couple moved to Chester (le Street) Deanery, while George Baker's country house underwent substantial renovations. The rebuilding of Elemore Hall illustrates how the gentry in the north-east were remodelling their country houses to meet the architectural standards of 'quality' found across Britain in the mid-eighteenth century. In many parts of England at this time, Tudor manor houses and medieval fortresses were yielding their place to the fashion for such innovative features as Palladian facades and sash windows. At Elemore, old chimneys were demolished, and Venetian windows and balconies were added to north and south wings. The south front received a new Gibbs surround. The interior was refurbished with Italian stuccoes by Guiseppe Cortese, who was at that time doing a lively trade in remodelling the

---

[66] PGL/68/224i and xvi. Fragments of letters from Judith Baker to her sister Mrs Chapeau at Haworth [n.d.].

[67] Genevieve Lloyd argues that Hume's reformulation of reason as 'the slave of the passions', rather than loosening the classical alignment between maleness and reason, presented a 'subtle reinforcement of the older pattern' in the eighteenth century through the development of a public/private dichotomy (public 'male' reason vs. private 'female' passion). In Lloyd, G. (1993), *The Man of Reason: 'Male' and 'Female' in Western Philosophy*, 2nd edn, London, pp. 51-6.

conservative interpretation of the national taste for 'British Palladian', which was often copied from pattern books at the time. Mrs Baker's room & the Great Dining Room overlooked newly-landscaped gardens. New fire places, a 'marble water closat' and a 'marble table made by Mr Cortese' were installed, together with fine apricot coloured plasterwork, cornices and moulding. The dining room ceiling was decorated with Cupid & Psyche in an oval frame, with motifs of masks, flowers & musical instruments. Neptune in the clouds formed the centrepiece of the Great Staircase, also by Cortese. The grounds received temples and a terrace walk, with a winding tree-flanked carriage drive. 'William Joyce, nurseryman of Gateshead', provided vegetable and flower seeds, fruit trees and bushes, 160 limes, a thousand elms, a thousand hornbeams and many shrubs'. George Baker spent a total of £3,000 (equivalent to £180,000 today) renovating his house for his new bride. Mary Noel wrote to her niece Sophia that she thought Elemore a 'comfortable House' with 'a remarkable good Staircase of Stone' and 'a pretty walk to the clearest cold Bath I ever saw'.[69]

The Bakers expressed their taste for good living through the renovations to their estate and country house in county Durham, but for the twenty-five years of their married life, they looked south to London and Bath for shopping and serious entertainment. Whether out of habit or personal preference, Judith's expeditions to London continued after she was widowed in May, 1774. In April 1776, for example, she departed from Elemore to London for just over one month, and calculated in her account book of that year that her 'Exp[ense]s in London[,] Bills pocket money &c. the whole sum I charge together £50'.[70] Surviving vouchers from the same trip indicate that the three day journey alone cost Judith an extra £17 (one way) in horses, lodgings, food and drink for herself and her servants.[71] For the purposes of comparison, it took a year for a coal hewer in county Durham to earn the latter amount alone.[72] Once Judith had arrived in the capital, lodging with her family at Hill Street, the spending began in earnest. From previous trips to London, the bills of Mr Christopher Law, Dean Street Holborn, near Red Lion Square, for example, indicate that Judith bought satin shoes – in white, pink and black, for herself and her daughter, to the value of £11 19s, on nine separate occasions between July 1767 and March, 1769.[73] She evidently had her favourite places to

---

Sedgfield, Co. Durham. See Gosden, J. (1982), 'Elemore Hall Transformed, 1749-1753', *Transactions of the Architectural & Archaeological Society of Durham & Northumberland*, new series, 6, p. 33. On the rebuilding of country houses in general, see Wilson, R.G., and Mackley, A.L. (1999), 'How Much Did the English Country House Cost to Build, 1660-1880?', *Economic History Review*, 2nd series, 52:3, pp. 436-468.

[69] Elwin, *Noels and Milbankes*, p. 181.

[70] PGL/BB45/26/fol. 28.

[71] PGL/BB80/42/1-52. April-May 1776. Vouchers for a journey to London & back.

[72] Wrightson, *Earthly Necessities*, p. 318, gives the example of the coal hewer John Brabbon who in 1752 earned almost £19 as a hewer at Northbanks Colliery in Whickham– and that was a good year.

[73] PGL/BB77/35/53.

shop, and visited them year on year. There is a particularly fine handbill from James Smyth & Nephews, Perfumers to His Majesty, At the Civet Cat, in New Bond Street. In April, 1768, Judith visited the shop, and spent £1 on scents & cosmetics. Almost exactly one year earlier, she visited the same perfumery (24 March 1767) and stocked up on similar items, spending £1 2d.[74] Like that other provincial gentlewoman, Jane Austen's Mrs Bennet, she knew all the best warehouses in London in which to buy her Florentine silks, old gold lace, and velvet.[75] Judith Baker's account books indicate that when she was in London she used the opportunity to do favours for her female neighbours from the north-east in paying their bills, and arranging to have goods sent to them. This may be characterised as a frequently overlooked aspect of the 'residual loyalty' of county gentry in London towards their own county, observed by Lawrence and Jeanne Fawtier Stone.[76] One of Judith's closest friends was Lady Windsor, née Alice Clavering, a member of the Clavering family of Axwell, Northumberland, whose kinsman the Bakers had supported in his bid to become MP for Durham city.[77] When either of them happened to be in London, each conveyed to the other the latest gossip about society engagements and forthcoming marriages, and predicted the arrival in town of other gentry families from the north-east.[78] Judith instructed her servant Thomas Core to wait upon Lady Windsor and offer his services in her absence.[79] They paid each others' shop bills, and exchanged produce from their estates as gifts. At the foot of a bill for a 'White Sack hoop' from Ann Wright, 'Hoop-maker to Her Majesty' in Union Street, Hanover Square, was a note to the effect that Mrs Baker 'Paid at the same time of the Rt Honble Lady Windsor the full contents and all Demand'.[80] At the haberdasher's, J & R Harrop's, located in the cloak and hat warehouse at the Sun and Peacock in Coventry Street near Piccadilly, Mrs Baker paid off several bills: Lady Windsor's for 10s 6d, Lady Beauchamp's for £1 18s, and a considerable bill of her own for £5 9s 10d.[81] The payment of friends' bills had an element of largesse that marked Judith's status and affluence, and confirmed her credit among both peers and social inferiors, notwithstanding that she expected to be recompensed at a later date. Consumption in London thus cemented bonds of friendship and affection between gentlewomen from north-east England through this informal system of mutual assistance. While

---

[74] PGL/BB77/35/22.

[75] Austen, J. (1813 reprinted Penguin edn 1972), *Pride and Prejudice*, London, p. 304. I am grateful to Julia Berry for drawing my attention to this comparison.

[76] Stone, L. and Fawtier, J. (1986), *An Open Elite? England, 1540-1880* (Oxford, 1986), p. 28.

[77] See PGL/Clavering MS/K485.

[78] PGL/BB13/46 Alice Windsor to Judith Baker, London, 13 February 1770.

[79] PGL/BB77/35/47 Thomas R. Core to Mrs Baker, London, 20 June 1769, 'Am Favoured with yours of the 12th Inst. and will wait on Lady Windsor the first opportunity'.

[80] PGL/BB77/35/64.

[81] PGL/BB77/35/24 [n.d.].

this pattern was by no means unique to women from county Durham and Northumberland, it does illustrate the universality of this practice among English provincial gentlewomen. Those living at a greater distance from the metropolis would no doubt have been especially reliant upon such networks.

Another of Judith's London correspondents was Mrs Tempest, wife of the MP for Durham, who thanked Judith for sending her 'all the Durham witt', and apologised that she had no witty riposte with which to reciprocate due to a lack of 'that comodity in this place'.[82] News and gossip were as much part of the exchange of 'commodities' as material goods. Mrs Tempest reported the activities of the defeated parliamentary candidate Gowland in London, impugning his character as someone who 'never means to honour you with his company again in the North unless there shoud be some very dirty work to do'. Notably, Durham is referred to by Judith's friends in London, not by name, but as 'the North' or 'the Country'.[83] Likewise, a receipt from Mrs Deval in Barton Street, Berkley Square, confirms that she was paid £1 9s 3d by Mrs Baker for 'doing up some Linnen' for 'a lady in the North'.[84] When she was not in London, Judith's purchases were channelled through personal contacts such as Lady Windsor – but more particularly via her widowed sister Mrs Bland, who obtained a wide range of goods for Judith, from books and printed ephemera, to hair cushions, china and comestibles. Mrs Bland also arranged for these goods to be packed and transported from London to county Durham. For example, in 1783, Mrs Bland bought Wedgwood ware for Judith in London, who reimbursed her for the expense and for the carriage to Elemore.[85] An account from 26 April, 1781 indicates that Mrs Bland bought the following items for her sister: a bottle of salts, a hoop, '7yds stuff', 'A Clock' from 'Mr. Consett' (£1 11s 6d), '6 yds Ribbon', '1st Royal Kalender for 1782' and the 'Polite Repository' (3s 6d), 'A reading glass' (5s), several quires of paper, and '2 Plays' (6s). The total, including £12 10s 2d that she already owed her, came to £23 10s 7d.[86]

Judith consistently ordered items from her favourite shops, sometimes over a period of twenty or more years, and patronised an ever-widening network of businesses in London, in particular milliners and dressmakers.[87] It is notable that, despite the greater size and variety of shops available in London, Judith does not seem to have preferred to shop around, but instead built up a close network of personal contacts and tradespeople in the West End to whom she was personally known. Her pattern of consumption in the metropolis thus mirrored her strategy for doing business in her local towns in the north-east: it was predicated upon a system of patronage, personal acquaintance, and credit. The types of services which Judith

---

[82] PGL/BB11/83 Mrs John Tempest to Judith Baker, Argyll St, 23 February 1762.

[83] PGL/BB11/83 Mrs John Tempest to Judith Baker, Argyll St, 23 February 1762. In reference to a snowstorm, Mrs Tempest comments 'I hope you have not suffered by it in the Country'.

[84] PGL/BB77/35/56. The bill was paid on 16 January 1770.

[85] PGL/BB45/29 Account book entries for May and October 1783.

[86] PGL/BB85/49B/30.

[87] See Pullin, N. (2000), ''Business is Just Life': Gender, Skill, Ideology and the Eighteenth-Century Business Woman', unpublished University of London PhD thesis.

required in London were frequently offered by the female sex, in particular those relating to dress and fashionable apparel. Her hair, clothing, shoes and cosmetics were supplied via women she knew in London, a peculiarly feminised form of luxury which depended upon female taste for procurement and purchase, but the services of a sea captain bound for Sunderland for delivery. A letter from Mrs Beauvis, milliner, of Jermyn Street, St James Square to Mrs Baker at Elemore, records that Judith ordered dresses from London in the latest style.[88] She received detailed advice from 'S. Newlin' (a milliner?) in a very poorly-written note concerning fashions in ladies' caps ('at present ferdinand caps are a jenerall fashon which I will describe as well as I can') together with a description on how to arrange borders, trimmings, ribbons and feathers.[89] Like the Newcastle ladies who pressurised Josiah Wedgwood to let them have the latest designs before they reached London, Judith was reassured by the tradesmen and women with whom she dealt that they would keep her informed of the latest fashions.[90] William Barlow, a haberdasher in London, thanked Mrs Baker for settling her bill of £14 13s 6d in February, 1782, and promised her that 'when the summer silks come out of the Loomes you many depend on my sending an elegant collection of patterns'.[91]

Another example of repeat buying was that of food. When supplying provisions for their Durham house, the Bakers habitually 'exported' certain edible luxuries back to the north-east. They ran up an enormous grocery bill in London during March, 1766 at Blakiston Myles & Co. in the Strand, for (among other things) 'green tea, bohea tea, sugar, chocolate, coffee, black pepper, currants, mace, "maccorony", raisins, cinnamon, ginger, vermicelli, hair powder', to a total of £39 4s 5d. The groceries were 'Shipt on board the Hearts of Gold Captain Bywater for Sunderland'.[92] The order from Blakiston & Myles was obviously not a one-off, but an annual trip to stock up on luxury foodstuffs. Judith continued to shop at Blakiston and Myles long after her husband's death. Another bill dated London, 14 April 1783, is for £32, and presents almost exactly the same list and in the same order as 10 years earlier, including 'Corriander seeds, sugar, tea, chocolate', etc.[93] Judith's collection of recipes indicate the family's fondness for luxury foods, and that a lively exchange of information about the best dishes took place between gentry families in the north-east, such as a hearty recipe from Mr Lambton for beef

---

[88] 'Madam, I have According to your Orders sent the first of Crepe Linen 2 dresses Caps & a token [?] for the Young Ladies & 2 dresses negligeed all which I hope will be to your Liking as they are made in the present fashion they are wore [sic].' PGL/BB77/35/73. Mrs Beauvis to Mrs Judith Baker, 27 April 1770.

[89] PGL/BB11/3, S. Newlin to Mrs Baker, 11 March 1760.

[90] See also McKendrick, Brewer and Plumb, *Birth of a Consumer Society*, ch. 3, 'Josiah Wedgwood and the Commercialisation of the Potteries'.

[91] PGL/BB85/49B/22.

[92] PGL/BB77/35/80.

[93] PGL/BB86/51D/16.

soup.[94] The Baker family's food was another dimension of their participation in the evolving national culture: the appearance of certain dishes, such as Apple Charlotte (famously popularised by the queen), was a mark that they were attuned to a form of fashion that extended to the dinner table. Another recipe, for chicken curry was copied from the cook who worked for Judith's titled relatives, the Milbankes: the spices were sent to Durham from London, and were the edible proofs of Empire.[95]

The lifestyle of the Bakers typifies the mobility and consumer behaviour of a rich gentry family in the last decades of the eighteenth century. It also illustrates the range of urban pleasures they enjoyed. While in London, Judith found time in between her shopping trips to go to Ranelagh gardens, to the theatre, and to Sadler's Wells (originally a health spa).[96] In a small marble-covered exercise book, Judith kept a meticulous account of the expenses that she, her husband and their daughter Elizabeth incurred on a trip to Bath during the 1760s. In addition to the journey expenses, room hire, and washing bill, Judith recorded additional expenditure on ball tickets, sedan chairs, play tickets, and purchase of consumables such as gloves, hair powder, washballs, six breakfast plates, a jeweller's bill for Miss Baker, a pair of silver tea tongs. On a single day, she bought 'a Prayer Book Miss B[aker]', a map of Bath, 'a Bill for Hats, gave her husband 11s cash, bought raffle tickets, paid the milliner and servants' bills, and went to an exhibition and the opera. She also spent nearly six shillings on prints. In total, their trip to Bath, which lasted over a month, came to a grand total of over £144.[97]

The dimension of 'luxury' in the comforts, leisure and entertainment the Bakers enjoyed at Bath and London is evident. Their wealth also enabled them to spend much of the year at various provincial racecourses, with Judith constantly taking meticulous notes and accounts of their expenditure at each. The whole family was fond of horse racing, and their son George was, according to the *Sporting Magazine*, one of the most noted horsemen in England. He won his first race on his own horse Blacklegs, in 1782.[98] Although the 'sport of kings' was largely a male domain, Judith enjoyed going to the races, and adopted the enthusiasm of her husband and son. A private memorandum by Judith illustrates how the language associated with this expensive hobby must have permeated her speech. In a memo about a protracted legal wrangle with a neighbour, Mr. Lambton, over deeds relating to the purchase of her family's estate at Dinsdale, Judith recorded that her children were '*of[f] on legs* to know the consequence'.[99]

Widowhood brought Judith's greater participation in running the family businesses, although her personal expenditure in the long term did not alter

---

94 PGL/BB68/225.

95 PGL/BB68/225. A classic work on the changing English diet is Drummond J.C. and Wilbraham, A. (1939 reprinted 1994), *The Englishman's Food: Five Centuries of English Diet*, London, 2nd edn, pp. 210-18 on the diet of eighteenth-century gentry.

96 See PGL/80/42/27; sundry expenses 'paid to M. Marsden in London, [17]76' and PGL/BB46/31/ff. 24-6, expenses in London, June 1787. See also Porter, R. (1994), *London: A Social History*, London, p. 122.

97 PGL/BB65/178.

98 Extract from the *Sporting Magazine*, August 1837, pp. 319-24.

99 PGL/BB128/106/o (1771-3).

significantly after her husband's death. While at Elemore, she made small purchases of tea, fabrics and everyday household items from shopkeepers in Durham and Newcastle. Old age brought increasing reliance upon smaller local towns, including Tynemouth, her place of retirement after her son's marriage. In 1784, she spent just over 16 shillings buying 'fine Souchong Tea' and miscellaneous small items such as 'silk twist' from Thomas Chipchase of Durham.[100] Ten years later, we find her buying miscellaneous paper, wax and wafers from the Durham stationer Ann Clifton, who also fed Mrs Baker's continued love of politics with a copy of 'The Wars of Westminster'.[101] Local newspapers and trade directories confirm that by the last quarter of the eighteenth century, the urban centres of the north-east were amply supplied with luxury goods, which were advertised 'hot' from London, specifically 'To the Ladies'. Shops such as Mr Buckle's haberdashery, opposite the High Bridge, sold silk brought 'by the Manufacturer from London' to Newcastle, while Jameson's china showroom boasted a 'very elegant Assortment' of 'India China, Blue and Green edg'd Cream colour'd ware &c... this week received from London'.[102] Mrs Lisle's tea shop in Newcastle sold 'TEA of the best Quality, neat as from the India House; also COFFEE, CHOCOLATE, COCOA, and HARD SUGAR', supplied 'from her connections in London' (the advertiser declared her intention to sell these 'upon as good terms as any shop in Newcastle or London').[103] We may only guess at the gentry's evaluation of the status-claims of shopkeepers with regard to the prestige of their goods. What is evident is that luxury *was* locally available, but for as long as was practicably possible into old age, Judith supplemented the purchases she made at home with items she imported directly from London herself.

Prudence

Time and again, historians of the eighteenth century conflate the values of 'industry, frugality, prudence, inner resourcefulness, integrity and generally an orientation towards productivity and utility' with middling status.[104] Yet it is less frequently noted that, among the ranks of the gentry, the attitude towards money could be one of meticulous stewardship rather than profligacy. It is axiomatic that the impetus at this level of society was to preserve and pass on the family estate to future generations. Nevertheless, the engagement of eighteenth-century gentlewomen in meticulous daily management of the minutiae of account-keeping too

---

[100] PGL/BB86/51c/13.

[101] PGL/BB86/51e/22.

[102] *Newcastle Courant*, 19 October 1771; 4 August 1781; 28 September 1782. See also Whitehead, W. (1778), *Whitehead's Newcastle Directory for 1778*, Newcastle.

[103] *Newcastle Courant*, 20 August 1791.

[104] Klein, L. (1995), 'Politeness for Plebes: Consumption and Social Identity in Early Eighteenth-Century England', in A. Bermingham and J. Brewer (eds), *The Consumption of Culture, 1600-1800: Image, Object, Text*, London, p. 363.

often slips from view in the current historiography.[105]

As a newly-married woman, Judith's earliest account book, a vellum-bound exercise book, kept in small, hesitant handwriting, recorded the perfunctory details of household and personal expenditure, amounting to between £8 and £12 per month.[106] After her husband's death in 1774, Judith started to keep a much larger ledger, with a monthly running total, and credit and debit columns on facing pages. Here was estate management in its proper sense, extending beyond the sphere of a housekeeper. It would be rash to speculate about the Bakers' total annual income without systematic analysis of the various sources in rents and business ventures (such as the alum trade). Judith's account books for the early 1780s do however illustrate the considerable sums of money that she was monitoring. She calculated that in 1781 the total income from rents, the sale of livestock, and estate profits, came to just over £3,260, a profit of £173.[107] Over the next three years, both income and expenditure rose steadily, rather than spectacularly. The year 1784 saw an income of £3,432, and a profit of £211.[108] A planned quantitative analysis of the full range of business papers in the Baker Baker archive will no doubt yield more clues regarding the family's income, fixed and capital assets.

As we have seen, Judith's managerial and financial responsibilities increased considerably after her widowhood. In a private memorandum to herself, Judith recorded the exact date of her husband's death (15 May 1774), the date her son came of age (5 October 1775) and the day her mother died (4 December 1775). Within a year, she had become the widowed matriarch of the family. Following her husband's death, Judith inherited many of his debts, perhaps as much as £6,000. While her son was in his minority – for approximately a year, they lived very frugally. Unlike her predecessor in County Durham, the widowed Lady Bowes, who handed over the management of the Gibside estate as soon as her son reached his majority,[109] Judith continued to keep the accounts for Elemore for a further twelve years, until George married in 1787.[110] Her son showed none of his mother's aptitude for prudent financial management: he spent huge sums on his horses and kept his stablemen in expensive livery. Although George was now the master of Elemore, it was his mother who regulated the household finances and

---

[105] There is no mention of gentlewomen working in business, or operating as consumers, for example, in Sharpe, P. (1996), *Adapting to Capitalism: Working Women in the English Economy, 1700-1850*, London. The survey is largely concerned with the wage labour of female servants, agricultural labourers and industries that responded to 'fashion trends in the domestic market', but nowhere is the *source* of the demand for silk, commercial lace embroidery, straw-plaiting, shoe-binding and tailoring (p. 38) anatomised. Similarly, there is no attention to the business activities of eighteenth-century gentlewomen in Simonton, D. (1998), *A History of European Women's Work, 1700 to the Present*, London.

[106] PGL/BB45/1.

[107] PGL/BB45/28. Income for 1781 was £3260 17s 2 ½ d, a profit of £173 19s 1d.

[108] PGL/BB45/28. Income for 1784 was £3432 8s 2 ½ d.

[109] Wrightson, *Earthly Necessities*, p. 278.

[110] The fortune of Isabella Dalton, George's bride, is listed in PGL/BB127/87.

determined the cash flow — when to pay bills, balancing the estate income and expenditure. Perhaps this was not so unusual for an unmarried man of George's rank: his preference for field sports over business, and his mother's acumen would have made it a logical and commodious arrangement. There is little evidence that Judith resented her displacement when her son married, but if George thought that his mother would be any less precise in calculating her own financial dues than in maintaining his accounts, he was mistaken. In a memorandum written when she moved to take up the life of a dowager in Tynemouth, Judith calculated what was owed to her by her son from her husband's legacy and her jointure from the Wingate Grange and Crook estates.[111] Not only this, but she added interest for the time that had passed in between, less the cost of her living expenses for the previous eleven years, which she estimated at £200 per annum. In total, she calculated that her son owed her £2,237, 17 shillings and sixpence.[112]

Judith's approach to the payment of bills while she was mistress of Elemore was to pay tradesmen as late as she could, a common practice among the gentry, but one which she pushed to its limits, no doubt taking advantage of her geographical remove from London. There are several letters of complaint in the Baker archives from irate tradesmen to whom they owed money. Joseph Green, a London gloveseller, reminded Mrs Baker in November 1769, that she had ordered over sixty pairs of gloves from him since April 1768, none of which had been paid for. He added peevishly 'I can assure you my profit is so small on Womans Gloves that I am a looser by them at so long Credit.' He finally received payment in December that year.[113] Judith's comfortable lifestyle should not be confused with idleness: time was not a luxury she enjoyed, as the note scribbled in haste and slipped into the pocket of a visiting servant for delivery to her sister Hester indicates.[114] She was paradoxically frugal in some habits, free in others: she treated her maids to plays during race week, but kept an eye on the smallest expenses. Like other members of the gentry, she passed on second hand clothing to tenants and servants, a conscientious and charitable act that cemented ties of patronage and personal loyalty in the neighbourhood, as a somewhat pitiful letter from the son of one of her tenants, William Dodds, testifies.[115] She checked every ha'penny in her accounts. Thomas Core sent to Mrs Baker, informing her that he had posted 'The

[111] PGL/BB17/49d.

[112] PGL/BB17/49d.

[113] PGL/BB77/35/48.

[114] PGL/BB/68/224 [xvi]. Letter from Judith Baker to her sister Mrs Chapeau at Harworth (n.d.): 'My dear Sister . . . I go to Tynemouth on Friday to Bradley on Saturday back here Monday – I have today my dressing room hanging anew & Mr Mrs. & little Miss Conyers down here so farewell dear sister to you & yr Husband with affection, JB.'

[115] Letter from William Dodds to Judith Baker, 21 March 1785: 'Madim, I Receved your Good preasint of the Cloaths but indead I have not words to Express your Goodne's but after all its my duety to Humbley thank you indeade thay fit just as well as if I had taken measure on for them...' PGL/BB/17/49.

Paper and Gowns in Three Parcells [from London]'. The letter was addressed to General Lambton at Elemore Hall, Durham, since he was an MP and could receive post without charge.[116] This was common practice, but it is noteworthy that as far as saving money was concerned, Judith did not miss a trick. She kept meticulous handwritten memoranda of her business meetings as well as a detailed account book right up to her death, aged over 80, in 1810. She stitched bills together so she would not have to pay more than tuppence per sheet for the stamp, and bartered to re-sell second hand household items such as kitchen utensils when she bought new ones. We also find evidence that she closely scrutinised bills: one, addressed to her son George in 1768, recorded that he had bought a 'Small Red Leather trunk, 2s'. In Judith's small, sharp hand on the back of the bill is the note 'Pray what was this Trunk? Where did you get this [note] don't pay it.'[117]

Conclusion

The desirability of obtaining luxury goods from London did not diminish by the end of the eighteenth century, notwithstanding the growth of provincial urban centres with expanding tertiary and service industries. The case of Judith Baker has illustrated the importance of networking to affluent eighteenth-century gentlewomen, and provided precise details of how a steady flow of goods was mediated through personal contacts, via London, and urban centres in north-east England. Consumption emerges as the primary means by which Judith became a stakeholder in the urban life of the metropolis, a less overtly political role than the one she assumed in Durham city, but never the less underpinned by a tightly-woven system of credit and patronage that bound the gentry from north-east England together, even when they were 'abroad' in London. Far from being the 'physically and psychologically very isolated' group characterised by Lawrence Stone, we have seen how the gentry of north-east England were well informed about national affairs, and were able to exploit their unusually high degree of communication with the metropolis via the coastal shipping trade.[118]

The orientation of Judith's urban life is also instructive. One of the most obvious questions, yet one of the most difficult to answer, is why she chose London, rather than Edinburgh (by then a thriving commercial town, and practically on her doorstep).[119] Instead, the trouble she took to transport goods from London to 'the country' illustrates how the 'old' English landed gentry was

[116] See for example a letter from the Bakers' agent, Mr Core, to Mrs Baker, addressed to General Lambton at Elemore Hall, Durham, 2 August 1770. PGL/BB/77/35/77.

[117] PGL/BB77/35/47.

[118] Stone, *Open Elite?* p. 39. The reference is of course to the Northumberland gentry, but the geographical proximity of county Durham makes this a reasonable extrapolation.

[119] See for example Joseph Plumptre's eyewitness account of the flourishing Scottish capital in his 'Prospect of Edinburgh', written in 1799, in I. Ousby (ed.), *James Plumptre's Britain: the Journals of a Tourist in the 1790s*, London, pp. 106-7. See also Nenadic, 'Print collecting', p. 208 and *passim*.

orientated towards the south rather than the north, even those who lived on the peripheries of England. As Susan Whyman has highlighted, the growing professionalisation of government and regulation of parliamentary sittings increasingly drew English country gentlemen into London at certain times of the year, an annual ritual in which they were often accompanied by their female family members.[120] As a relative of MPs and former MPs, and political patron in her own right, Judith persisted in her annual visits to London, perhaps as a residual habit after the death of her husband, but certainly to maintain contact with relatives who lived there permanently, and to keep her finger on the pulse of national life.

Yet what, if anything, was new about the sort of life that Judith Baker experienced in the mid- to late eighteenth century? Besides the relative neglect of north-eastern archives, there may on the surface be little of novelty to merit the rescue of Judith's case history from the obscurity in which it has hitherto languished. Recent work by Alice T. Friedman, for example, reminds us that the purchase of luxury items in London had been a feature of the lives of provincial gentlewoman since the days of Bess of Hardwicke.[121] It may indeed be the case that Judith Baker was exhibiting a long-established and deeply traditional pattern of gentry behaviour in favouring London as the source of many luxury goods, with the only distinct advantage that she had above her ancestors being the speed with which she could obtain them, and the variety of her choice. What more has this Durham gentlewoman to offer?

First, Judith Baker's history has subtle but none the less remarkable differences in nuance and focus from her Lancashire counterparts, as studied by Amanda Vickery. While it is true that her choices were bound by the obligations of family and responsibilities to a host of tenants and servants, her life 'on the town', in comparison to that of a sixteenth- or seventeenth-century gentlewoman, was remarkably free. Her patterns of expenditure and frequent extended journeys to the metropolis suggest she was able to exercise choice. The influence she exerted as the manager of her son's estates and the family businesses was also considerable. In saying this, I am not equating consumerism and account-keeping with 'freedom', still less with 'happiness', but highlighting the palpable difference between the ideological confinement of gentlewomen to the household and the pragmatic compromise of this 'ideal' in the outworking of eighteenth-century women's lives. Also, Judith's experience is another example of the variation in interpretation of patriarchal authority, particularly if one were married to a sickly husband who fathered only two children, and had a son who was more interested in spending money on horses than in augmenting the family fortune. In Judith's patterns of expenditure, there was evidently a tension between the social requirement for herself and her family to exhibit a lifestyle that enhanced and proclaimed their status, and the prudence required of a gentlewoman if she were to

---

[120] Whyman, *Sociability and Power*, pp. 87-109 and *passim*.

[121] Friedman, A.T. (2000), 'Inside/Out: Women, Domesticity and the Pleasures of the City', in L. Cowen Orlin (ed.), *Material London, ca.1600*, Pennsylvania, pp. 232-50.

be a capable household manager and guardian of her family's welfare. It may have been the case that one of the marks of a true gentleman was that he never knew his bank balance, but it was more than likely that his wife did.

The life of Judith Baker reminds us that certain 'gentleman's daughters' could act as agents in the public sphere of local politics and business — and were not thought exceptional for doing so. What is more, even as writers and commentators railed against the likely pernicious effects of luxury, Judith continued her seasonal round of lavish expenditure and counting of ha'pennies. A combination of filial, wifely and maternal duties bred into her a responsibility for managing household affairs, but her personality — her love of precision, her shrewdness and calm assertion of all that was due to her, in terms of respect and legal entitlement, also emerges from among the dusty columns of figures and occasional marginalia that are her main historical legacy.

Chapter 8

Women in Towns as Keepers of the Word: The Example of Warwickshire During the 1780s to 1830s

Denise Fowler

Dr Parr (1747-1825) of Warwick, a pedagogue and a controversial and nationally known Anglican clergyman with Dissenting sympathies, expressed a well-established consensus amongst the more enlightened portion of the population when he admired women for 'the excellence which some have displayed in the elegant accomplishments of painting, music and poetry, in the nice discrimination of biography, in the broader researches of history and in moral compositions'.[1] To his list we can add the ubiquitous novels, the letters, diaries, children's books and primers, commonplace books and scrapbooks. Women were involved in all these literate endeavours as readers, writers, copyists, domestic educators, teachers, printers, booksellers, owners of circulating libraries, publishers, advertisers in the local press, and school benefactresses. This paper stresses the importance of the urban environment in shaping the role of women in print culture. If radical Unitarian women loom large here it is only because nonconformity was mostly concentrated in towns and especially, outside London, in the towns of the Midlands and the North.[2] It is also significant that Unitarians believed strongly in the humanising effect of literature for both sexes, and were actively involved in intellectual endeavours.

Towns offered women an ideal outlet for these roles as 'keepers and agents' of the word in the developing urban culture of the period, when communication was essential to the sustenance and maintenance of public life. Women helped forge the tools which allowed the citizens of the town to survive in the market place, in the shops and workshops, in the assembly rooms, on the promenade, and in the newsrooms; in short, in most places in town where the language of the grammar school was not a requirement. Proximity and the greater availability of reading matter in the urban environment were essential to the establishment of a culture in which women could take an active part, play a predominant role, and even develop

---

1 Field, W. (1828), *Memoirs of the Reverend Samuel Parr*, vol. 2, London, p. 159.

2 Seed, J. (1986), 'Theologies of Power: Unitarianism and the Social Relations of Religious Discourse, 1800-1850', in R.J. Morris (ed.), *Class, Power and Social Structure in British Nineteenth-Century Towns*, Leicester, pp. 107-57, especially p. 119.

a certain professionalism.[3] Proximity facilitated the establishment for women of networks whose importance in the culture of print has been well described, for instance by Jane Rendall, or by Kathryn Hughes. Their accounts focus on the period a few decades after ours but their findings are of considerable relevance.[4] As we shall see, towns were not only a space of concentrated opportunities for women, but urban development itself, with its new industries and services, was a fascinating theme which inspired some of the women writers from the Midlands, long before Dickens or Elizabeth Gaskell.

There were more ancient reasons why women were prominent as agents of the written word. For centuries, particularly up to the seventeenth century and before protestant iconoclasm in England, Mary as Keeper of the Word was a familiar image, communicated in the iconography of the countless Annunciations where she is surprised by the angel Gabriel and depicted against a background of books propped up on a lectern or lying on a shelf. Thus was created the most ancient role of women as readers. This influence of religion on women in their role as readers merits special attention. The essentiality of the sacred word in girls' education was still the norm in the early nineteenth century, as the 'Rules and Regulations of the Coventry Lancastrian Girls' School' made clear in 1822: 'No book except the Holy Scripture of the authorised version shall on any account whatever be introduced into the school; reading lessons shall consist exclusively of extracts from the authorised version of the Holy Scripture.'[5] This rule was particularly restrictive, but at the same time the churches did give women a crucial role as Bible and catechism readers. Their ability to read and/or memorise the catechism and other pious literature and teach it to their children was the guarantor of the development of their own virtue and that of those to whom they were transmitting the sacred word.

From the eighteenth century the iconography of women reading became more secular, and so did the Word itself, a remarkable process to which women have contributed greatly as avid readers, interpreters, propagators, and creators in the domain of the written word. Indeed, the apprenticeship to literacy might have been steeped in the Scriptures, but the vastly expanding market for books, especially children's books, in the late eighteenth century, reflected a commercial and secularising trend. Such a trend had its origin partly in the nonconformist idea of reading as an exploratory process but, more importantly, it offered women a platform which put them at the centre of print culture.

---

[3] Fergus, J. and Farrar Thaddeus, J. (1987), 'Women, Publishers, and Money, 1790-1820', *Studies in Eighteenth-Century Culture*, 17, pp. 191-207.

[4] Rendall, J. (1989), 'Friendship and Politics: Barabara Leigh Smith Bodichon (1827-91) and Bessie Rayner Parkes (1828-1925)', in S. Mendus, and J. Rendall (eds), *Sexuality and Subordination*, London; Hughes, K. (1998), *George Eliot*, London.

[5] Coventry Record Office (hereafter CRO), 495/3/1.

Opportunities for Reading

Just like Anna Larpent in London, as described by John Brewer,[6] women in the towns of Warwickshire had plenty of opportunity for reading. A varied literature was distributed and abundantly available on the market place, in the form of cheap tracts, handbills, primers, chapbooks, etc. Sunday Schools, Schools of Industry like the one in Warwick which had a lending library attached to it in 1818, and other such, all had their libraries. Towns provided many new spaces and opportunities for women readers outside the privacy of their homes. By the early 1800s, reading rooms had become quite common on the high streets, and market places of towns. In the *Warwick Advertiser* of 4 January 1817, Heathcote the bookseller and printer on the Market Square 'respectfully informs' his public that 'he has opened a commodious ROOM in which are received two Daily Newspapers, with the *Warwick Advertiser, Birmingham Gazette, Liverpool Mercury*, the *London Price Current*, and several Periodical Publications. Terms of Subscription one guinea per year. Room open to Subscribers from Ten in the morning until Eight in the Evening.' In his *Descriptive Guide to Leamington Priors*, James Bisset advertised his very own 'Ladies and Gentlemen's Reading and News Room' as well as Mr Olorenshaws's and Mr Perry's Rooms, both of them also combined with circulating libraries.

The presence of a strong nonconformist community in the Midlands ensured that reading was on offer, and towns in Warwickshire saw a remarkable development of Public Libraries and circulating libraries.[7] Circulating libraries contributed, more or less exclusively and relatively cheaply, to the diffusion of the 'lighter' kind of literature. By 1800, there were 1000 in England, mostly attached to bookshops in towns, and fiction represented seventy per cent of their stock.[8] Enterprising booksellers like Elizabeth Angel in Stratford-on-Avon kept their stock up to date and advertised in the local press and by the diffusion of handbills, and were fully aware that circulating libraries were a good outlet for the 'three decker novels' on their shelves. During the period between the late 1750s to 1840, there were seventy-six circulating libraries in Birmingham, twenty of them run by women. Women also had access to the Birmingham New Library for Dissenters (1796), the Friends Reading Room, as well as Book Clubs. Coventry boasted twenty circulating libraries, five run by women, as well as two girls' charity schools with libraries. Leamington, coming later on the scene of leisure culture, had twenty-eight libraries by the first decades of the nineteenth century, four of which were run by women. Warwick had eight, one run by a woman, and Stratford

---

[6] Brewer, J. (1996), 'Reconstructing the Reader: Prescriptions, Texts and Strategies in Anna Larpent's Reading', in J. Raven, H. Small and N. Tadmor (eds), *The Practice and Representation of Reading in England*, Cambridge, pp. 162-74.

[7] See Hurwich, J. (1970), 'Nonconformists in Warwickshire, 1660-1720', unpublished University of Princeton PhD thesis; Money, J. (1977), *Experience and Identity, Birmingham and the West Midlands, 1760-1800*, Manchester.

[8] Gregory, P. (1984), 'The Popular Fiction of the Eighteenth-Century Circulating Libraries', unpublished University of Edinburgh PhD thesis.

eight also, with three run by women.[9] The fact that some of these libraries were run by women meant that women who might have been discouraged from frequenting circulating libraries because of the public opprobrium attached to them, felt they could use them with impunity.[10] Jan Fergus tells us that the best clients of booksellers' circulating libraries in the Midlands were women from a professional and commercial background, rather than from country gentry.[11] Booksellers' subscription lists show that novels and especially magazines were popular among women, mostly widows and spinsters who were mistresses of their budgets, and this readership cut through class lines. Although, according to booksellers' records, male readership of fiction was still superior, there is of course no knowing whether their subscriptions were taken on behalf of their wives.[12] There were many widows and spinsters in Warwick, many women of property, and we can assume that they were avid readers of fiction, and probably their servants also, although according to Jan Fergus servants tended to borrow manuals or plays rather than novels.[13]

Fortunately, some of the catalogues of the sometimes ephemeral circulating libraries remain to tell us what was on offer and therefore what was popular; indeed these circulating libraries were a commercial venture, they took careful notice of public demand, and we can assume that their catalogues are fair indicators of what people actually read. Elizabeth Angel's advertising handbill for her circulating library in Stratford in the 1800s sums up pretty well what must have been generally liked. She 'respectfully informs the Inhabitants' of her new 'well-selected stock', 'consisting already of nearly three Hundred Volumes, recently published, Poetry, Plays, Novels, Romances, and Miscellaneous Works, and many other Volumes, written by Authors of Merit and Celebrity, are binding, and a Catalogue is printing.' The 1796 catalogue of John Lowe's circulating library in Birmingham advertised 'many thousand volumes', 1500 of them novels. Warwick, it appears, was a more frivolous town: by 1810, William Perry's circulating library on the Market Place offered well over 2500 titles, many of which showed that there must have been a demand in the town for steamy romances, scabrous stories, and other fiction: *Parson's Wife, Perplexed Lovers, Nunnery for Coquets, Oriental Anecdotes, Fille de Chambre, French Lady, Religious Courtship, Wife and Mistress, Old Wife and Young Husband*, and so on. The kind of circulating library

---

[9] These statistics are available for all counties of England from: www.r-alston.dircon.co.uk/library.htm.

[10] For a good summary of the controversy surrounding circulating libraries at the time, and the negative stereotypes attached to them, see Pearson, J. (1999), *Women Reading in Britain 1750-1835*, Cambridge.

[11] Fergus, J. (2000), 'Women Readers: a Case Study', in V. Jones (ed.), *Women and Literature in Britain 1700-1800*, Cambridge, pp. 155-78.

[12] Fergus, J. (1992), 'Women Readers of Prose Fiction in the Midlands 1746-1800', *Transactions of the Eighth International Congress on the Enlightenment*, Oxford, pp. 1108-12. Interestingly, Fergus says that women who took out subscriptions to magazines, were not the same as those who borrowed books, who were different again from those who bought books. The buyers of books were more likely to be widows and spinsters.

[13] Fergus, J. (1996), 'Provincial Servants' Reading in the Eighteenth Century', in J. Raven, H. Small and N. Tadmor (eds), *The Practice and Representation of Reading in England*, Cambridge, pp. 202-25.

which probably prompted Mr Showell of Birmingham to reassure his public (of women?) that:

> It is much to be regretted that circulating libraries are too frequently the receptacles of demoralizing works, and many complaints have been made that, so few Books, comparatively speaking, are to be obtained from these sources that are worthy of the attention of the Reader whose object is information and instruction as well as amusement.[14]

What these catalogues show is the popularity of women authors, especially in the domain of novels, memoirs and histories, letters, poetry and educational works: Maria Edgeworth and Harriet Martineau, for instance, are as much represented in Showell's catalogue as Walter Scott. Most catalogues also advertise the ubiquitous Mme de Genlis's *Tales of the Castle* and other educational works by her. Like Anna Larpent, some women readers of Warwick also favoured books about women: out of 800 titles of fictional works in William Perry's library, over 200 refer to a woman in the title; there are scores of Amanda, Elvina, Christiana, etc. The Parkes of Warwick, a Unitarian family of drapers turned worsted manufacturers from the late 1790s, were at the centre of a local elite of readers and letter-writers. Their bequest to the Warwick Free Public Library (mentioned in its catalogue of 1866)[15] contained many books written by women such as Lady Montague, Maria Edgeworth and Harriett Martineau again, and many historical memoirs by women, including the popular volumes of histories written by Kate Thomson who, with her sisters, had been a teacher in the town. Her sister Frances, also a writer, married one of the Parkes' sons and wrote under the name of Mrs Parkes.[16] Surprisingly, the bequest does not include Kate Thomson's three volume novel *Constance*; was this because it was too controversial owing to its hardly veiled portraits of Warwick inhabitants?[17] We shall see later what Phoebe Parkes, the daughter of the family, actually read, especially in the way of more ephemeral literature as recorded in her scrapbook.

What women chose to read, however, why they chose to read what they read, and how they read all this literature on offer are problems which still nag historians of reading. On the whole, diaries and letters are mostly silent about the reading habits of their authors, but one modest mine of information, however, is provided by commonplace books and scrapbooks. It is a modest mine because there are not many which have survived, and those that have are not necessarily a true reflection of what was actually read. We are presented only with a selection of what was deemed to be commendable, of lasting interest, and 'worthy': 'the commonplace book did not constitute a record of everything that an individual read, but only of the "beauties" that a reader chose to transcribe'.[18] By means of the commonplace

---

[14] [1832?] Catalogue of Showell's Select Circulating Library, Birmingham.

[15] The 1847 Catalogue of the Warwick Public Library does list the book.

[16] Parkes, Mrs William (1825), *Domestic Duties; or Instructions to Young Married Ladies*, London.

[17] Thomson, K. (1830), *Constance*, 3 vols, London.

[18] Colclough, S. (1998), 'Recovering the Reader, Commonplace Books and Diaries as Sources of Reading Experience', *Publishing History*, 44, pp. 5-38.

books, the great availability of reading matter in towns fostered another role of women as readers, that of contributors to the 'manuscript culture' of the time. As we shall see, women participated assiduously to the transmission of works of literature through selecting and copying excerpts in their commonplace books or scrapbooks.

Women as Writers

But what is of greater interest to us here is that these manuscripts reveal a fascination for the urban setting and the ferment of ideas circulating there. Although Stephen Coulclough gives us examples of other types of serious readers in Lowestoft and Halifax, for instance, not surprisingly most of the few commonplace books which have survived in Warwickshire were kept by nonconformist women, not only because the seriousness of the reading and writing enterprise was part of their education and religious commitment, but also because towns were where Unitarians lived, and towns offered unique opportunities for reading and finding a network of like-minded readers. Like Miss R. of Lowestoft's commonplace book quoted by Colclough, the scrapbook of the Unitarian Phoebe Parkes, whom we have already mentioned, gives us an interesting insight into the urban culture in which she was interested and participated.[19] It is a scrapbook with a theme, that of the urban environment. We are told that Phoebe's parents were eclectic readers and prolific letter-writers,[20] and they probably gave her a good education at home and/or at the school in the High Street of the Misses Byerleys, who were good family friends.[21]

Phoebe's scrapbook contains views of Warwickshire towns, especially Warwick, Leamington, Coventry, and Birmingham, drawn by her or engraved by local artists such as James Bisset and William Rider; writings and portraits of Matthew Boulton and James Watt; newspaper cuttings from the *Gentleman's Magazine*, the *Literary Gazette*, and the *New Monthly Magazine*, as well as one from what might be the *Birmingham Aris Gazette* telling of the celebrations in the town for the opening of the Warwick and Birmingham, and the Warwick and Napton canals in December 1799; articles on nonconformist worthies, especially Joseph Priestley; an article from the *Birmingham Post* on the discovery of oxygen by Priestley; articles on Samuel Parr, the radical Anglican scholar and friend of the family, as well as a description of him written in her hand. The scrapbook also contains a letter from Parr to her, which indicates that he provided her with books and had an interest in her education; it has some lines about Sarah Siddons, the London actress who had been resident in Warwick, as well as a poem by Garrick

[19] Warwick County Record Office (hereafter WCRO), Par, A. (1824), Phoebe Parkes' Scrapbook.

[20] WCRO, Bertie Greatheed's Journals, e.g. 27 October 1805; Field, *Memoirs of The Reverend Samuel Parr,* vol. 2, London.

[21] Two of them, in fact, became the already mentioned authors Kate Thomson, and the other Mrs William Parkes. Kate Thomson also became Elizabeth Gaskell's step-aunt and was consulted by her upon literary matters, see Uglow, J. (1993), *Elizabeth Gaskell*, London.

complaining about the poor hospitality he was given at Warwick Castle; and it has a cutting recounting the visit of Charles Fox to the Warwick monthly meeting of the Whig club at the Crown and Anchor. Finally, Phoebe relates an anecdote which might have been told to her and her family either by Parr himself, or by another family friend, the Reverend William Field, author of the *Memoirs of Samuel Parr*. It relates how Parr sarcastically put down a zealous Church of England man who was querying Parr's flirtation with the Dissenters. We are given here a compendium of urban culture, focused on the local community as affected by wider issues ranging from antiquarian interests to politics, science, and industry. It is suggestive of an active engagement in the culture of the town, and a strong sense of identification with it. It could be said that this scrapbook is a prefiguration of the early feminist interests of Phoebe's niece Bessie Rayner Parkes in Birmingham and London, a generation later.[22] Bessie's ideas, like Phoebe's, would have been influenced by William Field, a Warwick Unitarian minister and friend of the family, to whose school in Leamington Bessie was sent as a boarder from Birmingham.

Sarah Moody Breedon's Commonplace Books in six volumes, each over 600 pages long, give another impressive sample of a serious nonconformist woman reader and writer at work.[23] She was probably related to James Moody, an Independent minister in Warwick in the later part of the eighteenth century, whose letters were published after his death in 1806. Sarah's first and third volumes consist essentially of a collection of sermons preached in Coventry by the charismatic George Burder, a Congregationalist minister and friend of James Moody.[24] Tens of thousands of copies of his sermons were published by the Religious Tract Society, which he himself founded in 1799. There are also a few sermons preached by Quaker women in Evesham and Kenilworth in 1795, and other sermons preached in different towns of Warwickshire. The second volume of her commonplace book contains a cut out and moveable 'geographical clock showing the hour in any part of the world', finely hand-drawn, as well as many astronomical, astrological, and philosophical extracts and notes on gravity, natural phenomena and much more. Volume four is entirely devoted to over 160 extracts on 'The Religious Rites, Ceremonies, and Creeds of every Denominations'. This again shows her eclectic, non-sectarian interests and personal quest. Volumes five and six contain a collection of extracts on a wide variety of subjects, with an accent on philosophical and theological matters, and also notes on animals, music, geology, gas light and such like. Interestingly, she sums up an essay by Mr Dawson 'upon the importance of reading', which is 'not getting through books, but their repeated perusal, until the reader could write a correction to their contents, or an abstract of the design of the writer [...] Nothing worth having is to be obtained except by hard work; and there is no character so truly honourable as that of the *hard worker*.' She has underlined 'hard worker'; not only did she approve, but her

[22] On Bessie Rayner Parkes see Rendall, 'Friendship and Politics', pp. 136-170. See also Hughes, *George Eliot*; Gleadle, K. (1995), *The Early Feminists, Radical Unitarians and the Emergence of the Women's Rights Movement 1831-1851*, New York.

[23] Birmingham Library Archives (hereafter BLA).

[24] Munden, A. (1999), 'George Burder, An Able Minister of the New Covenant', *Warwickshire History*, 1, pp. 37-53.

voluminous books are a testimony that she took the advice seriously. Reading according to the protestant ethic was a hard but ambitious and emancipating task. In fact, in the same volume she copied(?) a short essay of a gently feminist character on woman versus man, and another by Lady Morgan on the necessity of women's emancipation. The Introduction to volume six gives us a very modest explanation of the purpose of these books: 'The 6 Volumes of Gleanings, commenced in the year 1793 were by S.M.B, mainly as references to refresh a treacherous memory. They consist of a confused medley of extracts from some of the best authors, upon various subjects, and might be found useful for private inspection. But by no means to be exposed.'

Here again is the work of a woman reader which reflects the general, ungendered and proto feminist interests of the period and, above all, of her milieu of committed nonconformism which thrived in the towns of the Midlands as well as in London. As is the case for Phoebe Parkes, the influence of Joseph Priestley is obvious in Sarah Moody Breedon's choice of subjects, and also that of George Burder who was himself very interested in science, and electricity in particular. The Mr Dawson whose ideas on reading she is interested in must be George Dawson, another Unitarian radical figure, a preacher in Birmingham and 'a great hero of the Coventry radicals'.[25] She read carefully, she abstracted, and thus transmitted 'some of the best authors'. But her choice is also a reflection of the ideas being debated in the urban fora of Warwickshire, and in the capital, by a network of the radically minded of the time, and at a period which predates even Kathryn Gleadle's 'early feminists'.

The notebook of another Warwickshire young woman around 1810, Henrietta Newsham of Whitnash near Leamington,[26] brings us somewhat nearer to the type of literature offered by the circulating libraries. It starts with a list of expenditure which comprises food, candles, and ribbons, but also three books, pens, ink, pensil [*sic*], and paper. Then follow her 'Notes on books read'. Out of the quite long list of books borrowed over the year — an average of three a month — the works written by women are the majority. Like Sarah, she is an exacting and religious young woman, although the works she quotes are of a lighter kind than those promoted by the former. She has read four metrical historical romances, three of them by women, Miss Seward's letters, three volumes of 'Miss Edgeworth', and she has copied poems by Walter Scott. There is a novel by Mme Cottin which she describes as an 'interesting and moral tale'. She judges the poetry of Crabbe as 'interesting but rather laboured and stiff', and Lord Byron's *Satire upon the Scotch Believers* to be 'very severe if not malignant, some parts rather witty'. Her greatest praise goes to *Lectures on some passages of the Acts of the Apostles* by John Dick, who was a theological writer of considerable standing at the time; she finds him 'very excellent indeed'.

Another commonplace book by a nonconformist woman is that of Mary Russell of Birmingham.[27] Her manuscript starts in October 1790 with a sermon by Doctor

---

[25] Gleadle, *The Early Feminists*, esp. p. 42.

[26] WCRO, Notebook etc. of a young lady, c.1810.

[27] BLA, Commonplace Book of Mary Russell of Showell Green, Birmingham, c.1790.

Priestley: 'a funeral sermon for my dear mother' whom he described as 'an excellent member of this congregation'; a Latin poem 'On a mother' follows, with an 'imitation' of it in English, all written in a beautiful hand, then more poems either copied from books or cut out from newspapers, some of them well known names like Pope, Swift, Ben Johnson, and Gibbon. There is Benjamin Franklin's *Epitaph Written by Himself*, and many more epitaphs and poems on death; epitaphs were then considered as a good moral lesson on the ephemeral character of life. This commonplace book was obviously helping her to grieve over the loss of her mother, a process which was directing the selection of her reading, and which sheds an interesting light on the whole process of what and how readers read.[28]

From these instances we begin to distinguish a type of one kind of readership involving women: they took their task seriously, followed their own inclinations, and probably also the recommendations of conduct books like the eight volumes of *Domestic Duties or Instructions to Young Married Ladies* (1825), written by Phoebe Parkes's sister-in-law, Mrs William Parkes, who recommended her readers to start the day with two hours of serious reading and studying, including 'languages, literature and science'. For the afternoon, she recommended lighter reading such as 'our best novels, biography, poetry, travels, and several of the periodical works'. She also advised that servants should have access to books, but only 'books of an improving nature [should be] put into their hands'. This is a serious programme of reading, and it would seem that the commonplace books we have reviewed were the fruit of the morning type of reading. The afternoon reading is the leisure type offered by the circulating libraries. Mrs Parkes also recommended reading as a social and pleasurable activity, especially if the reading is done by men while women are at their needlework. For us, the commonplace books are a fruit of this approach to reading, as well as a repository of the contemporary urban interests which women were acquainted with and fostered. They show us that, even though women were officially debarred from much of the civic and public life of the town, they were *de facto* interested and active participants.

Engagement with the Urban Environment

The subject of women as writers in the period has been fairly extensively studied in recent years.[29] An interesting aspect of the women writers of the Midlands, however, which we have already found in the commonplace books they kept, is the place they gave to the town in their works. This is no wonder really, as it was the

---

[28] See Brewer, 'Reconstructing the Reader', and Klancher, J.P. (1987), *The Making of English Reading Audiences, 1790-1832*, Wisconsin, for an account of the debate around the reader and the reader's voice.

[29] See for instance Todd, J. (1989), *The Sign of Angellica, Women, Writing and Fiction 1660-1800*, London; and especially Turner, C. (1992), *Living by the Pen, Women Writers in the Eighteenth Century*, London, which contains a good catalogue of women's fiction published in book form. Devine Jump, H. (ed.) (1997), *Women's Writing of the Romantic Period, 1789-1836, An Anthology*, Edinburgh, contains a very extensive bibliography.

development of provincial urban life and culture which, as the other chapters in this volume show, gave women new roles and opportunities. Lady Montague, for example, is the heroine of Mrs Prickett's historical romance *Warwick Castle*, written in the fashionable epistolary style of the time, and published in 1814.[30] Her interest in politics gives us pages full of the debate upon Catholic emancipation which Lady Montague favours. However as the subtitle of her novel indicates, 'With some Account of Warwick, Birmingham, Leamington, Kenilworth, Stratford upon Avon', towns are important protagonists in her romance. Lady Montague went to Leamington to take the waters, which she describes in great scientific details; she also made the best of the town's circulating libraries and Reading Rooms. She found Birmingham even more fascinating: she admired the fact that 'The humblest of its artisans is well-informed', that it had an intelligent philosophical society, and that 'a general sentiment of benevolence...here actuates all ranks'. She describes with enthusiasm the manufactories they visited there. In a bold use of intertextuality, she wrote a romance which is also a guide to the towns of Warwickshire and a guide to other guides, as she recommends James Bisset's just published *Descriptive Guide to Leamington Priors*, with a disclaimer that she was innocent of having seen it before. The town as a setting and protagonist of fiction was then only in its clumsy infancy.

Sarah Medley is one of the very few women of her time to have written a guidebook, which was in fact a town guide. After writing her *Memoirs of Samuel Medley* (1800) about her father, a well-known Liverpool Baptist Minister and writer of hymns, she joined the important nonconformist congregation in Leamington and wrote one of the first guides to the town, *The Beauties of Leamington Priors*, published in Coventry in 1813. In it, she advertised the 'rational' pleasures to be found in a town 'where we find the friends of intellect and liberal mind'. Later, in her 1821 *Visitor's Guide to Leamington Spa*, she added a chapter called 'Reading', where she listed all the Reading Rooms and libraries which by then had appeared in the town.[31]

Kate Thomson, whom we have already met, also chose a town, Warwick, disguised as 'Newberry', as the main setting to her novel *Constance*. Although *Constance* contains endless scenes depicting foreys into country life, Kate Thomson's more sympathetic heroines and heroes are mostly urban inhabitants — a departure from the eighteenth-century trend for romances about country gentry. She is explicit about it:

> The Society at Newberry at this period [the 1780s-1790s] differed in no respect from that of most country town...saving that it was more genteel [...] The younger branches of aristocratic families, retired clergymen, and physicians without practice, of whom its inhabitants were partly composed, looked with contempt upon the commercial portion of their fellow-townsmen, who had, however, the superiority of wealth, and perhaps intelligence, over their haughty neighbours...

---

[30] Prickett, Mrs (1814), *Warwick Castle*, 3 vols, London.

[31] Other examples for town guides by women include Watt, S. (1804), *A Walk Through Leicester*, Leicester; Harvey, J. (1794), *A Sentimental Tour Through Newcastle*, Newcastle.

Unlike the trading middling classes these 'haughty neighbours' had 'no public spirit; no desire for improvement; no taste for innovation...'. Constance's future husband, the Reverend Bouverie, praises the middling classes to her, as opposed to the 'highest and the lowest classes, whose reasoning powers are the least cultivated, their passions the most strongly indulged'.[32] The town was the place where the 'commercial portion' of society and its culture thrived; it was the place where Sarah Medley's 'friends of intellect and liberal mind' could be found. But unlike Sarah Medley, Kate's agenda was not to identify herself with the Warwick urban life which she found too dull and gentrified; she wrote from London where she was leading an active and successful life as a writer. She certainly identified herself with the political language of the new urban middle class which, as described by Dror Wahrman, believed itself to be the 'repository of intelligence', and to be 'associated with social change and in particular the growth of industry'.[33]

Educational Literature

We have seen nonconformist women in their role as serious readers, and as writers about towns. They wrote also for the children who were the future of this urban society. Indeed, they were the most prolific writers of educational literature and generally of literature for children. The urban environment provided women with an increasing demand for such literature, since parents from the middling classes, 'the commercial portion' of the inhabitants, wanted educational books, and general reading matter for their children.[34] It was generally the case that this 'commercial portion' not only allegedly possessed 'superior intelligence', but also comprised many Nonconformists, especially Unitarians eager to promote education amongst young people.

Women who were teachers, or mothers, or both (which was often the case), frequently wrote their own primers and textbooks of stories and poems, according to their requirements, and also for reasons of economy. Many of these texts have been lost, but amongst those authors who wrote for their families and who were published, some wrote under their own name like, for example, Mrs Trimmer, Anna Barbauld, or Mrs Sherwood; others remained anonymous, or occasionally published under their own name when their work had given them the security of success, like Elizabeth Hill the writer of hymns and poems for children, or the teacher and writer Jane Arden.[35] The period we are covering was a period during which a formidable array of women wrote moral tales for the betterment of children, and shaped important areas of the print market in which they could be

[32] Thomson, K. (1830), *Constance*, London, vol. 1, pp. 31-2.

[33] Wahrman, D. (1995), *Imagining the Middle Class*, Cambridge, p. 289.

[34] See Clarke, N. (1997), 'The Cursed Barbauld Crew', in M. Hilton, M. Styles and V. Watson (eds.), *Opening the Nursery Door*, London and New York, pp. 91-103.

[35] Tsurumi, R. (2000), 'Between Hymnbook and Textbook', *Paradigm*, 1, pp. 24-9; Skedd, S. (1997), 'Women Teachers and the Expansion of Girls' Schooling in England, c.1760-1820', in H. Barker and E. Chalus (eds), *Gender in Eighteenth-Century England: Roles, Representations and Responsibilities*, London, pp. 101-25.

described as pioneers. The list is long, but they formed a fairly close-knit network of authors who often pirated but also advertised each other. Maria Edgeworth has young Harry in *Early Lessons for Children* (1809) read 'Mrs Barbauld's little books [...] with which Harry was very much pleased', and Mrs Barbauld, in her own *Lessons for Children* (first published in 1778) has Mary choose Mrs Trimmer's *Natural History* as the book to read in one day, to impress her father. It was thus that we find, among the subscribers to Berquin's *L'Ami des Enfants*, the names of Mrs Barbauld, Mrs Fenn, Miss Burney, and Hannah More.[36] Apart from Thomas Day and William Godwin in England, and Arnaud Berquin in France, male authors were not able to compete. Although Isaac Watt's *Divine and Moral Songs*, a collection of hymns written for children, was still popular, Elizabeth Hill's *The Poetical Monitor* (1796), another collection of hymns, was a remarkably successful successor to it, and went into thirteen editions until the 1830s.[37] It can be safely surmised that all this literature was widely used, and by nonconformist academies and families in particular.

A remarkable trait of this literature, whose clientele were mostly the middle classes, is that it was often written for the lower ranks, the poor, and for girls and mothers. Elizabeth Hill wrote for Protestant Dissenters' charity schools, and praised the Shakespear's [sic] Walk Charity School in London for the children's mental improvement which, in her opinion resulted from the 'female management' of the school.[38] Evangelical Anglican women like Sarah Trimmer and Hannah More wrote principally for Sunday Schools. And if their books were mostly bought by the middling classes, they also found their way into poor homes in the form of tracts and cheap reprints, and they greatly contributed to domestic literacy. These texts, especially those emanating from nonconformist authors, were principally non-devotional, with a moral agenda. In fact, it could be said that women fashioned a new language, a secular language, as part of popular education. It was not the language of Latin grammar, but a language in the spirit of William Cobbetts's *Grammar* (1819), in which he condemned the 'False Grammar', that is the pomposity and verbosity of Latin grammar. Eleanor Fenn, for instance, wrote her *Mother's Grammar* (1804) under the pseudonym of Mrs Lovechild; it addressed itself to mothers and preceptresses, and its author also hoped that 'it will not be unacceptable to those ladies also engaged in tuition'.

Women were the main users of this literature and the pillars of the education of children of all classes, in the home of course,[39] but also in the innumerable Dame Schools, charity schools, Sunday Schools, factory schools, workhouse and prison schools, and Schools of Industry, as well as in the private academies and seminaries, which altogether occupied a sizeable portion of a town's economy and culture; Warwick had them all, and Coventry had something in the order of one

---

[36] Holtom, C. (1997-98), *Catalogue of Children's Books of Instruction and Entertainment from 18th to 20th Century*, St.Teath, Cornwall.

[37] Tsurumi, 'Between Hymnbook and Textbook', pp. 24-9.

[38] Tsurumi, 'Between Hymnbook and Textbook', p. 25.

[39] Vincent, D. (1997), 'The Domestic and the Official Curriculum in Nineteenth-Century England', in M. Hilton, M. Styles and V. Watson (eds.), *Opening the Nursery Door*, London and New York, pp. 161-69.

hundred Dame Schools in our period.[40] We know of the existence of some of these establishments through advertisements in the local press, or through guides and town directories where women teachers are listed under 'Professional Gentlemen' and far outnumber the male teachers. We see the relentless increase in the place of women in education throughout the early decades of the nineteenth century. By the 1830s, Leamington had over fifteen academies — of which two were for gentlemen— run by women, as opposed to five run by men (Pigot's Directory of Warwickshire, and Fairfax', New Leamington Guide, 1832). In Coventry, out of twenty-eight academies and schools, eighteen were run by women. In Birmingham, out of one hundred academies, sixty were run by women (Pigot, 1828-29). In fact, day and boarding private schools for girls were the most numerous, especially in spa towns where the population of girls in need of education far outnumbered that of boys, because they came with their parents or just their mothers, to take the waters while their brothers were in their boarding schools or more prestigious public schools.[41]

Purveyors of the Word

The manuals used in these schools were the sort of texts printed by provincial printers, and in their role as transmitters of the word, women did occupy another public office, beyond teaching, that was in the domain of printing and bookselling, a trade which had traditionally been viewed as acceptable for women. Many women who were wives of printers, booksellers and stationers, often ran circulating libraries attached to the business, for example the twenty women owners of circulating libraries in Birmingham. There also were women who were printers and booksellers either as widows or in their own right, like Elizabeth Angel in Stratford who was also 'patent medicine vender, perfumer etc.'. She was the successor to Mr Keating who had been a printer and bookseller of good repute, and printer of the first Stratford newspaper. Also in Stratford, and roughly at the same time, Elizabeth Walford registered a press in 1799 and the same year published *A Brief Account of Stratford*, while a Mrs Wilkes ran a bookshop.[42]

Coventry also had an important tradition of women printers and booksellers, probably because of the town's long established nonconformist community with its culture of print and reading, and its educational drive with its demand for tracts, sermons, hymns and books.[43] There were eleven recorded women printers and booksellers in the town during the second half of the eighteenth century and the

---

[40] Leinster-Mackay, D.P. (1976), 'Dame Schools: a Need for a Review', *British Journal of Educational Studies*, 34, pp. 33-48.

[41] Money, J. (1993), 'Teaching in the Market-Place: the Importance of Education in the Economy of the English Leisure Towns', in J. Brewer and R. Porter (eds), *Consumption and the World of Goods*, London, p. 343. On the general expansion of girls' schooling see Skedd, 'Women Teachers and The Expansion of Girls' Schooling'.

[42] WCRO, and Stratford Record Office, Morgan, P. (1951), 'Early Booksellers, Printers and Publishers in Stratford-upon-Avon', unpublished document.

[43] Seed, J. (1985), 'Gentlemen Dissenters', *Historical Journal*, 28:2, pp. 299-325.

early nineteenth.[44] In London, women were involved in the most mainstream genres of the period and many women were involved in the print trade.[45] As for most provincial printers at the time, however, the work of these women printers was mostly of the 'jobbing' sort, the kind generated by the administrative and cultural life of towns; but they also printed catalogues, works of local interest, sermons, hymns, and primers in great quantities for the local, especially Sunday Schools; more rarely they might publish and print local newspapers, as in the case of Elizabeth Jopson in Coventry High Street with her very successful *Jopson's Coventry Mercury*. On 27 February 1764 she placed an advertisement in her newspaper to promote her circulating library: 'To be lett [*sic*] out to Read...the following entertaining Books.' Her list of twenty-five works is of the fairly light kind, like *Almira, or the History of a French Lady of Distinction*, or *Genuine Memoirs of Maria, an admired Lady of Rank and Fortune and some of her friends*, 'just published'. There were four volumes of the *Tatler* for good measure, and she also advertised for a New Edition of *Reading made Compleatly [sic] Easy*. She sold wholesale or retail to the local charity schools. Not only did she print in the 'neatest and most expeditious Manner', she also bound, gilt, and lettered books.

Another successful printer in Coventry was Mary Luckman, who printed popular titles such as Bunyan's *Pilgrim Progress*, John Gray's *Fables*, and many such others delightful one penny chapbooks for children, and primers 'written for the amusement of Good Boys and Girls, embellished with cuts', like the popular *Goody Two-Shoes* and Dr Watts' *Songs*. Like Mary Luckman, Ann Rollason took over the business of her husband, Noah Rollason, printer, bookseller and stationer in 1813, and became the owner of the *Coventry Mercury* (no longer the *Jopson's Coventry Mercury*). Her son Charles joined the business in 1820, but it was she who kept it running until 1847, thus going against the London trend which showed a decline in the number of women printers after 1800. Like the Jopsons before her, she was stationer for the Bayley Charity School and its provider of hymn books and Bibles. Elizabeth Jopson, Mary Luckman, and Ann Rollason bear out Hannah Barker's observation that the ease with which widowed women took over a business at the death of their husbands shows that they must have been actively involved in its running before.[46]

Finally, another public involvement of women in the print culture of the time was their role as founders or benefactors of educational charities, especially for girls. In Warwick, for instance, Sarah Greville provided for the education in reading, writing, and arithmetic of the girls in St Peter's Charity School. In Coventry, the first benefactor of the Blue Coat School for girls was a woman, and almost half of the benefactors of the school were in fact benefactresses; the same was true of the Fairfax Charity School, a Quaker school founded by Mrs Southern

---

[44] WCRO, Chamberlaine-Brothers, R. (1990), 'Warwickshire Printers and Booksellers of the 18th Century', unpublished document.

[45] McDowell, P. (2000), 'Women and the Business of Print', in V. Jones (ed.), *Women and Literature in Britain, 1700-1800*, Cambridge, pp. 135-154; Barker, H. (1997), 'Women, Work, and the Industrial Revolution: Female Involvement in the English Printing Trades, c.1700-1840', in H. Barker and E. Chalus (eds), *Gender in Eighteenth Century England: Roles, Representations and Responsibilities*, London, pp. 81-100.

[46] Barker, 'Women, Work and the Industrial Revolution', pp. 94-95.

and Mrs Craner for teaching reading and writing to 36 poor girls in the town. In the Bailey Charity School, founded by Kate Bailey, children were taught reading, writing, arithmetic and 'other branches of secular education'.[47] The Coventry Lancastrian Girls School was founded and run by a committee of women whose task was also to solicit donations or subscriptions.[48] The spinsters and widows of the Warwickshire towns not only used their money to buy books and subscriptions to libraries and magazines, but they also ensured that there would be schools to employ women teachers to teach girls and boys how to read, and eventually, maybe, to enjoy the literature they themselves had read.

Conclusion

We can conclude that in towns, more women than men were involved in teaching and general educational activities in their role as mothers, teachers, and preceptresses. This put them at the centre of the towns' cultural, educational, and commercial life as much as the books they read, wrote, printed, sold, and circulated. As we have seen, towns in the Midlands gave women a better chance for this role than in some other parts of the country because of the concentration of Nonconformists, and because the nonconformist creed fostered literate culture as a means of self-improvement for both sexes. Finally, urban women were 'keepers' of the word in a wide and generous sense because, thanks to the demands and opportunities of urban life, not only did they transmit and interpret the word in various ways and roles but, as we have seen, they also fashioned a new style of written language, simpler, more direct, and less analytical than the Latin English of their educated male counterparts. This is the language which became the language that went into the schools when mass education was finally established later in the century, a token of the creative and pioneering role of women as participants in urban culture.

---

[47] Poole, B. (1870), *Coventry, its History and Antiquities*, London. All these schools were founded in the first half of the eighteenth century and were still going strong into the second half of the nineteenth century.

[48] CRO, 'Rules and Regulations of the Coventry Lancastrian Girls School', [1822-1872].

Chapter 9

Mary Chandler's *Description of Bath* (1733): A Tradeswoman Poet of the Georgian Urban Renaissance*

David E. Shuttleton

Mary Chandler's *A Description of Bath...in a letter to a friend* (1733) is one of the earliest examples of a sustained urban topographical poem by a woman.[1] It is a substantial prospect poem surveying the geographical, historical, social and moral topography of a provincial, urban landscape in which she herself was an economic participant. It is also, as I shall argue, an overtly political poem, and as such represents a significant attempt by an early-Georgian woman to assume a public role in civic mapping. The poem itself is discussed in some detail in the latter half of this chapter. In the first half, after this brief introduction, I provide some biographical, historical, and literary contexts within which we should read Chandler's representation of Bath.

Chandler's *Description of Bath* was originally published anonymously, but was expanded and re-titled from a third edition of 1734 onwards as *The Description of Bath: a Poem, Humbly Inscribed to Her Royal Highness the Princess Amelia, by Mrs Chandler to which are added several poems.* With amendments, in this form it reached an eighth edition by 1767, over twenty years after the poet's death. Unlike many Bath-inspired poems of the period — what Steele pejoratively dubbed, Bath's 'Water Poetry' — Chandler's *Description* is not merely a jeu-d'esprit by an occasional visitor, but a substantial piece of civic propaganda by a propertied local

* This essay is a substantially revised version of 'Mary Chandler's *Description of Bath (1733)*; the poetic topographies of an Augustan tradeswoman', *Women's Writing*, 7:3, (2000), pp. 447-67. I must thank the editors for permission to reproduce parts of that essay, and in particular the special-issue editor Sarah Prescott, for her editorial and critical support.

[1] Mary Chandler's shorter poems are represented in Lonsdale, R. (ed.) (1989), *Eighteenth-Century Women Poets: An Anthology*, Oxford, pp. 151-54; an extract from her 'Description of Bath' is reprinted in Lonsdale, R. (ed.) (1984), *The New Oxford Book of Eighteenth Century Verse*, Oxford.

resident.[2] Mary Chandler (1687-1745), was herself a commercial participant in the spa town's rapid expansion in the early decades of the century. In a sketchy account of his sister, her brother Samuel noted that family financial pressures had demanded that his eldest sister was trained from a young age for 'trade'.[3] In about 1705 she had opened a millinery shop 'opposite the Pump Room Bath', at the town's social hub.[4]

Chandler developed an interest in poetry in childhood, but only received a limited home education and to her own frustration she was only able to read the classical poets in translation (she particularly admired Horace). As she acknowledges, her principal poetic model was Alexander Pope, but his work of the 1730s adopts an increasingly oppositional political stance, whereas Chandler occupies an Old Whig, pro-Hanoverian position in accordance with her nonconformist family background. Her father, Henry Chandler, a leader of Bath's Presbyterian community, was described by anecdotalist John Nichols as a learned man who, 'descended from ancestors heartily engaged in the cause of Nonconformity' and whose own father, a Taunton tradesman, had 'much injured his fortune by his principles.'[5] This activist nonconformist tradition was to be maintained by Mary Chandler's brother Samuel, briefly a London bookseller, but latterly a minister and author of numerous, influential works of nonconformist exegesis and polemic. He was to become, in the words of Paul Langford, 'the uncrowned patriarch of Dissent in the latter part of George II's reign'.[6] As both shopkeeper and poet Mary Chandler benefited from this west-country, nonconformist family network with firm London connections. When poor health finally forced her to retire from business in 1745, she not only owned 'a well and long-accustom'd Milliners Shop', but she had also paid for the building of a substantial lodging-house in a dissenter-owned enclave just off Bath's fashionable Orange Grove.[7]

---

[2] *The Guardian*, 174, 30 September 1713.

[3] Chandler, S. (1753), 'Life of Mary Chandler', in *An Account of the Lives of the Poets of Britain and Ireland,* 5 vols, R. Shiells (ed.), London, i, pp. 345-54 (p. 348), (misleadingly attributed to Theophilus Cibber). Also Lonsdale, *Eighteenth-Century Women Poets*, pp. 151-2.

[4] For Bath history see Barbauld, A. (1906), *Life and Letters at Bath in the Eighteenth Century*, London; Borsay, P. (1989), *The English Urban Renaissance: Culture and Society in the Provincial Town, 1660-1770*, Oxford; Neale, R.S. (1981), *Bath 1680-1850: A Social History*, London. According to Neale, the number of houses in Bath approximately doubled between 1700 and 1743, and the population tripled by 1800 (Table 2.i, p. 44).

[5] Nichols, J. (1812), *Literary Anecdotes of the Eighteenth Century*, 6 vols, London, v, pp. 304-5.

[6] Langford, P. (1989 reprinted 1992), *A Polite and Commercial People: England 1727-1738*, Oxford, p. 85.

[7] Advertisement in *The Bath Journal* for 8 April 1745. For her lodging-house, subsequently the Grove Tavern, (demolished), which had 'two large kitchens, five rooms at parlour level, another five at dining level, five atticks and six garretts', see Fawcett, T. and Inskipp, M. (1994), 'The Making of Orange Grove', *Bath History*, 5, pp. 24-50.

Chandler's poetic career coincides with the first public construction of the professional English woman writer.[8] Feminist literary historians have recently been concerned to recover the terms upon which late seventeenth- and early eighteenth-century women poets achieved a measure of linguistic and political legitimacy.[9] Carol Barash, in her excellent study of *English Women's Poetry, 1649-1714*, offers a substantial account of a predominantly pro-Stuart, High-Church, courtly poetic tradition traceable back to Phillips, Behn and Killigrew; one which, following political marginalisation in the 1690s, and as later manifest in the work of Anne Finch, Countess of Winchilsea, sought further legitimacy through the symbolic authority of Queen Anne.[10] But Barash, of necessity, tends to exclude women from a low-church, Williamite and whiggish tradition associated with Locke's notions of political and religious 'Liberty'.[11] It is within this tradition — yet to find a comparable historian — of a younger, post-Revolution generation of pro-Hanoverian women poets active after 1714, that Chandler belongs.

Women and 'the Town': Gender, Trade and Poetry

The post-Revolution period saw a flowering of urban descriptive poetry, largely about London and predominantly produced by men; a sub-genre, as represented by Jonathan Swift's so-called 'Town Eclogues' (1709), John Gay's *Trivia: or the Art of Walking the Streets of London* (1716), Alexander Pope's *Dunciad* (1728; 1742)

---

[8] Some key studies include, Spencer, J. (1986), *The Rise of the Woman Novelist: from Aphra Behn to Jane Austen*, Oxford; Hobby, E. (1988), *Virtue of Necessity: English Women's Writing, 1649-1688*, London; Todd, J. (1989), *The Sign of Angellica: Women, Writing and Fiction 1649-1800*, London; Shevelow, K. (1989), *Women and Print Culture: The Construction of Femininity in the Early Periodical*, London and New York; Ballaster, R. (1992), *Seductive Forms: Women's Amatory Fiction from 1684-1740*, Oxford; Turner, C. (1992), *Living by the Pen: Women Writers in the Eighteenth Century*, London and New York.

[9] Barash, C. (1993) '"The Native Liberty...of the Subject": Configurations of Gender and Authority in the Works of Mary Chudleigh, Sarah Fyge Egerton and Mary Astell', in I. Grundy and S. Athens (eds), *Women, Writing and Authority 1640-1799*, Carbondale, pp. 55-69; Mermin, D. (1990), 'Women Becoming Poets: Katherine Philips, Aphra Behn, Anne Finch', *English Literary History*, 57, pp. 335-55; and Greer, G. (1995), *Slip-Shod Sybils: Recognition, Rejection and the Woman Poet*, Harmondsworth.

[10] Barash, C. (1997), *English Women's Poetry, 1649-1714: Politics, Community, and Linguistic Authority*, Oxford.

[11] Whilst Barash does give a brief account of women's poetry under William and Mary she quickly turns to the figure of Mary's sister, Anne (Barash, *English Women's Poetry*, pp. 209-216). As Barash remarks, any account would need to give careful consideration to the ambivalent status accorded Locke by feminist historians, and the identification of women poets with William's martial exploits.

and Samuel Johnson's *London* (1738). Such poems frequently employ the ironic tropes of mock-Virgilian pastoral to draw a contrast between corrupt modern town manners and traditional rural virtues. Thus in Gay's *Trivia* the seasonal round of country life in Virgil's Georgics finds a parodic parallel in the diurnal and seasonal rhythms of London life. Augustan urban poetry is essentially satirical, often echoing the tirades against the luxurious, effeminate and vicious manners of urban life by the Roman poet Juvenal, even if, as certainly is the case with Gay, the poetry can evince a certain delight in the social jumble of the Georgian urban scene.

As a seasonal recreational retreat for the Hanoverian elite, Bath suggested a 'town away from town'; one which increasingly promised both pastoral pleasures *and* town luxuries. Chandler's gender, her provincial context and her commercial, dissenter background, all served to place her urban vision at a certain critical tangent from that of her male, London-based, and predominantly Tory poetic contemporaries. One obvious point of comparative reference might be Lady Mary Wortley Montagu's own series of 'Town Eclogues' (written c. 1714-15, some in collaboration with Gay), one for each day of the week, which satirise life in and around the Court at St James's Palace. Until recent feminist re-appraisal, even these lively satires have occupied a rather tenuous place at the borders of a masculine Augustan canon, being largely mentioned in passing in the context of Pope's later, mysteriously rebarbative estrangement from Lady Mary, a one-time friend. Though Chandler and Lady Mary were both staunch Hanoverians, the former, as a parochial nonconformist shopkeeper was writing from a very different social position to that of the scholarly and well-connected Whig aristocrat. A noted wit, Lady Mary exercised considerable influence as the Turkish ambassador's wife who promoted variolation for small-pox and as the eventual mother-in-law to a prime minister (Bute).[12] In old age Lady Mary complained to her daughter that 'the confounding of all Ranks and making a jest of order has long been growing in England, and I perceive by the books you sent me, has made a very considerable progress. The Heros and Heroines of the age are Coblers and Kitchin Wenches'. The measure of the age, Lady Mary insisted, could be gained from such 'Triffling authors' who 'write merely to get money'.[13] So whilst Chandler, like Lady Mary, published poetry in a society with highly proscriptive conceptions of respectable female positioning and social mobility, it was also in the face of such contested class assumptions regarding who had claims on literary representation and authority.

In the work of Chandler's male contemporaries (Pope, Swift and Gay), the term 'trade', particularly through its association with the debased values of a Grub Street world of 'modern' commodified literary production, is often brought into pejorative conjunction with the feminine as a common, transvaluated target of satirical repudiation. In *The Dunciad*, for example, contemporary women writers

---

[12] Grundy, I. (1999), *Lady Mary Wortley Montagu: Comet of the Enlightenment*, Oxford; for her 'Town Eclogues' see Chapter 7.

[13] Montagu, Lady Mary Wortley, (1997), *Selected Letters*, in I. Grundy (ed.), Harmondsworth, pp. 388-89.

like 'Corinna', the proto-feminist poet Elizabeth Thomas (1675-1731) and author of her own urban satire, *The Metamorphoses of the Town: or A View of the Present Fashions* (1730), are portrayed negatively, as literary whores and as such symptomatic of the collapse of classical, patrician values.[14] More broadly, in much post-Restoration writing (by both men and women), by the very nature of their purportedly unruly sexuality, women are prone to trade in the derogatory sense of sexual "trafficking" and, given their purported vanity, they are vulnerable to new consumer desires. To pick an obvious example, in William Wycherley's Restoration stage-comedy of London manners, *The Country Wife* (1675), despite her jealous husband's sadistic efforts to the contrary, the eponymous heroine transforms from an innocent country-girl to a sexually knowing woman of the town. In the play's bawdy 'China Scene', the humour depends upon some blatant double-entendres through which the rivalry of the 'Virtuous Gang' of fashionable town women haggling over buying porcelain serves to thinly disguise their sexual voracity as they fight for the sexual favours of the rake Horner. Similarly in Pope's depiction of Belinda as a vain, flirtatious young girl at the court of Queen Anne, in *The Rape of the Lock* (1714) (Canto I), her very heart is shown to be nothing more than a 'Toy-Shop' full of superfluous trinkets. Indeed throughout the century women were targeted as the promoters of an effeminising Luxury. It was within this potentially hostile critical climate that Chandler, herself a tradeswoman selling fancy trimmings to the *beau monde*, presumed to publish her Bath poem.

Unlike her male contemporary Gay, Chandler's gender precluded her from adopting his lone urban persona as a fascinated proto-flaneur who dirties his shoes and coat-tails as he makes his mock-heroic journey through the dangerous streets of London. This image of a street-walker was obviously to be avoided by a woman poet aspiring to gentility.[15] Rather, as she 'dares to raise her Voice, and stretch her Wings', Chandler's pervasive metaphor is of poetic flight and as such renders her *Description* more appropriately comparable with a disembodied journey into 'Virtual Reality', as she imaginatively constructs a refined city fit for a self-consciously genteel female poet.[16]

---

[14] Pollack, E. (1985), *The Poetics of Sexual Myth: Gender and Ideology in the Verse of Swift and Pope*, Chicago; McWhir, A. (1995), 'Elizabeth Thomas and the Two Corinnas: Giving the Woman Writer a Bad Name', *English Literary History*, 62, pp. 105-19.

[15] Nokes, D. (1995), *John Gay: A Profession of Friendship*, Oxford; 'Trivial Pursuits', pp. 197-230.

[16] Chandler's immediate model for her use of this metaphor is the opening of John Denham's, *Cooper's Hill*. My 'virtual' image is borrowed from Shoemaker's comment that 'the new form of public space created by the proliferation of printed literature, [was] a kind of eighteenth- and nineteenth-century virtual reality in which works created in private could be distributed throughout society'. Shoemaker, R.B. (1997), *Gender in English Society, 1650-1850: The Emergence of Separate Spheres?*, Harlow, p. 315.

Perhaps inevitably Chandler felt obliged to offer extended formal gestures of apology for her social presumption in entering the masculine world of letters. In a typically self-effacing 'Dedication' added to her *Description of Bath*, and so common in women's poetry anthologies of this period, she declares that she is 'far from assuming any airs on account of this mean performance; but would rather chuse [sic] to be taken notice of as one who deals honestly in trade, and behaves decently in the relations of life, than as a writer; since I am conscious I have a better right to the first, than the last character.'[17] But despite this disclaimer, which reverses the terms of many aristocratic women poets, like Lady Mary — who typically resorted to manuscript circulation, and anonymity or pseudonyms in order to distance herself from the stigma of literary commerce — Chandler clearly did claim some 'right' to a place in the public realm of genteel poetry, whilst unashamedly declaring, if sometimes bemoaning her dependence upon trade.[18] Highly conscious of insisting upon his sister's gentility, her brother Samuel posthumously emphasised a conflict in his sister's career wherein 'the hurries of the life which her circumstances at Bath threw her, sat frequently heavy upon a mind so entirely devoted to books and contemplation' so that Bath 'especially in the Season, but too often furnished her with characters in her own sex that were extremely displeasing to her.'[19] He is at some pains to shift the emphasis away from shopkeeping and onto poetic activity — here a signifier of gentility — as he foregrounds the assumed incompatibility of his sister's pious literary sensibilities with her necessary contact with Bath's world of commodified pleasure. Here it might be noted that milliner's shops in particular where commonly portrayed as mere fronts for brothels.

Samuel Chandler's improper women were presumably those bounty hunters and pleasure-seekers who were drawn to Bath, which increasingly functioned as both marriage market and gambling-den. Chandler's complex relationship with this fashionable world was also influenced by the fact that, in the words of her brother, she 'had nothing in her shape to recommend her, being grown, by an accident in her childhood, very irregular in her body'.[20] Elsewhere I have discussed the often conflicted images of embodiment in Chandler's occasional poetry within the context of her doubly marginalised, subject-position of being self-consciously marked as both a 'cripple' and a spinster.[21] Chandler consciously chose to remain single, pursuing a life characterised by self-education, financial independence,

---

[17] Chandler, *Description of Bath*, p. i (added to post 1734 editions). Unless otherwise stated, subsequent references, in brackets, are to the 1734, 3rd edn.

[18] By one estimate, half of the women's poetry prefaces published between 1667 and 1750 make apologies for the author's sex; see R.G. Gibson, '"My Want of Skill": Apologies of British Women Poets 1660-1800', in F.M. Keener and S.E. Lorsch (eds) (1988), *Eighteenth-Century Women and the Arts*, New York and London, pp. 79-81, as cited by Shoemaker, *Gender in English Society*, p. 283.

[19] Shiells, *An Account of the Lives of the Poets of Britain and Ireland*, p. 346.

[20] Shiells, *An Account of the Lives of the Poets of Britain and Ireland*, p. 348.

[21] Shuttleton, D.E. (1998), '"All Passion Extinquish'd": The Case of Mary Chandler (1687-1745)', in I. Armstrong and V. Blaine (eds), *Women's Poetry of the Enlightenment: the Making of the Canon, 1730-1820*, London, pp. 33-49.

piety and a genteel poetic reputation. Both Claudia Thomas and Linda Veronica Troost have recently noted the obvious parallel with Pope, who was similarly deformed, and who reputedly 'favoured her [Chandler] with his friendship at Bath, and complimented her for her poem on that place.'[22] Thomas observes that 'Chandler's image of herself as a sickly, ill-shaped, female Horatian recluse, who prefers her distinguished friendships and her muse to marriage, recalls Pope's frequent autobiographical references to his own stature, friendships, hospitality, and bachelor status', though she rightly adds that to do so 'was a bolder stroke for an unmarried milliner than a genteel male poet'.[23] But whilst, as Helen Deutsch has recently analysed, Pope's monstrous frailty supposedly accounted for his barbed satires, Chandler's deformity and consequent valetudinarianism was used to explain an 'extreme sensibility', and a life characterised by her brother as one of long-suffering self-control, ending in ascetic renunciation.[24]

Chandler's poems support her brother's claim that she accepted early in life that 'the disadvantages of her shape' removed her from the marriage market which formed the basis for Bath's social season, but upon which, as milliner and hotelier she was nevertheless economically dependent. 'A True Tale' in particular, presents a self-parodic explanation of why she has refused a proposal of marriage made by an elderly man of substance entering her shop, ostensibly to buy gloves, around 1741 (when she was 54).[25] The poem amounts to a forthright declaration of emotional and intellectual independence as Chandler publicly offers a distinctly anti-romantic account of being treated like a commodity in her own shop-window or, given her physical condition, perhaps like someone in a provincial freak-show exposed to public curiosity. Whilst she uncomfortably joins in the public laughter at a man who walks 'Fourscore miles, to buy a crooked wife/Old too! I thought the oddest thing in Life', she then exposes his selfish, patronising motives (he needed someone 'to help life glide more smoothly near its end', and assumed she needed economic rescue). Chandler wittily subverts the accepted meanings of physical mobility and ownership by declaring that she would 'rather walk alone my own slow pace', than be 'imprision'd' in a six-horse coach when 'Sir...may hold the string [rein]'. After all, she can easily afford to hire a chariot when she needs one, though she prefers to 'ramble and retire' away from the social gaze.

---

22 Shiells, *An Account of the Lives of the Poets of Britain and Ireland*, p. 345; Thomas, C. (1994), *Alexander Pope and His Eighteenth-Century Female Readers*, Carbondale and Edwardsville, pp. 98-102; Troost, L.V. (1996), 'Geography and Gender: Mary Chandler and Alexander Pope', in D.C. Mell (ed.), *Pope, Swift and Women Writers*, Newark and London, pp. 67-85. Pope left no verifiable comments on Chandler.

23 Thomas, *Alexander Pope*, p. 199.

24 Deutsch, H. (1996), *Resemblance and Disgrace: Alexander Pope and the Deformation of Culture*, Boston, *passim*, but especially Chapter 1, where she illustrates how, for many of the poet's literary enemies, 'Pope's body explicates the evil within', p. 23.

25 Reprinted in Lonsdale, *Eighteenth-Century Women Poets*, p. 152.

Of several retirement poems expressing a desire for pastoral retreat, Chandler's 'My Wish' is the most closely modelled upon Horace's *Beatus Ille.* It constructs a consoling fantasy of an independent life of spiritual and literary study with 'A Mind from Bus'ness free' and 'A Fortune from Incumbrance clear, /About a Hundred Pounds a Year' (p. 66). 'My Wish' was later reprinted alongside 'A True Tale' in the poetry column of *The Gentleman's Magazine* in 1770, where an anonymous correspondent offered the following framing, narrative comment:

> Mr Urban, I send you what I think a literary curiosity, viz, a copy of verses formerly written by an old maid, who kept a glove shop at Bath, which had the good effect to procure a real courtship; but tho' the writer was old and crooked, she had yet fortitude enough to withstand the tempting offer of her admirer, and to prefer competancy and independence to splendid wealth and senile submission![26]

Discussing Mary Chandler in the 1920s, Oswald Doughty with equal condescension imagined the 'quiet and monotonous existence' of his apparently loveless subject, and he was clearly thrilled to find that she was belatedly blessed by the romantic attentions of a man.[27] He grossly misreads 'A True Tale' as merely a tragic story of 'Mr Right' arriving too late. More sympathetically Thomas has recently cited 'My Wish', 'A True Tale' and Chandler's other poems espousing independent spinsterhood, as illustrative of a feminocentric adaptation of the Horatian model, concluding that Pope functions as an 'alter-ego', as Chandler 'identifies herself with his professional and political integrity, but protects her feminine identification with private life.'[28] This is an important revision, but the emphasis upon psychology does run some risk of suggesting that Chandler's poetry is exclusively concerned with a feminine 'private life', whereas in her eponymous *Description of Bath*, as we shall see shortly, Chandler engages with a public world of civic history and dynastic politics. [29]

The local success of her *Description of Bath* clearly brought Chandler some public visibility within the literary, economic, and civic landscape of early-Georgian Bath, but as suggested above, her shorter, more personal poems largely confirm her own eagerness to repudiate a world of fashionable female consumption

---

[26] *The Gentleman's Magazine*, 40, 1770, pp. 433-34.

[27] Doughty, O. (1925), 'A Bath Poetess of the Eighteenth Century', *The Review of English Studies*, 1:4 , pp. 404-420.

[28] Thomas, *Alexander Pope*, pp. 197-8. She discusses 'A Letter to the Right Honourable the Lady Russell...', in which Chandler rejects a suggestion from condescending patrons that she should marry one 'C----', a farmer, because, 'Two Bodies so exactly paired ! 'tis plain/ "Heav'n made the Match, and destin'd him the Man"'. I find no justification for Thomas's suggestion that this might allude to Pope.

[29] For the notion of 'separate spheres' see: Riley, D. (1988), "*Am I that Name?" Feminism and the Category of Woman in History*, Basingstoke, pp. 44-51; Klein, L. (1995), 'Gender and the Public/Private Distinction in the Eighteenth Century: Some Questions About Evidence and Analytic Procedure', *Eighteenth-Century Studies*, 29, pp. 97-109; recent debates reviewed in Shoemaker, *Gender in English Society*, ch. 8.

and embrace a pious, pastoral retreat. In all its later editions her *Description of Bath* itself is accompanied by several shorter pastoral poems attesting to Chandler's gratitude for the therapeutic relief from the pressures of the commercial world of Bath to be gained in the gardens and landscaped grounds on the country estates of a circle of landed west-country patronesses, with whom she seems to have been on more intimate terms than her position as a milliner might at first suggest.[30] But whilst much Augustan pastoral poetry celebrates retreating from the pressures of court life — as in, for example, the work of Chandler's younger, aristocratic contemporary, Anne Finch, author of 'The Petition for an Absolute Retreat' — Chandler strikes a middle-class note in celebrating rural retirement as a respite from shopkeeping. Chandler's is not a celebration of that self-sufficient, paternalistic rural economy described in earlier Cavalier country-house poems, but rather it suggests an emergent bourgeois 'structure of feeling', identified by Raymond Williams in Pope's early *Epistles*, in which the country house is less a symbol of a purportedly received and natural feudal social order, but of 'productive investment' and 'the creation rather than the celebration of Nature'.[31] For, as Williams notes, now in this post-Glorious Revolution settlement a house in the country is the reward for a life which demands time spent in the commercial bustle of the town or city. As Chandler herself celebrates, these new country houses are placed, 'at an easy distance from the Town' (Bath or Bristol), and the view from Old Sodbury manor, home of her patroness 'Mrs Stephens', is of new suburban villas and the commercial river-traffic of the Bristol Channel.[32]

'To Sing the Town Where Balmy Waters Flow...'

Linda Veronika Troost has recently observed that Chandler's Bath poem 'follows a well established tradition of topographical poetry' which effectively combines various classically derived forms: the journey poem, the town poem, the country house poem, the satiric spa poem, and the meditative local poem. For Troost, in *A Description of Bath*, Chandler 'avoids the linear organization of space even though her imagination seems to move from the city to the country', for 'she favours

[30] Shiells, *An Account of the Lives of the Poets of Britain and Ireland*, p. 346-7. Several poems record these retreats; see 'To Mrs Boteler' or less obscurely to 'Mrs Jacobs on Her Seat Called The Rocks, in Gloucestershire' or 'To Mrs Stephens at Sodbury', near Bristol. Other patrons included Elizabeth Rowe and Frances Seymour, Countess of Hertford. See Prescott, S. and Shuttleton, D.E. (2001), 'Mary Chandler, Elizabeth Rowe and "Ralph's Miscellany": A Coincidental Biographical and Bibliographical Note', *Notes and Queries*, 246:1, pp. 31-4.

[31] Williams, R. (1973), *The Country and the City*, London, p. 69.

[32] Chandler, 'To Mrs Jacob on Her Seat Called The Rocks', *The Description of Bath*, p. 74.

instead, circular or ring structures (typical of "feminine" romance)', and passing 'linearly through the streets of Bath to Prior Park' she 'meanders, only to return to where she started'. Moreover, noting Chandler's (in fact, somewhat sceptical) allusion to the physico-theologian, Thomas Burnet's cyclical theories of geological time in his *Sacred Theory of the Earth* (1684), Troost also claims that Chandler's 'organization of time sequences...eschews the linearity of the chronological', because she apparently, 'chooses circles and spheres for divinity, elevating the circle where Pope elevates the phallic line'.[33]

Such a formalist reading, which — despite Troost's initial use of quotation marks — assumes an untenable, reductive equation between circularity and 'the feminine', between 'linearity' and phallicism is problematically based upon an essentialist, ahistorical, and universalising conception of femininity rooted in the corporeal rhetoric of French feminism.[34] Nevertheless Troost alerts us to the significance of female authorship and provides some valid classical and neo-classical formal precedents for Chandler's poem, including the importance of John Denham's topographical model in *On Cooper's Hill* (1642), as once noted by Samuel Johnson:

> [Denham] seems to have been...the [original] author of a species of composition that may be denominated local poetry, of which the fundamental subject is some particular landscape, to be poetically described, with the addition of such embellishments as may be supplied by historical restrospection or incidental meditation.[35]

For my materialist reading, I want to emphasise the word 'embellishments' here. This might deceptively suggest the merely aesthetic or ornate: but like Denham's *Cooper's Hill*, Chandler's *Description of Bath* does not merely describe a pre-existent reality, but does so through a not fully transparent language loaded with rhetorical embellishments which seek to naturalise her particular version of the spa-town. Chandler's *Description of Bath* offers a historically, politically and indeed gender-specific ideological intervention in so far as it actively constructs an ethically prescriptive topography of sociability, portraying Bath as a model landscape for the enactment of an emerging, enlightenment ideal of civilised, consumerist pleasure.

Discussing traditional accounts of the social organisation of space in Georgian Bath as simply expressions of 'the Age of Reason', the Marxist social historian R. S. Neale asserts that 'the space in Bath is an historical conjuncture and a social

---

[33] Troost, 'Geography and Gender', pp. 67-8.

[34] Troost, 'Geography and Gender'. Troost's footnote refers to Luce Irigaray and Jaques Derrida on 'the phallus as transcendental signifier' in Toril Moi's *Sexual/Textual Politics*. I can see nothing particularly 'feminine' in the cyclical theories of post-Newtonian physico-theology: theories produced by male virtusoi but used by male poets like Thomson as much as by women.

[35] Samuel Johnson, *Lives of the Poets*, 'Denham', as quoted by Troost, 'Geography and Gender', p. 67.

form deriving its meaning from the social processes expressed through it.'[36] Chandler's *Description* belongs to a particular historical juncture, but as already suggested, is also significant in being produced by a woman. Introducing *Engendering the City* (1997), a collection of essays on contemporary women's urban photography, Marsha Meskinnon notes that 'space is neither empty nor neutral', but rather 'a central organising metaphor for all forms of social discourse'. As a consequence 'space is neither empty of cultural forms, like some pre-existent *tabula rasa*, nor is it a gender-neutral stage on which people act.'[37] Thus, Chandler's use of the urban prospect poem can be read as a peculiarly female exercise in what Frederic Jameson has influentially described as 'cognitive mapping'; but whereas Jameson is concerned with a shift from a modern to post-modern spatiality, Chandler's poem records the imaginative negotiation of a shift not so much, in my reading, from abstract linear to circular structures, but from pre-capitalist feudal town to a modern resort based upon early market-led, entrepreneurial capitalism.[38]

I want to preface my own reading of Chandler's *Description* with an entry from Bath's City Council minutes for 1738-9 which casts a quaintly quotidian light upon Mary Chandler's proprietary relationship with the historical fabric of the city eulogised in her poem:

> It is ordered by the Corp[aratio]n that Mrs Mary Chandler of the City of Bath, spinster, shall forthwith repair or cause to be repaird Under the Inspection of the mayor, Justices & Chamberlain of the said City The Townwall that she hath made use of near the Eastgate whereon she has ordered some buildings - and shall keep the said Wall in substantial repairs for ever after and also pay for all such Stones that her workmen have made use of belonging to the Townwall af[or]s[ai]d or other Incroachments these together with such fine as shall be impos'd on her or her assigned at any time hereafter...[39]

---

[36] Neale, *Bath 1680-1850*, p. 174.

[37] Meskinnon, M. (1997), *Engendering the City: Women Artists and Urban Space* [*Nexus I: Theory and Practice in Contemporary Women's Photography*], London, p. 1. Inspired by Walter Benjamin's 'Arcades Project', theoretical studies have tended to focus upon the modern city, but students of the English Enlightenment have made much critical use of Jurgen Habermas's (1989) now much-discussed model in *The Structural Transformation of the Public Sphere*, translated by T. Burger and F. Lawrence, Cambridge. For how attention to gender difference has been crucial in questioning to any simplistic notion of seperate spheres see Shoemaker, *Gender in English Society*.

[38] Jameson, F. (1991), *Postmodernism: or the Cultural Logical of Late Capital*, London, pp. 50-54; pp. 409-17. Jameson derived the term 'cognitive mapping' from Klein, K. (1960), *The Image of the City*, Cambridge Mass.

[39] Bath Council Minute Books. I must thank Colin Johnstone for transcribing references to Chandler in the Bath City Archive.

The members of the Council had in fact already decided that Mary Chandler 'shall have no Liberty to build on the Town wall nor make any Windows in the same', and had actually gone in person to examine these encroachments onto the fabric of the incorporated City boundary. The poet was subsequently fined five guineas 'for the Stones she had caused to be taken' and ordered to pay 'ten Shillings and Sixpence per annum for the said Incroachments'. This vandalism, aimed at letting in light, had been perpetrated by the builders employed by Chandler to construct her aforementioned lodging-house adjoining the City Walls on a desirable plot between the Abbey Church and the Orange Grove.

This amusing local property issue encapsulates the tensions being generated by the rapid process of modernisation which was transforming Bath in the 1730s, but as such it probably reflects less any proto-conservation movement, but rather the anxieties of an established municipal authority over the spread of buildings beyond, if not actually through the Old Town Walls, and therefore out with their ancient jurisdiction (here, Chandler found herself in good company: amongst others a 'Rev'd Kennet' was similarly fined).[40] The illicit gleaning of stones from the walls also posed a threat to the profits of the council's leading member, the entrepreneur and stone-quarry owner, Ralph Allen. All-told, this incident must have been mildly embarrassing for the author of *A Description of Bath* which closes with a eulogy to Allen's architectural and landscaping improvements at nearby Prior Park.

Chandler's *Description* was frequently raided for specific images, serving to fix an emerging canon of established tourist sites. The printer-novelist Samuel Richardson, for example, who printed most editions of the poem for his own brother-in-law, the Bath bookseller James Leake, then nepotistically added her complimentary poetic description of Leake's bookshop to his own 1742 revised edition of Defoe's *Tour Through the Whole Island of Great Britain*.[41] But it was Chandler's closing eulogy to Allen which drew most attention amongst the London *literati*. In 1733 Allen had instigated work on a Palladian house and landscaped grounds at Prior Park on his Widcombe estate above Bath. Based upon the designs of his business partner, the architect John Wood, who was about to have such an impact upon Bath's urban landscape, this palatial show-house, self-consciously constructed as a form of civic self-advertising, and in particular to prove the strength of Bath freestone, was far from being complete when Chandler's *Description* first appeared.[42] In his biography of Allen, Benjamin Boyce rightly reads Chandler's poetic portrait of the postal officer and quarry-owner as a response to Pope's satirical picture of Timon and his vulgarly ostentatious villa in

---

[40] I must thank Peter Borsay for his kind help with Bath historical references and a conversation which prompted my ideas in this paragraph.

[41] Richardson, who knew Mary Chandler's family in London, printed all editions of her poem between 1734 and 1755.

[42] For Allen's relations with Wood see Varey, S. (1990), *Space and the Eighteenth-Century Novel*, Cambridge, pp. 73-5; 111-16. Varey provides evidence for Prior Park being designed specifically as a 'show-house' at p. 111.

the *Epistle to Burlington* (1731).[43] Chandler hails Allen as a 'Mighty Genius' born to implement patriotic social reform, and 'Virtue's Exemplar in degen'rate Days', but in echoing Pope's claims for her own disinterest, as a woman she has to face up to the specific charge of sexual transgression:

> You chide the Muse that dares your Virtues own,
> And, veil'd with Modesty, would live unknown;
> An honest Muse, no Prostitute for Gain,
> Int'rest may court her, but shall court in vain:
> But ever pleas'd to set true Worth in View,
> Yours shall be seen, and will, by All but You
> (pp. 17-18).

In Chandler's 'prophetic' description, Allen's landscaped estate will implicitly form a counter-example to Pope's caricature of Timon's vulgar misuse of riches, and thus serves as advance publicity for Allen as an example of how new wealth can be produce good taste. Chandler transforms the fruits of capitalist accumulation into the personal expression of a new cultural aesthetic; one with an almost magical ability to transform 'Nature'. Allen's profitable capitalisation of the postal service (gained in 1715 as reward for intercepting a Jacobite plot), is sentimentally figured in the poem as a charitable means of oiling the wings of pastoral romance, whilst his quarrying of freestone is similarly mystified as merely an act of civic philanthropy. In the later editions, this can be read alongside Chandler's poem 'On Mr. B---'s Garden. To Mrs S....', another imitation of Pope's *Epistle to Burlington*, in which enacting such wise improvements to an estate are actually figured as a rehearsal for entering heaven: 'Sterling Truth, calm Temperance, and Love/Lead from these pleasing Scenes to those above, /To nobler Structures built by Hands divine' (pp. 72-3). This suggests a particularly pious contribution to what Raymond Williams terms 'the new morality of improvement' in which 'the neglect of charity is now not only a moral and theological example' but also 'a default of use'.[44] In addition, Chandler's reference to the 'noble manly Joy of doing Good', suggests the contemporary reconfiguration of manliness in terms of a traditionally feminine-marked propensity for benevolence.

Chandler's portrait of Allen as this type of exemplary 'new-man' marks the start of a process of mythologisation which includes Fielding's version of Allen as Squire Allworthy of 'Paradise Hall' in *Tom Jones* (1749). With the original's express permission, it was also promulgated by Pope in *One Thousand Seven Hundred and Thirty Eight* in which Allen represents the exception to what the poet bewails as a prevalent cultural corruption: 'Let low-born ALLEN, with an aukward Shame, /Do good by stealth, and blush to find it Fame' (perhaps conscious of

[43] Boyce, B. (1967), *The Benevolent Man: a Life of Ralph Allen*, Boston, pp. 56-9.
[44] Williams, *The Country and the City*, p. 59.

condescension, Pope later amended the epithet to 'humble').[45] Chandler's promotion of Allen thus encapsulates a devolving shift in the perceived locus of civic virtue away from the traditional aristocracy and high Anglican episcopal establishment. She had some access to Allen's powerful local circle of largely self-made men who included scholarly figures like Bishop William Warburton and the fashionable physician Dr William Oliver. In *To Doctor Oliver who corrected my Bath Poem*, for example, Chandler claims (in the third person), that, 'Ev'n Pope approv'd, when you had tun'd her lyre.' Pope might well have approved a poem which ends with an overt compliment to his own poetic mastery.

Chandler's commencement as milliner (c.1705) coincided with the arrival of Richard 'Beau' Nash, who as 'Master of Ceremonies' had a crucial part in establishing Bath as a polite resort which underwent a rapid process of urban improvement exactly coeval with Chandler's career.[46] Her *Description* celebrates this burgeoning city by painting an idealised portrait of the resort as a utopia reminiscent of ancient Athens where in 'comely Order, Rows of Buildings stand' and 'Squares, and Hospitals, and Temples rise'. This is a therapeutic urban pastoral space where palaces and fountains 'o'erspread the verdant Ground' and where clean water and fresh produce are in abundance (pp. 11-12). In a useful essay on the commodification of nature in spa societies Barbara M. Benedict examines how the literature of these 'consumptive communities' figured taking the waters as a type of gentlemanly pastoral retreat in which healthy consumption promises a cure for corrupted sociability.[47] Chandler's *Description* was originally sold in James Leake's bookshop alongside other contemporaneous 'prospects' of the city, such as Samuel and Nathaniel Buck's engraved print of *The South East Prospect of the City of Bath* (1734), which, in viewing the city from a distant down, similarly emphasises Bath's pastoral setting, whilst foregrounding a group of rustic peasants bearing produce, and two genteel couples in a fête champêtre.[48] Similarly Chandler's poem borrows traditional tropes from Classical eclogues and pastorals to figure Bath as, in Benedict terms, a 'sympathetic society' divested of labour and based upon 'natural' social exchange rooted in pleasurable, if regulated desire.

In Chandler's poem these newly refined pleasures are both materially and symbolically overlaid on the site of older, pastoral recreations: 'Where the smooth Bowl was wont to skim the Green,/Now stately Rooms for Pleasure change the Scene' (a footnote explains that 'Where Lindsey's New Room now stands, was a Bowling-Green not long since'). Similarly 'Harrison's Banqueting-House' is figured as 'a fair Pavilion' placed amidst an English version of an Arcadian landscape, reminiscent of Poussin, 'where Nature sports romantic' and the poet can

---

[45] *The Twickenham Edition of the Poems of Alexander Pope* (1961), (general ed.) J. Butt, New York, iv, p. 308.

[46] In his 'Life of Nash', Goldsmith actually dates Bath's tranformation from 1705: see *Collected Works of Oliver Goldsmith*, A. Friedman (ed.) (1966), 4 vols, Oxford, iii, p. 302.

[47] Benedict, B.M. (1995), 'Consumptive Communities: Commodifying Nature in Spa Society', in *The Eighteenth Century*, 36:3, pp. 203-19.

[48] Reprinted in Hyde, R. (1994), *A Prospect of Britain: The Town Panoramas of Samuel and Nathaniel Buck*, London.

find an inspirational retreat from crowds and 'empty noise' (p. 17). As originally type-set, Chandler's poem visually enacts a certain tension between the manifest poetic pastoral abstractions of the main text and the latent, though precise commercial referencing of her footnotes ('Lindsey's New Room' etc.); a tension which encapsulates the text's transitional reworking of older courtly codes for new bourgeois, proprietorial purposes. These footnotes, which suggest the poem's barely disguised commercial unconscious, can be equated with the similar use of 'keys' on decorative contemporary prints offering pastoral prospects of Bath, whilst drawing attention to local businesses.[49] Chandler's *Description* is therefore just one example of a product of an emergent 'Culture Industry', as described by Max Horkheimer and Theodor Adorno and as such was soon competing for attention within a burgeoning market in poems, novels, prints, health treatises, guides and pamphlets which aimed at endorsing or contesting their interested image of Bath as an ideal resort.[50] Chandler's polite, Horatian survey was read alongside more Juvenalian, 'realistic' or dystopian accounts like the anonymous verse-satire *The Diseases of Bath* (1737) (also sold by Leake), which paints Bath as a filthy, dangerous, disease-ridden cess-pit run by insolent chair-men and death-dealing, mercenary quacks; complaints which characterise Christopher Anstey's popular poetic satire in *The New Bath Guide* (1766) (later illustrated by Cruikshank), which itself informed Matthew Bramble's splenetic accounts in Smollett's novel *The Expedition of Humpry Clinker* (1771).

Chandler's *Description* represents a significant, early contribution to the ideological work underpinning what social historian Peter Borsay has influentially described as Georgian England's 'urban renaissance'.[51] As evidence for the reputation of Georgian resorts as 'melting-pots of society', Borsay cites Chandler's description of Lindsey's Assembly Rooms as a place where, 'Pagan, Turk, the Papist, and the Jew,/And all mankind's epitome you view'.[52] Resorts like Bath played an important role in promoting new, liberal ideals of politeness, designed to promote free-trade, providing a forum in which a socially mobile, newly rich,

---

[49] See for example, the engraved 'Plan of the City of Bath' reproduced in Neale, *Bath 1680-1850*, p. 202-3. Published by Leake in October 1736, and devised by John Wood to advertise his (and Allen's) property developments, it includes a written advertisement extolling the virtues of the newly improved city. A key which directs the reader to all the points of geographical, historical, social and commercial interest as described in Chandler's *Description of Bath*.

[50] This point is made of spa literature by Benedict, 'Consumptive Communities', p. 216, footnote i, with reference to Horkheimer and Adorno's chapter (1972) on 'The Culture Industry: Enlightenment as Mass Deception' in M. Horkheimer, and T.W. Adorno, transl. J. Cumming, (2000), *Dialectic of Enlightenment*, New York.

[51] Borsay, P. (1989), *The English Urban Renaissance: Culture and Society in the Provincial Town, 1660-1770*, Oxford.

[52] Borsay, *The English Urban Renaissance*, p. 271.

entrepreneurial class-fraction, exemplified by Allen, could consolidate their own power-base, largely through appropriate marriages, in close proximity to, if not actually within the established landed aristocracy. But, as Borsay notes, behind this early eighteenth-century emphasis upon conviviality, lay 'a deep apprehension about the well-being of society', born out of the memories of the Civil War, and sectarian factionalism. Moreover, in so far as such anxieties continued to inform English politics after the Restoration, through the compromises of the Glorious Revolution, and the 'rage of party' which marked the early decades of the new century 'the mission to civilize and socialize the gentry may be seen as part of a subtle campaign to reunite a divided elite'. Sociability was thus encouraged through the provision of what Borsay terms 'controlled contexts in which people of different persuasions could mix together', whilst 'the new urban culture can...be seen as a balm to sooth and heal long-standing wounds, which if left untreated could threaten the health of the body politic'.[53] Borsay's use of a medical metaphor is particularly apt with regard to Chandler's encouragement of just such an accommodation through a poetic economy concerned with social as much as physical or spiritual healing. But in exploiting the metaphoric potential inherent in the claim for Bath's natural and divinely ordained therapeutic function she produces a mythology of a harmonious political and private body which is itself profoundly partisan. In this context we can turn to Chandler's re-dedication of the second edition of her *Description of Bath* to a female member of the Royal household: 'beauteous Princess' Amelia, the second daughter of George II.

By 1734 Bath's increasing status could already be measured in terms of royal visits; notably those of Charles II in 1663 and Queen Ann in 1702. The arrival of seventeen-year-old Princess Amelia Sophia Eleanora (1710-1786), in the spring of 1728 had given the spa a renewed stamp of Hanoverian approval: arriving by sedan chair, significantly she left for Bristol on a decorated barge down the newly navigable Avon just widened for commercial use by a stock-company headed by the resourceful Allen. She returned the next April, and on her birthday an arbour of greenery was erected in the mead outside her lodgings in the West Gate, where morris dancers serenaded her for an hour. This vestige of more elaborate Stuart court-pastorals is registered in Chandler's short encomium '...on the Princess Amelia. In Answer to Damon, who invited the Nymphs of Bath, to sing her Praise', which celebrates 'Brunswic's Line' as harbingers of 'Plenty, peace and Liberty' (pp. 33-4), and quellers of factionalism.[54] Similar sentiments are expressed through her revised opening to the *Description* itself where a 'humble' Chandler appeals to Amelia's 'True Royal Greatness' in providing protection for her 'Artless lays'. More than the waters themselves, Chandler is assured that Amelia can provide strength and protection to her weak and trembling muse and will 'awe the snarling Critics into Praise'. Just as Amelia has found strength and health from the waters,

---

[53] Borsay, *The English Urban Renaissance*, p. 279.

[54] There was an ox roast, and Allen was probably one of the council members who made speeches in her honour (see Boyce, *The Benevolent Man*, p. 25 and Barbauld, *Life and Letters*, p. 276, n. 5.).

so the female poet gains power from the princess's physical and political power through sisterly affinity.

In *Trivia*, Gay's mock-epic vision of London, there is a presiding female water-deity, the burlesque figure of Cloacina, goddess of the Fleet Ditch, an open sewer, from which she is seen arising, 'with wither'd turnip tops her temples crown'd', as the very embodiment of consumerist detritus (Book II, l. 196). Chandler's introductory account of Bath's origins also emphasises presiding female deities, but of a far more pure and benign nature:

> Long ere the Roman Eagle hither flew,
> Ere Albion's Sons their pow'rful Virtues knew;
> Brute's great Descendant rais'd them first to Fame,
> And, from their Use, assign'd the Town its Name.
> Pallas he chose Protectress of the Streams,
> Pallas the City her Protectress claims. (p. 3)

In a footnote, Chandler observes that 'The City of Bath is call'd in the British Language Caer Palludar' (from William Camden), and she later mentions that the Romans dedicated the baths to Minerva. Contemporary histories of Bath emphasised a traditional association between the efficacy of the waters and ailments identified as specifically female; in particular they were deemed to cure female infertility. So through its royal dedication and subsequent allusions to female tutelary goddeses, Chandler's *Description*, tends to feminise Bath as a place naturally ordained as a source of purification, healing and generation.

Chandler cites Milton's *History of Britain* (1670-1) and Thomas Guidot's *Treatises relating to the City and Waters of Bath* (1679; reprinted by Leake, 1725), as two specific sources for her account of the spa's ancient and mythic history, including the locally famous legend of its discovery by Bladud, the leperous son of King Lear.[55] Her interest in Bath's prehistory also suggests exposure to the quasi-mystical ideas of the architect John Wood, author of *The Origin of Building: or, the Plagiarism of the Heathens Detected* (1740) and *An Essay Towards a Description of Bath* (1742), where he claims that Bladud was a druid, and the same person as Abaris, a Hyperborean priest of Apollo who had conversed with Pythagoras.[56] As R.S. Neale notes, Wood's architectural project at Bath was rooted in an historical 'vision steeped in the Britannic myth of origin' which was 'heroic, noble, cultured and harmonious'. Whilst it chimed with some of the themes of the Augustan world view, in Wood's hands, it was Greek and Christianised, 'but,

[55] This legend, ubiquitous in Bath literature, is traceable to Geoffrey of Monmouth and William Camden's *Britannia* (1586).

[56] For Wood and the Bladud legend see Varey, *Space and the Eighteenth-Century Novel*, Cambridge, pp. 66-71; 96-110.

above all, it was British'.[57] Similarly in Chandler's poem Bath's waters are a font of native virtue; a distinctly Celto-British source of virtue pre-dating the Roman yoke:

The Romans well this ancient Story knew,
Minerva's Statues their Devotion drew;
Of curious Art her noble* Bust appears,
Safe from the Ruin of a thousand Years.
These salutary Streams alone can boast
Their Virtues not in thrice five Ages lost.
The floating Waters, from their hidden Source,
Thro' the same Strata keep unerring Course;
The flowing Sulphur meets dissolving Steel,
And heat in Combat, till the Waters boil:
United then, enrich the healing Stream,
Health to the Sick they give, and to the Waters, Fame.
Thus oft contending Parties rage and hate,
Malignant both, and push each other's Fate;
At last, their Fury spent, and cloy'd with Blood,
They join in Friendship for the Public Good

*Note: There is now an antique Bust in the Town-hall of Bath, supposed to belong to a Roman Statue of Pallas. (pp. 3-4)

Chandler's image of uniting streams echoes an extended metaphor in Denham's *Cooper's Hill* regarding Royalist magnanimity:

While luxury and wealth, like war and peace,
Are each the others ruine, and increase;
As Rivers lost in Seas some secret vein
Thence reconveighs, there to be lost again
(lls, 33-36).

But Chandler exploits the metaphoric potential of Bath's balneological chemistry to produce her own version of this politico-geological allegory; one which is not concerned with the just limits for Royal prerogative, but with fixing a post-Revolutionary ideal of party-political harmony. Elsewhere in her poem, such political stability, and its implicit mythic underpinning, is overtly linked to the consolidation of the Hanoverian settlement as symbolised by the dynastic marriage of George II's eldest daughter, the Princess Anne to William, the Prince of Orange. Thus *The Description of Bath* also functions as a royal epithalamium.[58]

---

[57] Neale, *Bath 1680-1850*, pp. 186-7.

[58] See Avery, E.L. (1956), 'A Royal Wedding Royally Confounded', *Western Humanities Review*, 10, pp. 153-64. The marriage, originally scheduled for 12 November 1733, was repeatedly postponed until 14 March 1734. Boyce found it incongruous that Chandler's *Description* should start with a royal dedication and end with the praise of Allen,

One of the more prominent additions to Bath's public space was an obelisk erected in 1734 to commemorate the Prince of Orange's recent recovery from the serious illness which had temporarily postponed his plans to marry the Princess Royal.[59] Chandler describes 'a verdant Square' with the Obelisk as 'the latest, proudest, Honour of the Place':

> To future Times this Monument shall show,
> How much all Britons, and all Belgians owe,
> To Springs which sav'd from Death the Great Nassau.
> From Him, and beauteous Anna, shall descend,
> Heroes like William, ready to defend
> Fair Liberty oppress'd, and trampled Laws,
> Or die with Pleasure in the glorious Cause.
> What less than this can Prophecy divine,
> When William's Blood is mix'd with George's Line?
> (p. 13)

Chandler concludes this pro-House of Orange polemic by praising Beau Nash for organising the subscription: 'What greater Honour can thy Pride receive, /Than that Thy Name with great Nassau shall live? (p. 13). This obelisk had been erected in the newly improved recreational and commercial space which soon became known as The Orange Grove. So far as the obelisk served to symbolise the success of the Prince of Orange's pre-marriage propaganda tour of the West Country, Chandler's poem forms a part of that project.

The Orange Grove was just one of a number of improved sites for polite sociability later described by Goldsmith who noted that when Nash first arrived, 'the nobility still preserved a tincture of Gothic haughtiness, and refused to keep company with the gentry at any of the public entertainments'.[60] As Borsay observes, 'the introduction of classical architecture into English towns would...have been seen as a humanizing and civilizing influence', particularly since 'the style which only recently preceded it, known pejoratively as gothic, was stigmatized as barbaric and chaotic'.[61] Chandler's *Description* noticeably contrasts these new arenas of public display with her account of Bath's 'ancient Abbey',

---

commoner, but the very fact that Chandler is comfortable with such a juxtaposition registers her ideological distance from Pope.

[59] Goldsmith's (1762), *Life of Richard Nash Esq*, describes Nash's monument as 'a small obelisk, thirty feet high' bearing the Prince's arms and this inscription: 'In memoriam sanitatis Principi Auriaco aquarum thermalium potu. Favente Deo, Ovante Brittania, Feliciter restituae, M. DCC. Xxxiv'. In 1738 Nash erected a similar obelisk to the Prince of Wales in Queen's Square for which Pope provided an anonymous inscription. See Goldsmith, O. (1966), *Collected Works*, (ed.) A. Friedman, 5 vols, Oxford, iii, p. 341.

[60] Goldsmith, *Collected Works*, p. 300.

[61] Borsay, *The English Urban Renaissance*, p. 260.

which occupies a central position within Chandler's survey, as Denham's description of the ruins of Chertsey Abbey does in *Cooper's Hill*. But whereas Chertsey prompts Denham to question the destruction reeked at the Reformation, for the True-Blue Protestant Chandler, 'The labour'd Work of superstitious Hands', is merely a remnant of a time when 'When Holy Craft supreme did guide the Helm,/And Gothic Darkness overspread the Realm' a time when 'The artful Priest amaz'd the gaping Croud,/And sacred Truth was veil'd in mystic Cloud':

> When Idol Images Devotion drew,
> And Idol Gods were worshipp'd as the true;...
> Welcome, fair Liberty, and Light divine!
> Yet wider spread your Wings, and brighter shine;
> Dart livelier Beams on ev'ry British Soul,
> And scatter slavish Darkness to the Pole (p. 10).

This symbol of Gothic barbarism provides a point of historical reference around which Chandler sets her account of the newly built sites of refined entertainment, the assembly rooms, terraces and avenues. Now restored to 'Pure Worship', nonetheless the Abbey Church is open to abuse as a place for another, more secular form of idolatry through which 'The Female Idol her Adorer knows', by 'meaning Looks, and cringing Bows' (the Abbey was notorious for such assignations partly because of its use as a pedestrian thoroughfare, the outside side alleyways being congested with market stalls). Ordering a moral clean-up, Chandler seeks to regulate the sexual relations which Bath's relaxed atmosphere permits, guiding her pious reader towards sites of acceptable social interaction: 'Fly hence, Prophane, nor taint this Sacred Place;/Mock not thy GOD, to flatter Cælia's Face.'

The availability of spaces where women are protected from the pressure of a sexualised male gaze forms a recurrent motif in Chandler's *Description*. The Baths in particular had long been a cause of moral anxiety, but Chandler cites the now regulated Cross Bath 'of gentler Heat', where 'The tender Virgin finds a safe Retreat/ From Sights indecent, and from Speeches lewd,/Which dare not there, with Satyr-Face, intrude' (p. 11). Likewise in Lindsey's New Assembly Rooms, 'Miss soon learns the Language of the Eyes' as 'The witless Beau looks soft, and swears he dies'. Chandler's scathing account of this world of trivial pursuits pays direct homage to *The Rape of the Lock*, but whereas Pope, through Clarissa's speech, simply encourages an attitude of passive obedience to a necessary evil, Chandler's muse actively calls her implied women readers to fly with her away from 'this enchanting Place', whilst pointing towards 'a safe Retreat' in Leake's bookshop and circulating library:

> There rest secure, amidst the Wise, and Great:
> Heroes of antient, and of modern Song,
> The bending Shelves in comely Order throng,
> Hither, ye Nymphs, attend the leading Muse,
> With her the Labours of the Wise peruse;
> Their Maxims learn, their Precepts be your Guide.

Think Virtuous Knowledge Woman's truest Pride:
One Hour thus spent, more solid Joys shall give,
Than the gay Idler knows, or Fools conceive (p. 16).

Chandler's faith in Leake's provision of 'virtuous knowledge' was somewhat naive, for, as Neale has remarked, ironically Leake's most reprinted publication was Thomas Stretzer's *A New Description of Merryland* (1740), a work of libertine erotica. *Merryland* is a counter-example of imaginative topography in which the ostensible author 'Roger Phfuquewell', descended from a 'Red-Headed' Irish family, 'of long-standing in the country', travels to 'Merryland', a 'Paradise of Pleasure, and Garden of delight', which is, of course, a woman's body.[62] Stretzer's libertine pastoral and Chandler's polite urban-pastoral, represent two ethical poles within Bath's culture of commodified pleasure. Where Stretzer produces the female body as a passive, paradisial land waiting for masculine conquest, Chandler imagines a garden-city where there is space, albeit heavily circumscribed, for unhindered female intellectual and poetic activity.

Conclusion

In conclusion, Chandler's concern with de-eroticised female space reminds us that the English Enlightenment was not merely a self-regulated process of reunification on the part of an aristocratic male elite.[63] As often argued, this process was also marked by the imposition of reconfigured normative conceptions of gender, as a bourgeoisie, eager to consolidate their cultural hegemony, appropriated values of moral virtue, sexual modesty, and religious piety, which had been labelled 'feminine' by an earlier masculinist, militaristic courtly code, rendering the regulation of female sexuality overdetermined as a necessary sign of social stability.[64] Discussing this process, Terry Eagleton succinctly observes how this 'feminization of discourse' was inherently contradictory in its impact upon the political power of actual women, 'for whilst "feminine" values relegated by the sexual division of labour to the private realm are now returning to transvaluate the ruling ideologies themselves', nevertheless, 'the feminization of discourse prolongs

[62] As quoted in Neale, *Bath 1680-1850*, p. 24 (I have not ventured to examine original in the BL).

[63] Borsay later remarks that 'the new urban culture...contributed to stability in practical ways by providing attractive contexts in which the traditional elite and the growing middling ranks could freely mix and acquire and exchange status and wealth, thereby neutralising the potentially most dangerous of all divisions in post-Restoration Britain', *The English Urban Renaissance*, p. 282.

[64] Todd, J. (1986), *Sensibility: An Introduction*, London, p. 60-64; and Barker-Benfield, G.J. (1986), *The Culture of Sensibility: Sex and Society in Eighteenth-Century Britain*, Chicago.

the fetishising of women at the same time as it lends them a more authoritative voice.'[65] Thus Mary Chandler's brother is keen to emphasise his sister's 'love of religion and virtue' and how she used her spare hours fruitfully, wishing not 'to lavish them away in fashionable, unmeaning amusements.' He casts her in the pious role as a virtuous, guardian spinster: 'the care she had of those young persons who were frequently committed to her friendship, put her upon her guard as to her own temper and conduct'.[66] So, in Eagleton's succinct formulation, we see how, whilst this sentimental model of a literary female 'travesties women as technicians of the heart, it is also a mechanism which partly readmits them to the public sphere'.[67] It was within these contradictory terms that as a propertied and politically self-conscious tradeswoman, Mary Chandler published a civic poem which, as her brother boasts, earned her the commendation of many in 'the first rank, for good sense and politeness'.[68]

[65] Eagleton, T. (1982), *The Rape of Clarissa: Writing, Sexuality and Class Struggle in Samuel Richardson*, Oxford, p. 13.

[66] Eagleton, *The Rape of Clarissa*, and *passim*.

[67] Eagleton, *The Rape of Clarissa*, p. 13.

[68] Shiells, *An Account of the Lives of the Poets of Britain and Ireland*, p. 349.

Bibliography

Aikin, J. (1795), *A Description of the Country from Thirty to Forty Miles Round Manchester*, London.

Andrew, D.T. (1989), *Philanthropy and Police: London Charity in the Eighteenth Century*, Princeton.

——. (1995), 'Female Charity in an Age of Sentiment', in J. Brewer and S. Staves (eds), *Early Modern Conceptions of Property*, London.

——. (1996), 'Noblesse Oblige: Female Charity in an Age of Sentiment', in J. Brewer and S. Staves (eds), *Early Modern Conceptions of Property,* London.

Andrews, C.B. (ed.) (1934-8), *The Torrington Diaries*, 4 vols, London.

Ankarloo, B. (1979), 'Agriculture and Women's Work: Directions of Change in the West 1700-1900', *Journal of Family History*, 4, pp. 111-20.

Aston, J. (1816), *A Picture of Manchester*, Manchester.

Austen, J. (1813, Penguin edition 1972), *Pride and Prejudice*, London.

Avery, E.L. (1956), 'A Royal Wedding Royally Confounded', *Western Humanities Review*, 10, pp. 153-64.

Ballaster, R. (1992), *Seductive Forms: Women's Amatory Fiction from 1684-1740*, Oxford.

Barash, C. (1993), '"The Native Liberty...of the Subject": Configurations of Gender and Authority in the Works of Mary Chudleigh, Sarah Fyge Egerton and Mary Astell', in I. Grundy and S. Athens (eds), *Women, Writing and Authority 1640-1799*, Carbondale.

——. (1997), *English Women's Poetry, 1649-1714: Politics, Community, and Linguistic Authority*, Oxford.

Barbauld, A. (1906), *Life and Letters at Bath in the Eighteenth Century*, London.

Barker, H. (1997), 'Women, Work and the Industrial Revolution: Female Involvement in the English Printing Trades, c. 1700-1840', in H. Barker and E. Chalus (eds), *Gender in Eighteenth-Century England: Roles, Representations and Responsibilities*, London.

Barker-Benfield, G.J. (1992), *The Culture of Sensibility: Sex and Society in Eighteenth-Century Britain*, Chicago.

Barrett, W. (1789), *The History and Antiquities of Bristol*, Bristol.

Barry, J. (1990), 'Provincial Town Culture, 1640-1780: Urbane or Civic?', in J.H. Pittock, and A. Wear (eds), *Interpretation and Cultural History*, Basingstoke.

——. (1994), 'Bourgeois Collectivism? Urban Association and the Middling Sort', in J. Barry and C. Brooks (eds), *The Middling Sort of People: Culture, Society and Politics in England 1550-1800*, Basingstoke.

——. (1995), 'I Significati della Libertà: La Libertà nell'Inghliterra del XVII e XVIII secolo', *Quaderni Storici*, 89, pp. 487-513.

——. (2000), 'Civility and Civic Culture in Early Modern England: The Meaning of Urban Freedom', in P. Burke, B. Harrison and P. Slack (eds), *Civil Histories*.

Essays Presented to Sir Keith Thomas, Oxford.

Bateson, M. (ed.) (1904-6), *Borough Customs*, 2 vols, London.

[Battye], T.A. (1800), *A Concise Exposition of the Tricks and Arts Used in the Collection of Easter Dues, with a List of Items which Compose this Divine Tax*. By TB, Manchester.

Benedict, B.M. (1995), 'Consumptive Communities: Commodifying Nature in Spa Society', in *The Eighteenth Century: Theory and Interpretation*, 36, 3, pp. 203-219.

Bennett, J. (1992), 'Medieval Women, Modern Women: Across the Great Divide', in D. Aers (ed.), *Culture and History 1350-1600: Essays in English Communities, Identities and Writing*, Hemel Hempstead.

Berg, M. (1988), 'Women's Work, Mechanization and the Early Phases of Industrialization in England', in R.E. Pahl (ed.), *On Work: Historical, Comparative and Theoretical Approaches*, Oxford.

——. (1993), 'What Difference Did Women's Work Make to the Industrial Revolution?', *History Workshop Journal*, 35, pp. 22-44.

——. (1993), 'Women's Property and the Industrial Revolution', *Journal of Interdisciplinary History*, 24, pp. 233-50.

——. (1994), *The Age of Manufactures, 1700-1820, Industry, Motivation and Work in Britain*, London.

Berry, A. (1995), 'Patronage, Funding and the Hospital Patient, c. 1750–1815: Three English Regional Case Studies', unpublished University of Oxford PhD thesis.

Berry, H. (forthcoming 2002) 'Consuming Passions: Shopping and Politeness', *Transactions of the Royal Historical Society*.

Bohstedt, J. (1988), 'Gender, Household and Community Politics: Women in English Riots, 1790-1810', *Past and Present*, 120, pp. 88-122.

Borsay, A. (1991), 'Cash and Conscience: Financing the General Hospital at Bath, c. 1738-50', *The Social History of Medicine*, 4, pp. 219-20;

——. (1991), '"Persons of Honour and Reputation": the Voluntary Hospital in an Age of Corruption', *Medical History*, 35, pp. 281-94.

Borsay, P. (1984), '"All the Town's a Stage": Urban Ritual and Ceremony, 1660-1800' in P. Clark (ed.), *The Transformation of English Provincial Towns*, London.

——. (1989), *The English Urban Renaissance: Culture and Society in the Provincial Town, 1660-1770*, Oxford.

Boyce, B. (1967), *The Benevolent Man: A Life of Ralph Allen*, Boston.

Brewer, J. (1996), 'Reconstructing the Reader: Prescriptions, Texts and Strategies in Anna Larpent's Reading', in J. Raven, H. Small and N. Tadmor (eds), *The Practice and Representation of Reading in England*, Cambridge.

——. (1997), *The Pleasures of the Imagination: English Culture in the Eighteenth Century*, London.

Brodsky Elliot, V. (1981), 'Single Women in the London Marriage Market: Age, Status and Mobility, 1598-1619', in R.B. Outhwaite, (ed.), *Marriage and Society: Studies in the Social History of Marriage*, London.

Brown, F.K. (1961), *Fathers of the Victorians*, Cambridge.

Burton, K.G. (ed.) (1950), *The Memorandums of John Watts Esq.: Mayor of Reading 1722-23 and 1728-29*, Reading.

Campbell, R. (1747), *The London Tradesman*, London.

Cappe, C. (1799), *An Account of Two Charity Schools for the Education of Girls, and of a Female Friendly Society in York*, York.

——. (1805), *Observations on Charity Schools, Female Friendly Societies, and Other Subjects Connected with the Views of the Ladies Committee*, York.

——. (1817), *On the Desireableness and Utility of Ladies Visiting the Female Wards of Hospitals and Lunatic Asylums*,York.

——. (1822), *Memoirs of the Life of the late Mrs Catharine Cappe, written by herself*, London.

Carmichael Stopes, C. (1894), *British Freewomen: Their Historical Privilege*, London.

Cavallo, S. and Warner, L. (1999), 'Introduction', in S. Cavallo and L. Warner (eds), *Widowhood in Early Modern Europe*, Harlow.

Cavanagh, D. and Kirk, T. (eds) (2000), *Subversion and Scurrility: Popular Discourse in Europe from 1500 to the Present*, Aldershot.

Centlivre, S. (repr. 1968), *The Gotham Election*, in *Collected Works*, vol. 3, London.

Chalkin, C.W. (1980), 'Capital Expenditure on Buildings for Cultural Purposes in Provincial England', *Business History*, 22, pp. 51-70.

——. (1998), *English Counties and Public Building 1650-1830*, London.

——. (2000), *The Rise of the English Town 1650-1850*, Cambridge.

Chalus, E. (1997), '"That Epidemical Madness": Women and Electoral Politics in the Late Eighteenth Century' in, H. Barker and E. Chalus (eds), *Gender in Eighteenth Century England: Roles, Representations and Responsibilities*, Harlow.

——. (1997), 'Women in English Political Life, 1754-1790', unpublished University of Oxford D.Phil thesis.

——. (1998) '"My Minerva at my Elbow": The Political Roles of Women in Eighteenth-Century England', in R. Connors, C. Jones and S. Taylor (eds), *Hanoverian Britain and Empire: Essays in Memory of Philip Lawson*, Cambridge.

——. (2000), 'Elite Women, Social Politics, and the Political World of Late Eighteenth-Century Britain', *Historical Journal*, 43, pp. 669-98.

——. (2000), 'Women, Electoral Privilege and Practice in the Eighteenth Century', in K. Gleadle and S. Richardson (eds), *Women in British Politics, 1760-1860: The Power of the Petticoat*, Basingstoke.

——. (2001), 'Lady Susan Woos the Voters', *BBC History Magazine* (June).

Chandler, M. (1734), *The Description of Bath: A Poem, Humbly Inscribed to Her Royal Highness the Princess Amelia*, London and Bath.

Chinnery, G.A. (ed.) (1967), *Records of the Borough of Leicester. vol. VI. The Chamberlain's Accounts 1688-1835*, Welwyn Garden City.

Churches, C. (1998), 'Women and Property in Early Modern England: a Case Study', *Social History*, 23, pp. 165-80.

Clark, A. (1919), *Working Life of Women in the Seventeenth Century*, London.

Reprint, London and New York, 1982.

Clark, J.C.D. (2000), *English Society 1660-1832*, revised edn, Cambridge.

Clark, P. (1995), 'Small Towns in England 1550-1850: National and Regional Population Trends', in P. Clark (ed.), *Small Towns in Early Modern Europe*, Cambridge.

——. (1983), *The English Alehouse: A Social History 1200–1830*, London.

——. (2000), *British Clubs and Societies 1580-1800: The Origins of an Associated World*, New York.

——. (ed.) (2000), *The Cambridge Urban History of Britain. vol. II 1540-1840*, Cambridge.

Clark, P. and Houston, R.A. (2000), ' Leisure and Culture 1700-1840', in P. Clark (ed.), *The Cambridge Urban History of Britain. vol. II 1500-1840*, Cambridge.

Clarke, N. (1997), 'The Cursed Barbauld Crew', in M. Hilton, M. Styles and V. Watson. (eds), *Opening the Nursery Door*, London and New York.

Clarkson, L.A. and Crawford, M. (1991), 'Life After Death: Widows in Carrick-on-Suir, 1799', in M. MacCurtain and M. O'Dowd (eds), *Women in Early Modern Ireland*, Edinburgh.

Climenson, E.J. (ed.) (1906), *Elizabeth Montagu: The Queen of the Bluestockings. Her Correspondence from 1720-61*, 2 vols, London.

Colclough, S. (1998), 'Recovering the Reader, Commonplace Books and Diaries as Sources of Reading Experience', *Publishing History*, 44, pp. 5-38.

Colley, L. (1992), *Britons: Forging the Nation*, London.

Collyer, J. (1761), *Parents & Guardians Directory and the Youth's Guide in the Choice of a Profession or Trade*, London.

Connors, R. (1997), 'Poor Women, the Parish and the Politics of Poverty', in H. Barker and E. Chalus (eds), *Gender in Eighteenth-Century England: Roles, Representations and Responsibilities*, London.

Corfield, K. (1986), 'Elizabeth Heyrick: Radical Quaker', in G. Malmgreen (ed.), *Religion in the Lives of English Women 1760-1930*, London.

Corfield, P.J. (1982), *The Impact of English Towns, 1700-1800,* Oxford.

Corfield, P.J. with Kelly, S. (1984), 'Giving Directions to the Town': the Early Town Directories', *Urban History Yearbook*, pp. 22-35.

Cozens Hardy, B. and Kent, E.A. (1938), *The Mayors of Norwich, 1403-1835: Being Biographical Notes on the Mayors of the Old Corporation*, Norwich.

Crafts, N.F.R. (1985), *British Industrial Growth During the Industrial Revolution*, Oxford.

Crawford, P. (1993), *Women and Religion in England 1500-1720*, London.

Craven, M. (1988), *An Illustrated History of Derby*, Derby.

Cromar, P. (1978), 'The Coal Industry on Tyneside, 1715-1750', *Northern History*, 14, pp. 193-207.

Cunningham, H. (1998), 'Introduction', in H. Cunningham and J. Innes (eds), *Charity, Philanthropy and Reform from the 1690s to 1850*, Basingstoke.

Cunnington, P. and Lucas, C. (1978), *Charity Costumes of Children, Scholars, Almsfolk and Pensioners*, London.

Davis, D. (1966), *A History of Shopping*, London.

D'Cruze, S. (1986),"'To Acquaint the Ladies": Women Traders in Colchester

c. 1750-1850', *Local Historian*, 17:3, pp. 158-62.

——. (1990), 'The Middling Sort in Provincial England. Politics and Social Relations in Colchester 1730-1800', unpublished University of Essex PhD thesis.

Dain, A. (1997), 'Assemblies and Polite Leisure in East Anglia', *Suffolk Review*, 28, pp. 2-22.

Davidoff, L. and Hall, C. (1987), *Family Fortunes: Men and Women of the English Middle Class, 1780 – 1850*, London.

Davies, G. and Bonsall, P. (1996), *Bath. A New History*, Bodmin.

Davies, N.Z. (1982),'Women in the Crafts in Sixteenth-century Lyon', *Feminist Studies*, 8:1, pp. 47-80.

de Mandeville, B. (1714), *The Fable of the Bees: or, Private Vices, Publick Benefits*, London.

Deering, C. (1751), *Nottinghamia Vetus et Nova*, Nottingham.

Defoe, D. (1726), *The Complete English Tradesman*, 2nd edn, London.

Dendy, F.W. (ed.) (1901), *Extracts from the Records of the Company of Hostmen of Newcastle upon Tyne*, Newcastle.

Derry, W. (1966), *Dr. Parr: A Portrait of the Whig Dr. Johnson*, Oxford.

Deutsch, H. (1996), *Resemblance and Disgrace: Alexander Pope and the Deformation of Culture*, Boston.

Devine Jump, H. (ed.), (1997), *Women's Writing of the Romantic Period, 1789-1836, an Anthology*, Edinburgh.

Dews, D.C. (1986), 'Ann Carr and the Female Revivalists', in G. Malmgreen (ed.), *Religion in the Lives of English Women, 1760-1930*, London.

Dickinson, H.T. (1995), *The Politics of the People in Eighteenth-Century Britain*, Basingstoke.

Doughty, O. (1925), 'A Bath Poetess of the Eighteenth Century', *The Review of English Studies*, 1:4, pp. 404-20.

Douglas, M. and Isherwood, B. (1996), *The World of Goods: Towards an Anthropology of Consumption*, 2nd edn, London.

Dresser, M. (1996), 'Sisters and Brethren: Power, Propriety and Gender Among the Bristol Moravians, 1746-1833', *Social History*, 21:3, pp. 304-29.

Drummond J.C. and Wilbraham, A. (1939 reprinted 1991), *The Englishman's History of Food: Five Centuries of English Diet*, London.

Drury, J.L. (1996), 'The Baker Baker Portfolio of Prints – its Content and Acquisition', *Durham County Local History Society Bulletin*, 56, pp. 3-20.

Eagleton, T. (1982), *The Rape of Clarissa: Writing, Sexuality and Class Struggle in Samuel Richardson*, Oxford.

Earle, P. (1989), *The Making of the English Middle Class: Business, Society and Family Life in London, 1660-1730*, London.

——. (1989), 'The Female Labour Market in London in the Late Seventeenth and Early Eighteenth Centuries', *Economic History Review*, 2nd series, 42:3, pp. 328-53.

Elliott, D.W. (1995), '"The Care of the Poor is Her Profession": Hannah More and Women's Philanthropic Work', *Nineteenth-Century Contexts*, 19, pp. 179-204.

Elliott, P. (2000), 'The Derby Philosophers: Urban Scientific Culture and Society in Provincial England, c. 1750-1850', unpublished University of Leicester PhD thesis.

Ellis, J. (2001), 'The "Black Indies": the Economic Development of Newcastle upon Tyne, c. 1700-1840', in R. Colls and W. Lancaster (eds), *Newcastle: A Modern History*, Chichester.

——. (2001), *The Georgian Town, 1680-1840*, Basingstoke.

——. (2000), 'Regional and County Centres, 1700-1840', in P. Clark (ed.), *The Cambridge Urban History of Britain. vol II, 1540-1840*, Cambridge.

——. (1995), '"On the Town": Women in Augustan England, 1688-1820', *History Today*, 45, pp. 20-27.

——. (1984), 'A Dynamic Society: Social Relations in Newcastle-upon-Tyne, 1660-1760', in P. Clark (ed.), *The Transformation of English Provincial Towns*, London.

Elwin, M. (ed.) (1967), *The Noels and the Milbankes: Their Letters for Twenty-Five Years 1767–1792*, London.

Erickson, A.L. (1993), *Women and Property in Early Modern England*, London.

Fawcett, T. and Inskipp, M. (1994), 'The Making of Orange Grove', *Bath History*, 5, pp. 24-50.

Feldman, D. (2000), 'Migration', in M. Daunton (ed.), *The Cambridge Urban History of Britain. vol. III. 1840-1950*, Cambridge.

Fergus, J. (2000), 'Women Readers: A Case Study', in V. Jones (ed.), *Women and Literature in Britain 1700-1800*, Cambridge.

——. (1996), 'Provincial Servants' Reading in the Eighteenth Century', in J. Raven, H. Small and N. Tadmor (eds), *The Practice and Representation of Reading in England*, Cambridge.

——. (1992), 'Women Readers of Prose Fiction in the Midlands 1746-1800', *Transactions of the Eighth International Congress on the Enlightenment*, Oxford.

Fergus, J. and Farrar Thaddeus, J. (1987), 'Women, Publishers, and Money, 1790-1820', *Studies in Eighteenth-Century Culture*, 17, pp.191-207.

Field, W. (1828), *Memoirs of the Reverend Samuel Parr*, vol. 2, London.

Finn, M. (1996), 'Women, Consumption and Coverture in England', *Historical Journal*, 39, pp. 703-22.

——. (2000), 'Men's Things: Masculine Possession in the Consumer Revolution', *Social History*, 25:2, p.135.

Fiske, J. (ed.) (1990), *The Oakes Diaries: Business, Politics and the Family in Bury St Edmunds*, Suffolk Record Society, 32, Woodbridge.

Fissel, M. (1991), *Patients, Power and the Poor in Eighteenth-Century Bristol*, Cambridge.

Foreman, A. (1998), *Georgiana: Duchess of Devonshire*, New York.

Forster, J.E. (ed.) (1890), *The Diary of Samuel Newton: Alderman of Cambridge 1662-1717*, Cambridge.

Fox, A. (1994), 'Ballads, Libels and Popular Ridicule in Jacobean England', *Past and Present*, 145, pp. 47-83.

Freifield, M. (1986), 'Technological Change and the "Self-Acting" Mule: A Study of Skill and the Sexual Division of Labour', *Social History*, 11:3, pp. 319-43.

Friedman, A.T. (2000), 'Inside/Out: Women, Domesticity and the Pleasures of the City', in L. Cowen Orlin (ed.), *Material London, ca.1600*, Pennsylvania.

George, M.D. (1992), *London Life in the Eighteenth Century*, London.

Gilbert, A.D. (1976), *Religion and Society in Industrial England. Church, Chapel and Social Change 1740-1914*, London.

Girouard, M. (1990), *The English Town: A History of Urban Life*, New Haven and London.

Gleadle, K. (1995), *The Early Feminists, Radical Unitarians and the Emergence of the Women's Rights Movement 1831-1851*, New York.

Gleadle, K. and Richardson, S. (eds) (2000), *Women in British Politics, 1760-1860: The Power of the Petticoat*, Basingstoke.

Goldsmith, O. (1966), *Collected Works of Oliver Goldsmith*, (ed.) A. Friedman, 5 vols, Oxford.

Gorsky, M. (1999), *Patterns of Philanthropy. Charity and Society in Nineteenth-Century Bristol,* Woodbridge.

Gosden, J. (1982), 'Elemore Hall Transformed, 1749-1753', *Transactions of the Architectural & Archaeological Society of Durham & Northumberland*, new series 6, pp. 31-6.

Gowing, L. (1996), *Domestic Dangers: Women, Words and Sex in Early Modern London*, Oxford.

——. (2000), '"The Freedom of the Streets": Women and Social Space, 1560-1640', in P. Griffiths and M.S.R. Jenner (eds), *Londinopolis: Essays in the Cultural and Social History of Early Modern London*, Manchester.

Gray, Mrs E. (ed.) (1927), *Papers and Diaries of a York Family*, London.

Greer, G. (1995), *Slip-Shod Sybils: Recognition, Rejection and the Woman Poet*, Harmondsworth.

Gregory, J. (1998), 'Gender and the Clerical Profession in England, 1660-1850', *Studies in Church History*, 34, pp. 235-72.

Gregory, P. (1984), 'The Popular Fiction of the Eighteenth-Century Circulating Libraries', unpublished University of Edinburgh PhD thesis.

Grindon, L.P. (1877), *Manchester Banks and Bankers*, Manchester.

Grundy, I. (1999), *Lady Mary Wortley Montagu: Comet of the Enlightenment*, Oxford.

Habermas, J. (1989), *The Structural Transformation of the Public Sphere*, translated by T. Burger and F. Lawrence, Cambridge.

Harding, V. (2000), 'Reformation and Culture 1540-1700', in P. Clark (ed.), *The Cambridge Urban History of Britain. vol. II 1500-1840*, Cambridge.

Harland, J. (ed.) (1866-7), *Collectanea Relating to Manchester and its Neighbourhood, at Various Periods*, 2 vols, Manchester.

Harvey, J. (1794), *A Sentimental Tour through Newcastle,* Newcastle.

Hayes, L.M. (1905), *Reminiscences of Manchester, and Some of its Local Surroundings from the Year 1840*.

Heath, J. (1979),'The Borough of Derby 1780-1810', *Derbyshire Miscellany*, 8, pp. 181-97.

Hecht, J.J. (1956), *The Domestic Servant Class in Eighteenth-Century England*, London.

Henstock, A. (ed.) (1980), *Diary of Abigail Gawthern of Nottingham 1751-1810*, Nottingham.

Hill, B. (1989), *Women, Work and Sexual Politics in Eighteenth-Century England*, Oxford.

——. (1996), *Servants: English Domestics in the Eighteenth Century*, Oxford.

Hobby, E. (1988), *Virtue of Necessity: English Women's Writing, 1649-1688*, London.

Hobson, M.G. (ed.) (1942), *Oxford Council Acts, 1752-1801*, Oxford.

Honeyman, K. (2000), *Women, Gender and Industrialisation in England, 1700-1870*, Basingstoke.

Hopkins, E. (1998), 'The Birmingham Economy During the Revolutionary and Napoleonic Wars, 1793–1815', *Midland History*, 23, pp. 105-20.

Huberman, M. (1987), 'The Economic Origins of Paternalism: Lancashire Cotton Spinning in the First Half of the Nineteenth Century', *Social History*, 12:2, pp. 177-92.

Hudson, P. (1992), *The Industrial Revolution*, London.

Hufton, O. (1981),'Women, Work and Marriage in Eighteenth-Century France', in R.B. Outhwaite (ed.), *Marriage and Society: Studies in the Social History of Marriage*, London.

——. (1984), 'Women Without Men: Widows and Spinsters in Britain and France in the Eighteenth Century', *Journal of Family History*, 9:4, pp. 355-76.

——. (1995), *The Prospect Before Her: A History of Women in Western Europe: Volume One 1500-1800*, London.

Hughes, E. (1952 reprinted 1969), *North Country Life in the Eighteenth Century. The North East, 1700-1750*, Oxford.

Hughes, K. (1998), *George Eliot*, London.

Humphries, J. (1990), 'Enclosures, Common Rights and Women: the Proletarianisation of Families in the Late Eighteenth and Early Nineteenth Centuries', *Journal of Economic History*, 1, pp. 17-42.

——. (1991), 'Lurking in the Wings ... Women in the Historiography of the Industrial Revolution', *Business and Economic History*, 20, pp. 32-44.

Humphries, J. and Horrell, S. (1995), 'Women's Labour Force Participation and the Transition to the Male-Breadwinner Family, 1790-1865', *Economic History Review*, 2nd series, 48, pp. 89-117.

Hunt, M. (1996), *The Middling Sort. Commerce, Gender and the Family in England 1680-1780*, Berkeley and London.

——. (2000), 'Wives and Marital "Rights" in the Court of Exchequer in the Early Eighteenth Century', in P. Griffiths and M.S.R. Jenner (eds), *Londinopolis. Essays in the Cultural and Social History of Early Modern London*, Manchester.

Hurwich, J. (1970), 'Nonconformists in Warwickshire, 1660-1720', unpublished University of Princeton PhD thesis.

Hutchinson, W. (1785), *History and Antiquities of the County Palatinate of Durham*, vol. II, Newcastle and London.

Hutton, W. (1783; 1976), *The History of Birmingham*, Birmingham.

Hyde, R. (1994), *A Prospect of Britain: The Town Panoramas of Samuel and*

Nathaniel Buck, London.

Innes, J. and Rogers, N. (2000), 'Politics and Government 1700-1840', in P. Clark (ed.), *The Cambridge Urban History of Britain. vol. II 1500-1840*, Cambridge.

Jameson, F. (1991), *Postmodernism: or the Cultural Logical of Late Capital*, London.

John, A.V. (ed.) (1986), *Unequal Opportunities: Women's Employment in England, 1800-1918*, Oxford.

Jones, R.W. (1998), *Gender and the Formation of Taste in Eighteenth-Century Britain: The Analysis of Beauty*, Cambridge.

Jordan, E. (1989), 'The Exclusion of Women from Industry in Nineteenth-Century Britain', *Comparative Studies in Social History*, 31, pp. 309-26.

Keast, J. (1989), *A History of East and West Looe*, Chichester.

Kent, D.A. (1989), '"Ubiquitous but Invisible": Female Domestic Servants in Mid-Eighteenth-Century London', *History Workshop Journal*, 28, pp. 111-28.

Kidd, A. (1993), *Manchester*, 2nd edn, Keele.

Kidd, A. and Nicholls D. (eds) (1999), *Gender, Civic Culture and Consumerism: Middle Class Identity in Britain 1800-1940*, Manchester.

Klancher, J.P. (1987), *The Making of English Reading Audiences, 1790-1832*, Wisconsin.

Klein, K. (1960), *The Image of the City*, Cambridge, Mass.

Klein, L. (1995), 'Politeness for Plebes: Consumption and Social Identity in Early Eighteenth-Century England', in A. Bermingham and J. Brewer (eds), *The Consumption of Culture, 1600-1800: Image, Object, Text*, London.

——. (1995), 'Gender and the Public/Private Distinction in the Eighteenth Century: Some Questions About Evidence and Analytic Procedure', *Eighteenth-Century Studies*, 29, pp. 97-109.

Koditschek, T. (1990), *Class Formation and Urban-Industrial Society: Bradford, 1750–1850*, Cambridge.

Kussmaul, A. (1981), *Servants in Husbandry in Early Modern England*, Cambridge.

La Rochefoucauld, F. (1995), *A Frenchman in England in 1784*, J. Marchand (ed.), translated by S.C. Roberts, London.

Lane, J. (1992), *Worcester Infirmary in the Eighteenth Century*, Worcestershire Historical Society, 6, Worcester.

Lane, P. (2000), 'Women, Property and Inheritance: Wealth Creation and Income Generation in Small English Towns, 1750-1835', in J. Stobart and A. Owens (eds), *Urban Fortunes: Property and Inheritance in the Town, 1700-1900*, Aldershot.

Langford, P. (1986), 'Tories and Jacobites, 1714-1751', in L.S. Sutherland and L.G. Mitchell (eds), *History of the University of Oxford*, v, Oxford.

——. (1989; revised 1992), *A Polite and Commercial People: England 1727-1783*, Oxford.

——. (1991), *Public Life and the Propertied Englishman: 1689–1798*, Oxford.

Laqueur, T.W. (1976), *Religion and Respectability: Sunday Schools and Working Class Culture, 1780 – 1850*, London.

Larson, E. (1986), 'A Measure of Power: The Personal Charity of Elizabeth

Montagu', *Studies in Eighteenth-Century Culture*, 16, pp. 197-201.

Leader, R.E. (1901), *Sheffield in the Eighteenth Century*, Sheffield.

Leinster-Mackay, D.P. (1976), 'Dame Schools: A Need for a Review', *British Journal of Educational Studies*, 34, pp.33-48.

Lemire, B. (1997), *Dress, Culture and Commerce: The English Clothing Trade Before the Factory*, London.

——. (1991), *Fashion's Favourite. The Cotton Trade and the Consumer in Britain, 1660-1800*, Oxford.

Lloyd G. (1993), *The Man of Reason: 'Male' and 'Female' in Western Philosophy*, 2nd edn, London.

Lloyd, S. (1996), '"Pleasure's Golden Bait": Prostitution, Poverty and the Magdalen Hospital in Eighteenth-Century London', *History Workshop Journal*, 41, pp. 50-70.

Lonsdale, R. (ed.), (1984), *The New Oxford Book of Eighteenth Century Verse*, Oxford.

——. (ed.) (1989), *Eighteenth-Century Women Poets: An Anthology*, Oxford.

Lown, J. (1990), *Women and Industrialisation: Gender at Work in Nineteenth-Century England*, Cambridge.

Malmgreen, G. (1985), *Silk Town: Industry and Culture in Macclesfield 1750-1835*, Hull.

——. (1986), 'Religion and Family life', in G. Malmgreen (ed.), *Religion in the Lives of English Women 1760-1930*, London.

Mandler, P. (1990), *The Uses of Charity: The Poor on Relief in the Nineteenth-Century Metropolis*, Philadelphia.

Martin, M.C. (1994), 'Women and Philanthropy in Walthamstow and Leyton, 1740-1870', *London Journal*, 19, pp. 119-50.

McClure, R.K. (1981), *Coram's Children: The London Foundling Hospital in the Eighteenth Century*, New Haven.

McDowell, P. (2000), 'Women and the Business of Print', in V. Jones (ed.), *Women and Literature in Britain, 1700-1800*, Cambridge.

McKendrick, N. (1974), 'Home Demand and Economic Growth: A New View of the Role of Women and Children in the Industrial Revolution', in N. McKendrick (ed.), *Historical Perspectives: Studies in English Thought and Society in Honour of J.H. Plumb*, London.

——. (1982), 'George Packwood and the Commercialization of Shaving. The Art of Eighteenth-Century Advertising or "The Way to Get Money and be Happy"', in N. McKendrick, J. Brewer and J.H. Plumb (eds), *The Birth of a Consumer Society: The Commercialisation of Eighteenth Century England*, Bloomington.

——. (1982), 'Introduction' and 'The Consumer Revolution of Eighteenth Century England', in N. McKendrick, J. Brewer and J.H. Plumb (eds), *The Birth of a Consumer Society: The Commercialization of Eighteenth Century England*, Bloomington.

McKendrick, N., Brewer, J. and Plumb, J.H. (1982), *The Birth of a Consumer Society: The Commercialisation of Eighteenth-Century England*, (new edn, London.

Mcleod, H. (1981), *Religion and the People of Western Europe, 1789-1970*, Oxford.

McWhir, A. (1995), 'Elizabeth Thomas and the Two Corinnas: Giving the Woman Writer a Bad Name', *English Literary History*, 62, pp. 105-19.

Meldrum, T. (2000), *Domestic Service and Gender 1660-1750: Life and Work in the London Household*, Harlow.

Mendleson, S. and Crawford, P. (1998), *Women in Early Modern England* Oxford.

Mermin, D. (1990), 'Women Becoming Poets: Katherine Philips, Aphra Behn, Anne Finch', *English Literary History*, 57, pp. 335-55.

Meskinnon, M. (1997), *Engendering the City: Women Artists and Urban Space* [*Nexus I: Theory and Practice in Contemporary Women's Photography*], London.

Midgley, C. (1992), *Women Against Slavery: The British Campaigns, 1780-1870*, London.

Money, J. (1977), *Experience and Identity, Birmingham and the West Midlands, 1760-1800*, Manchester.

——. (1993), 'Teaching in the Market-Place: The Importance of Education in the Economy of the English Leisure Towns', in J. Brewer and R. Porter, (eds) *Consumption and the World of Goods*, London.

Montagu, Lady Mary Wortley (1997), *Selected Letters*, in I. Grundy, (ed.) Harmondsworth.

Morgan, C.E. (1992), 'Women, Work and Consciousness in the Mid-Nineteenth-Century Cotton Industry', *Social History*, 17, pp. 23-41.

Morris, R.J. (1983), 'Voluntary Associations and British Urban Elites 1780-1850', *Historical Journal*, 26, pp. 95-118.

——. (1990), *Class, Sect and Party: The Making of the British Middle Class, Leeds 1820-1850*, Manchester.

Muldrew, C. (1998), *The Economy of Obligation: the Culture of Credit and Social Relations in Early Modern England*, London.

Munden, A. (1999), 'George Burder, an Able Minister of the New Covenant', *Warwickshire History*, 1, pp. 37-53.

Myers, S.H. (1990), *The Blue Stocking Circle: Women, Friendship and the Life of the Mind in Eighteenth-Century England*, Oxford.

Nash, S. (1984), 'Prostitution and Charity: The Magdalen Hospital, a Case Study', *Journal of Social History*, 17, pp. 617–28.

Neale, R.S. (1981), *Bath 1680-1850: A Social History*, London.

Neeson, J. (1993), *Commoners: Common Right, Enclosure and Social Change in England, 1700-1820*, Cambridge.

Nenadic, S. (1994), 'Middle Rank Consumers and Domestic Culture in Edinburgh and Glasgow, 1720-1840', *Past and Present*, 145, pp. 122-56.

——. (1997), 'Print Collecting and Popular Culture in Eighteenth-Century Scotland', *History*, 82, pp. 203-22.

Nicholas, R. (1998), *Crowds, Culture and Politics in Georgian Britain*, Oxford.

Nichols, J. (1812), *Literary Anecdotes of the Eighteenth Century*, 6 vols, London.

Nokes, D. (1995), *John Gay: A Profession of Friendship*, Oxford.

O'Brien P. and Quinault, R. (eds) (1993), *The Industrial Revolution and British*

Society, Cambridge.

Owen, D. (1965), *English Philanthropy, 1660–1960*, London.

Parkes, Mrs. William (1825), *Domestic Duties; or Instructions to Young Married Ladies*, London.

Pearson, J. (1999), *Women Reading in Britain 1750-1835*, Cambridge.

Pennell, S. (1999), 'Consumption and Consumerism in Early Modern England', *Historical Journal*, 42 pp. 549-64.

——. (2000), '"Great Quantities of Gooseberry Pye and Baked Clod of Beef": Victualling and Eating out in Early Modern London', in P. Griffiths and M.S.R. Jenner (eds), *Londinopolis: Essays in the Cultural and Social History of Early Modern London*, Manchester.

Phythian Adams, C. (1972), 'Ceremony and the Citizen: The Communal Year at Coventry, 1450-1550', in P. Clark, and P. Slack (eds), *Crisis and Order in English Towns, 1500-1700: Essays in Urban History*, London.

Pinchbeck, I. (1930), *Women Workers and the Industrial Revolution, 1750-1850*, London.

Pinches, S.M. (2001), 'Charities in Warwickshire in the Eighteenth and Nineteenth Centuries', unpublished University of Leicester PhD thesis.

Plumptre, J. (1992), 'Prospect of Edinburgh', in I. Ousby (ed.) (1799) *James Plumptre's Britain: the Journals of a Tourist in the 1790s*, London.

Pointon, M. (1997), *Strategies for Showing: Women, Possession, and Representation in English Visual Culture, 1665-1800*, Oxford.

Pollack, E. (1985), *The Poetics of Sexual Myth: Gender and Ideology in the Verse of Swift and Pope*, Chicago.

Poole, B. (1870), *Coventry, its History and Antiquities*, London.

Pope, A. (1961), *The Twickenham Edition of the Poems of Alexander Pope*, general editor J. Butt, New York.

Porter, R. (2000), *Enlightenment: Britain and the Creation of the Modern World*, London.

——. (1994) *London: A Social History*, London.

——. (1989), 'The Gift-Relation: Philanthropy and Provincial Hospitals in Eighteenth-Century England', in L. Granshaw and R. Porter (eds), *The Hospital in History*, London.

——. (1987), *Mind-Forg'd Manacles: A History of Madness in England from the Restoration to the Regency*, London.

Prest, W. (1994), 'One Hawkins, a Female Solicitor: Women Lawyers in Augustan England', *Huntington Library Quarterly*, 57, pp. 353-8.

Prickett, Mrs. (1814), *Warwick Castle*, 3 vols, London.

Prior, M. (1985), 'Women and the Urban Economy: Oxford 1500-1800', in M. Prior (ed.), *Women in English Society, 1500-1800*, London.

Prochaska, F.K. (1974), 'Women in English Philanthropy, 1790-1830', *International Review of Social History*, 19, pp. 426-45.

——. (1980), *Women and Philanthropy in Nineteenth Century England*, Oxford.

——. (1988), *The Voluntary Impulse*: Philanthropy in Modern Britain, London.

Pugin, A.W.N. (1836; 1841 edition republished 1969), *Contrasts*, Leicester.

Pullin, N. (2000), "Business is Just Life": Gender, Skill, Ideology and the

Eighteenth-Century Business Woman', unpublished University of London PhD thesis.

Rapapport, S. (1983), *World within Worlds Structures of Life in Sixteenth-Century London*, Cambridge.

Raven, J. (1995), 'Defending Conduct and Property: The London Press and the Luxury Debate', in J. Brewer and S. Staves (eds), *Early Modern Conceptions of Property*, London and New York.

Reeder, D. and Rodger, R. (2000), 'Industrialisation and the City Economy', in M. Daunton (ed.), *The Cambridge Urban History of Britain. vol. III. 1840-1950*, Cambridge.

Reeves, M. (1997), *Pursuing the Muses: Female Education and Non-conformist Culture 1700-1900*, London.

Rendall, J. (1989), 'Friendship and Politics: Barabara Leigh Smith Bodichon (1827-91) and Bessie Rayner Parkes (1828-1925)', in S. Mendus, and J. Rendall (eds), *Sexuality and Subordination*, London.

——. (1990), *Women in an Industrializing Society: England 1750-1880*, Oxford.

Richards, E. (1974), 'Women in the British Economy Since About 1700: An Interpretation', *History*, 59, pp. 337-57.

Richardson, S. (2000), '"Well-Neighboured Houses": The Political Networks of Elite Women 1780-1860', in K. Gleadle and S. Richardson (eds), *Women in British Politics, 1760-1860: The Power of the Petticoat*, Basingstoke.

Riley, D. (1998), *"Am I that Name ?" Feminism and the Category of Woman in History*, Basingstoke.

Roberts, M. (1990), 'Women and Work in Sixteenth-Century English Towns', in P.J. Corfield and D. Keene (eds), *Work in Towns 850-1850*, London.

Robson, R.J. (1949), *The Oxfordshire Election of 1754*, Oxford.

Roeder, C. (1905), *Beginnings of the Manchester Post-Office*, Manchester.

Roper, L. (1987), '"The Common Man", "The Common Good", "Common Women": Gender and Meaning in the German Reformation Commune', *Social History*, 12, pp. 1-21.

Rose, S. (1988) 'Gender Antagonism and Class Conflict: Exclusionary Strategies of Male Trade Unionists in Nineteenth-Century Britain', *Social History*, 13, pp. 191-208.

Sanderson, E.C. (1996), *Women and Work in Eighteenth-Century Edinburgh*, London.

Schwarz, L. (1999), 'English Servants and Their Employers During the Eighteenth and Nineteenth Centuries', *Economic History Review*, 2nd series, 52, pp. 236-56.

Scola, R. (1992), *Feeding the Victorian City: The Food Supply of Manchester, 1770-1870*, W.A. Armstrong and P. Scola (eds), Manchester.

Seed, J. (1986), 'Theologies of Power: Unitarianism and the Social Relations of Religious Discourse, 1800-1850', in R.J. Morris (ed.), *Class, Power and Social Structure in British Nineteenth-Century Towns*, Leicester.

Sekora, J. (1977), *Luxury. The Concept in Western Thought, Eden to Smollett* Baltimore.

Shammas, C. (1990), *The Pre-Industrial Consumer in England and America* Oxford.

Sharpe, P (2000), 'Population and Society', in P. Clark (ed.), *The Cambridge Urban History of Britain, vol.II 1500-1840*, Cambridge.

——. (1999), 'Dealing with Love: The Ambiguous Independence of the Single Woman in Early Modern England', *Gender and History*, 11.

——. (1995), 'Continuity and Change: Women's History and Economic History in Britain', *Economic History Review,* 2nd series, 48:2, pp. 353-64.

——. (1996), *Adapting to Capitalism: Working Women in the English Economy, 1700-1850*, Basingstoke.

Sheils, R.D. (1983), 'The Feminisation of American Congregationalism, 1730-1835', *American Quarterly*, 33, pp. 46-62.

Shesgreen, S. (1990), *The Criers and Hawkers of London*, Aldershot.

Shevelow, K. (1989), *Women and Print Culture: The Construction of Femininity in the Early Periodical*, London and New York.

Shiells, R. (ed.) (1753), *An Account of the Lives of the Poets of Britain and Ireland*, 5 vols, London.

Shipperbottom, R. (1997), 'Introduction' to Elizabeth Raffald, *The Experienced English Housekeeper*, Lewes.

Shoemaker, R.B. (1991), *Prosecution and Punishment: Petty Crime and the Law in London and Rural Middlesex c. 1660-1725*, Cambridge.

——. (1998), *Gender in English Society, 1650-1850: The Emergence of Separate Spheres?*, London.

Shuttleton, D.E. (1998), '"All Passion Extinquish'd": The Case of Mary Chandler (1687-1745)', in I. Armstrong and V. Blaine (eds), *Women's Poetry of the Englightenment: The Making of the Canon, 1730-1820*, London.

——. (2000), 'Mary Chandler's Description of Bath (1733): The Poetic Topographies of an Augustan Tradeswoman', *Women's Writing*, 7:3, pp. 447-67.

Simonton, D. (1998), *A History of European Women's Work, 1700 to the Present*, London.

Skedd, S. (1997), 'Women Teachers and the Expansion of Girls' Schooling in England, c.1760-1820', in H. Barker and E. Chalus (eds.), *Gender in Eighteenth-Century England: Roles, Representations and Responsibilities*, London.

Skinner, G. (2000), 'Women's Status as Legal and Civic Subjects', in V. Jones (ed.), *Women and Literature in Britain 1700-1800*, Cambridge.

Slugg, J.T. (1881), *Reminiscences of Manchester Fifty Years Ago*, Manchester.

Smail, J. (1994), *The Origins of Middle-Class Culture, Halifax, Yorkshire, 1660-1780*, Ithaca and London.

Smith, H.L. (1998), 'Women as Sextons and Electors: King's Bench and Precedents for Women's Citizenship', in H.L. Smith (ed.), *Women Writers and the Early Modern Political Tradition*, Cambridge.

Smollett, T. (repr., 1904), *Peregrine Pickle*, London.

Snell, K.D.M. (1985), *Annals of the Labouring Poor: Social Change and Agrarian England 1660-1900*, Cambridge.

Spencer, J. (1986), *The Rise of the Woman Novelist: from Aphra Behn to Jane Austen*, Oxford.

Staves, S. (1990), *Married Women's Separate Property in England, 1660–1833*, Cambridge, Mass.

——. (1998),'Investments, Votes, and "Bribes": Women as Shareholders in the Chartered National Companies', in H.L. Smith (ed.), *Women Writers and the Early Modern Political Tradition*, Cambridge.

Still, V.D.B. (1972), *The Blue Coat School, Birmingham, 1722-1972*, Birmingham.

Stobart, J. and Lane, P. (eds) (2000), *Urban and Industrial Change in the Midlands 1700-1840*, Leicester.

Stone, L. and Fawtier, J. (1986), *An Open Elite? England, 1540-1880*, Oxford.

Surtees, R. (1820), *History and Antiquities of the County Palatine of Durham*, vol. II, Durham.

Sutherland, L. (1986), Political Respectability, 1751-1771', in L.S. Sutherland and L.G. Mitchell (eds), *History of the University of Oxford*, v, Oxford.

Sweet, R. (1997), *The Writing of Urban Histories in Eighteenth Century England*, Oxford.

——. (1998), 'Freemen and Independence in English Borough Politics, c. 1770-1830', *Past and Present*, 161, pp. 84-115.

——. (1999), *The English Town. Government, Society and Culture, 1680-1840*, Harlow.

Thane, P. (1996), 'Old People and their Families in the Past' in M. Daunton (ed.), *Charity, Self-Interest and Welfare in the English Past*, London.

Thomas, C. (1994), *Alexander Pope and his Eighteenth-Century Female Readers*, Carbondale and Edwardsville.

Thomas, P.D.G. (1996), *John Wilkes: A Friend to Liberty*, Oxford.

Thomson, K. (1830), *Constance*, 3 vols, London.

Thwaites, W. (1984), 'Women in the Market Place: Oxfordshire, c. 1690-1800', *Midland History*, 9, pp. 23-42.

Tittler, R. (2001), *Townspeople and Nation: English Urban Experiences, 1540-1640*, Stanford.

Todd, J. (1986), *Sensibility: An Introduction,* London.

——. (1989), *The Sign of Angellica: Women, Writing and Fiction 1660-1800*, London.

Tomkins, A., 'Traditional Forms of Voluntary Charity: Oxford Almshouses in the Mid-Eighteenth Century', unpublished paper.

Troost, L.V. (1996), 'Geography and Gender: Mary Chandler and Alexander Pope', in D.C. Mell (ed.), *Pope, Swift and Women Writers*, Newark and London.

Tsurumi, R. (2000), 'Between Hymnbook and Textbook', *Paradigm*, 1, pp. 24-9.

Turner, C. (1992), *Living by the Pen: Women Writers in the Eighteenth Century*, London and New York.

Uglow, J. (1993), *Elizabeth Gaskell*, London.

Uitz, E. (1990), *Women in the Medieval Town*, London.

Valenze, D. (1985), *Prophetic Sons and Daughters: Female Preaching and Popular Religion in Industrial England*, Princeton.

——. (1995), *The First Industrial Woman*, Oxford.

Varey, S. (1990), *Space and the Eighteenth-Century Novel*, Cambridge.

Vickery, A. (1993), 'Golden Age to Separate Spheres? A Review of the Categories and Chronology of English Women's History', *The Historical Journal*, 36:2 pp. 383-414.

——. (1993), 'Women and the World of Goods: A Lancashire Consumer and Her Possessions, 1751-81', in J. Brewer and R. Porter (eds), *Consumption and the World of Goods*, London.

——. (1998), *The Gentleman's Daughter: Women's Lives in Georgian England*, Newhaven and London.

——. (ed.) (2001), *Women. Privilege and Power: British Politics 1750 to the Present*, Stanford, California.

Vincent, D. (1997), 'The Domestic and the Official Curriculum in Nineteenth-Century England', in M. Hilton, M. Styles and V. Watson (eds), *Opening the Nursery Door*, London and New York.

Wahrman, D. (1992), 'National Society, Communal Culture: an Argument About the Recent Historiography of Eighteenth-Century Britain', *Social History*, 17:1, pp. 43-72.

——. (1995), *Imagining the Middle Class*, Cambridge.

Walker, B. (1944), 'Note re Dowell's Retreat, Warner Street, Birmingham', *Transactions of the Birmingham Archaeological Society*, 65, pp. 142-3.

Wall, R. (1981), 'Women Alone in English Society', *Annales de Démographie Historique*, 16, pp. 303-17.

Walsh, C. (1995), 'Shop Design and the Display of Goods in Eighteenth-Century London', *Journal of Design History*, 8.

——. (1990), 'The Design of London Goldsmiths' Shops in the Early Eighteenth Century', in D. Mitchell (ed.) *Goldsmiths, Silversmiths and Bankers. Innovation and the Transfer of Skill, 1550-1750*, London.

Walton, J. (2000), 'Towns and consumerism', in M. Daunton (ed.), *The Cambridge Urban History of Britain. vol. III. 1840-1950*, Cambridge.

Watt, S. (1804), *A Walk through Leicester*, Leicester.

Watts, R. (1998), *Gender, Power and the Unitarians in England, 1760-1860*, Harlow.

Weatherill, L. (1986), 'A Possession of One's Own: Women and Consumer Behaviour in England, 1660-1740', *Journal of British Studies*, 25, pp. 131-56.

——. (1996), *Consumer Behaviour and Material Culture in Britain, 1660-1760*, 2nd edn, London.

Webb, S. and B. (1908), *English Local Government from the Revolution to the Municipal Corporations Act: The Manor and the Borough*, London.

White, J.E. (1815), *Letters on England*, 2 vols, Philadelphia.

Whyman, S. (2000), *Sociability and Power in Late-Stuart England: The Cultural World of the Verneys, 1660-1720*, Oxford.

Williams, Raymond (1973), *The Country and the City*, London.

Wilson, A. (1996), 'Conflict, Consensus and Charity: Politics and the Provincial Voluntary Hospitals in the Eighteenth Century', *English Historical Review*, 13, pp. 599-619.

Wilson, K. (1990),'Urban Culture and Political Activism in Hanoverian England: the Example of Voluntary Hospitals', in E. Hellmuth (ed.), *The Transformation of Political Culture: England and Germany in the late Eighteenth Century*, Oxford.

——. (1995), *The Sense of the People: Politics, Culture and Imperialism in England, 1715-1785*, Cambridge.

Wilson, R.G. and Mackley, A.L. (1999), 'How Much Did the English Country House Cost to Build, 1660-1880?', *Economic History Review*, 2nd series, 52:3, pp. 436-68.

——. (1980),'Georgian Leeds', in D. Fraser (ed.), *A History of Modern Leeds*, Manchester.

Wiskin, C. (2000), 'Women, Credit and Finance in England, c.1780–1826', unpublished university thesis, University of Warwick. Funded by studentship no. R00429634128 from the Economic and Social Research Council.

Withington, P. (2000), 'Citizens, Communities and Political Culture in Restoration England', in A. Shepard and P. Withington (eds), *Communities in Early Modern England: Networks, Place, Rhetoric*, Manchester.

Wood, A. (1999), *The Politics of Social Conflict: The Peak Country, 1520-1770*, Cambridge.

Wright Proctor, R. (1874), *Memorials of Manchester Streets*, Manchester.

Wright, S. (1989), 'Holding Up Half the Sky: Women and their Occupations in Eighteenth Century Ludlow', *Midland History*, 14, pp. 53-74.

Wrightson, K. (2000), *Earthly Necessities: Economic Lives in Early Modern Britain*, New Haven and London.

Wrigley, E.A. (1987), *People, Cities and Wealth: The Transformation of Traditional Society*, Oxford.

——. (1989), *Continuity, Chance and Change: The Character of the Industrial Revolution in England*, Cambridge.

Youngson, J.A. (1966), *The Making of Classical Edinburgh*, Edinburgh.

Index